Citizen Participation and Political Communication in a Digital World

The arrival of the participatory Web 2.0 has been hailed by many as a media revolution, bringing with it new tools and possibilities for direct political action. Through specialised online platforms, mainstream social media or blogs, citizens in many countries are increasingly seeking to have their voices heard online, whether it is to lobby, to support or to complain about their elected representatives. Politicians, too, are adopting "new media" in specific ways, though they are often criticised for failing to seize the full potential of online tools to enter into dialogue with their electorates. Bringing together perspectives from around the world, this volume examines emerging forms of citizen participation in the face of the evolving logics of political communication, and provides a unique and original focus on the gap which exists between political uses of digital media by the politicians and by the people they represent.

Alex Frame is Associate Professor in Communication Science at the University of Burgundy (Dijon, France) and TIL research group (EA4182). Recent publications include *Communication et Interculturalité* (2013) and *Communication and PR from a Cross-Cultural Standpoint* (edited with Valérie Carayol, 2012).

Gilles Brachotte is Associate Professor in Communication Science at the University of Burgundy, member of the CIMEOS/3S research team (EA 4177), and teaches in the web design department of Dijon-Auxerre Technological Institute (IUT Dijon-Auxerre). His research focuses on social change linked to ICT in society, among young people and in the political sphere.

Routledge Studies in New Media and Cyberculture

1 **Cyberpop**
Digital Lifestyles and
Commodity Culture
Sidney Eve Matrix

2 **The Internet in China**
Cyberspace and Civil Society
Zixue Tai

3 **Racing Cyberculture**
Minoritarian Art and Cultural
Politics on the Internet
Christopher L. McGahan

4 **Decoding Liberation**
The Promise of Free and Open
Source Software
*Samir Chopra and Scott D.
Dexter*

5 **Gaming Cultures and Place in
Asia-Pacific**
*Edited by Larissa Hjorth and
Dean Chan*

6 **Virtual English**
Queer Internets and Digital
Creolization
Jillana B. Enteen

7 **Disability and New Media**
Katie Ellis and Mike Kent

8 **Creating Second Lives**
Community, Identity and
Spatiality as Constructions of
the Virtual
*Edited by Astrid Ensslin and
Eben Muse*

9 **Mobile Technology and Place**
*Edited by Gerard Goggin and
Rowan Wilken*

10 **Wordplay and the Discourse of
Video Games**
Analyzing Words, Design, and
Play
Christopher A. Paul

11 **Latin American Identity in
Online Cultural Production**
Claire Taylor and Thea Pitman

12 **Mobile Media Practices,
Presence and Politics**
The Challenge of Being
Seamlessly Mobile
*Edited by Kathleen M.
Cumiskey and Larissa Hjorth*

13 **The Public Space of Social
Media**
Connected Cultures of the
Network Society
Thérèse F. Tierney

14 **Researching Virtual Worlds**
Methodologies for Studying
Emergent Practices
*Edited by Ursula Plesner and
Louise Phillips*

15 **Digital Gaming Re-imagines the
Middle Ages**
Edited by Daniel T. Kline

16 **Social Media, Social Genres**
Making Sense of the Ordinary
Stine Lomborg

17 The Culture of Digital Fighting Games
Performances and Practice
Todd Harper

18 Cyberactivism on the Participatory Web
Edited by Martha McCaughey

19 Policy and Marketing Strategies for Digital Media
Edited by Yu-li Liu and Robert G. Picard

20 Place and Politics in Latin American Digital Culture
Location and Latin American Net Art
Claire Taylor

21 Online Games, Social Narratives
Esther MacCallum-Stewart

22 Locative Media
Edited by Rowan Wilken and Gerard Goggin

23 Online Evaluation of Creativity and the Arts
Edited by Hiesun Cecilia Suhr

24 Theories of the Mobile Internet
Materialities and Imaginaries
Edited by Andrew Herman, Jan Hadlaw and Thom Swiss

25 The Ubiquitous Internet
User and Industry Perspectives
Edited by Anja Bechmann and Stine Lomborg

26 The Promiscuity of Network Culture
Queer Theory and Digital Media
Robert Payne

27 Global Media, Biopolitics, and Affect
Politicizing Bodily Vulnerability
Britta Timm Knudsen and Carsten Stage

28 Digital Audiobooks
New Media, Users, and Experiences
Iben Have and Birgitte Stougaard Pedersen

29 Locating Emerging Media
Edited by Germaine R. Halegoua and Ben Aslinger

30 Girls' Feminist Blogging in a Postfeminist Age
Jessalynn Keller

31 Indigenous People and Mobile Technologies
Edited by Laurel Evelyn Dyson, Stephen Grant, and Max Hendriks

32 Citizen Participation and Political Communication in a Digital World
Edited by Alex Frame and Gilles Brachotte

Citizen Participation and Political Communication in a Digital World

Edited by
Alex Frame and Gilles Brachotte

NEW YORK AND LONDON

First published 2016
by Routledge
711 Third Avenue, New York, NY 10017

and by Routledge
2 Park Square, Milton Park, Abingdon, Oxon OX14 4RN

First issued in paperback 2018

Routledge is an imprint of the Taylor & Francis Group, an informa business

© 2016 Taylor & Francis

The right of the editor to be identified as the author of the editorial material, and of the authors for their individual chapters, has been asserted in accordance with sections 77 and 78 of the Copyright, Designs and Patents Act 1988.

All rights reserved. No part of this book may be reprinted or reproduced or utilised in any form or by any electronic, mechanical, or other means, now known or hereafter invented, including photocopying and recording, or in any information storage or retrieval system, without permission in writing from the publishers.

Trademark notice: Product or corporate names may be trademarks or registered trademarks, and are used only for identification and explanation without intent to infringe.

Library of Congress Cataloging-in-Publication Data

Names: Frame, Alex, 1976- editor. | Brachotte, Gilles, 1971- editor.
Title: Citizen participation and political communication in a digital world / edited by Alex Frame and Gilles Brachotte.
Description: New York: Routledge, [2015] | Series: Routledge studies in new media and cyberculture; 32 | Includes index.
Identifiers: LCCN 2015024129
Subjects: LCSH: Communication in politics—Technological innovations. | Political participation—Technological innovations. | Internet in public administration. | Internet in political campaigns. | Online social networks—Political aspects. | Social media—Political aspects. | Political socialization.
Classification: LCC JA85 .C58 2015 | DDC 320.01/4—dc23
LC record available at http://lccn.loc.gov/2015024129

ISBN 13: 978-1-138-59796-9 (pbk)
ISBN 13: 978-1-138-93503-7 (hbk)

Typeset in Sabon
by codeMantra

Contents

*Foreword: 'Ideologies' and 'Utopias' in the Discourses
and Practices of Digital Politics*　　　ix
SIMEON YATES

Introduction　　　1
ALEX FRAME

PART I
Participation and Political Communication: The Perspective of Politicians and Parties

1 Talking to Themselves: A classification of *Facebook*'s Political Usages and Representatives' Roles Among Israeli Members of Knesset　　　13
SHARON HALEVA-AMIR

2 Two Step Flow Twitter Communication in 2013 Italian Political Election: A Missed Opportunity for Citizen Participation　　　25
GUIDO DI FRAIA AND MARIA CARLOTTA MISSAGLIA

3 Ad Hoc Mini-Publics on Twitter: Citizen Participation or Political Communication? Examples from the German National Election 2013　　　42
JESSICA EINSPÄNNER-PFLOCK, MARIO ANASTASIADIS, AND CAJA THIMM

4 Is Twitter Invigorating Spanish Democracy?: A Study of Political Interaction through the Accounts of The Prime Minister and The Leader of the Main Opposition Party　　　60
ELENA CEBRIÁN GUINOVART, TAMARA VÁZQUEZ BARRIO AND DAVID SARIAS RODRÍGUEZ

5 Candidate Orientation to ICTs in Canadian Municipal Elections　　　81
ANGELIA WAGNER

viii *Contents*

6 "I show off, therefore I am": The Politics of the Selfie   95
CHRISTELLE SERÉE-CHAUSSINAND

PART II
Emerging Forms of Digital Media-based Political Participation by Citizens and Civic Activists

7 Re-Imagining the Meaning of Participation for a Digital Age   109
DARREN G. LILLEKER

8 Who's Afraid of Clicktivism? Exploring Citizens' Use of Social Media and Political Participation in the Czech Republic   125
JAROMÍR MAZÁK AND VÁCLAV ŠTĚTKA

9 Twitter as a Counterpublic Sphere: Polemics in the Twittersphere During French Electoral Campaigns   139
ARNAUD MERCIER

10 Cultural Creation and Political Activism in the Digital World   153
LLUÍS ANYÓ AND IASA MONIQUE RIBEIRO

11 The Mediatization of Politics and the Digital Public Sphere: The Dynamics of Mini-Publics   167
CAJA THIMM

12 Alternative Media Spaces: The Case of Russian LGBT News Blogging Community   184
EVGENIYA BOKLAGE

13 Online Lobbying of Political Candidates   202
PAULA KEAVENEY

Concluding Note   217
GEOFF CRAIG

Contributors   221
Index   227

Foreword

'Ideologies' and 'Utopias' in the Discourses and Practices of Digital Politics

Simeon Yates

As Alex Frame notes at the start of this volume the development and implementation of new media digital technologies is a core element in economic and social change in many spheres of society. This dynamic, dialectic and sometimes simply confusing process often moves on at a pace that is hard for social researchers to keep up with. This has felt ever more the case over the last two decades in which new communications media forms and technologies appear to arrive almost constantly. It is in such circumstances that volumes such as this are important. First, the media 'revolution' that is underway needs to be documented – both the changes themselves and perceptions of them. Second, at some future point our use of digital media will be as general and ubiquitous as writing and print are now (or rather were in the late twentieth century). We will need points of reference such as this volume to remind us of the stages, conflicts, possibilities and concerns that made the digital world.

All the contributions to this volume speak to the great promise that lies in the use of the Internet and digital media for new forms of politics and for the regeneration of existing political systems. Indeed, for those of us with long memories, many pages of academic research and many hours of conference discussions in the early 1990s focused on the benefits and potential of the use of the Internet for deliberative politics. This was exemplified by the journalistic enthusiasm over online fora such as the WELL whose activities underpinned Howard Rheingold's (1993) seminal study "The Virtual Community". Digital media could seemingly address issues of political disengagement and maybe deadlock in our 'analogue' representative democracies. At the same time, long before the web or social media were mainstream, others were documenting the darker sides of digital media. Their use to control, limit and survey debate is examined in Shoshanna Zuboff's (1988) "In the Age of the Smart Machine". The potential for digital media to polarize behaviour and opinion, and foster conflict can be found in one of the first ever studies of online interaction - Keisler, Seigel and Macquire's (1984) "Social Psychological Aspects of Computer-Mediated Communication". As Frame points out in the introduction, current academic debate is still engaged in an exploration of these two themes – though with more nuanced takes on the arguments and with ever greater amounts of empirical data to hand.

x *Simeon Yates*

Politicians and the political process are of course aware of these debates, from activist movements to the slow change of UK parliamentary process. For examples, the recent UK Speaker of the House of Commons Commission on Digital Democracy (http://www.parliament.uk/business/commons/the-speaker/speakers-commission-on-digital-democracy/) engages with the possibilities and pitfalls of digitally mediated politics.

In this brief foreword I would like to argue that we see debate and conflict around the 'ideologies' and 'utopias' of digital politics in both examples of digital media use and in their analyses. Mannheim's (1936) foundational sociological work "Ideology and utopia" set up a particular model in which 'ideologies' and 'utopias' were 'ideas' held by different social groups; ways of seeing the world or how the world could be. Importantly he argued that 'ideologies' function predominantly to explain, justify or reinforce present social and political structures, and that 'utopias' were the forward looking 'hoped for' visions of a society that had changed or transcended current forms. Mannheim's work has of course been heavily criticized and discussed in the interceding near century – but I wish to use this specific idea of 'ideologies' and 'utopias' to explore the understandings we have of the transformative potential or actuality of digital media. In this analysis the idea of 'ideologies' and 'utopias' (note the lowercase form) refer to systems of ideas invoked to reinforce or to challenge contemporary social structures and norms – they are ideas about what is and what should be as articulated by different social groups. Such a definition encompasses the grand 'ideologies' 'utopias' of the last decade from liberal democracy to socialism. It also applies to contemporary political debate and action from environmentalism to LGBT rights and on through to the more reactionary political groups of the far right or religious intolerance. I also want to distinguish between 'ideologies' and 'utopias' of 'the digital' and these political 'ideologies' and 'utopias' of the kind Mannheim himself analysed. Of course, and I will return to this later, many contemporary social and political 'ideologies' and 'utopias' invoke the digital in various ways.

What do I mean by these distinctions? More importantly how do rather grand ideas such as 'ideology' and 'utopia' play out in the realities of everyday political action? We are often told in both academic and public discussions that the potential of digital technologies has been 'hyped up' – taken beyond the reasonable to provide visions of unrealistic futures. It then often feels like the 'hyped up' reality becomes the actual reality as the technology arrives in our homes. I would argue that we are today surrounded by 'ideologies' and 'utopias' of the digital. In which both those with great power in the digital realm provide 'ideologies' of its use and others point to the 'utopian' potentials of the technology. We are presented 'utopian' visions in the possibilities that it may bring to all aspects of life – inside and outside of politics – from the freeing up of access to information and education, new routes to political engagement, limitations to state and religious power, greater opportunities for free speech and so forth. We also see the

Foreword xi

growth of particular individualised, consumerist forms of digital media – not least Twitter and Facebook – whose formats and 'ideologies' of interaction underpin much of our everyday engagement with digital media. True or not, buried within such visions is a strong sense of technological determinism or at least technicism as described by Grint and Woolgar (1997) – the assumption that the future of our society is being determined by technology implementations. The idea that technology might not be the determinant of our social futures, that it is not the prime mover nor the solution, does not usually enter this discourse.

At the same time the everyday of political life, of conflict and resolution, elections and law-making continues. In this context ideas of what is the political, how it should function, who has or should have power, and how it is exercised are still under debate. Here we find political 'ideologies' at work in the context of national and international politics – be they about spread of democracy, neo-nationalisms, economic policy, personal freedom, privacy and so forth. We may also identify Mannheim's 'utopias' in the discourses of marginalized groups, activists and even in the arguments of reactionary political groups. Today the digital operates as a dissemination route for such ideas outside of the obvious control of states and national governance. At the same time the digital operates as a tool for states to survey and curtail debate, as well as a route for the dissemination of dominant 'ideologies'. It is in this complex interplay of both digital **and** political 'ideologies' and 'utopias' that contemporary **day-to-day political participation** takes place. As is noted in the introduction to this volume, what is key here is how citizens make use **and** sense of contemporary political practices within online and offline frames of reference. Yet the realities of these day-to-day uses point out the limitations, both social and technical, of digital media use in politics and the extent to which politics as a social system determines the implementation and uses of technologies.

To borrow from Bakhtin (1981) there seem to be forces acting on the 'voices' of both those who use and those who study digital political media. Bakhtin argued that utterances are inflected with the 'centripetal' forces that seek to expand beyond existing norms, and the 'centrifugal' forces that seek to constrain to given norms what is said. When articulating our understandings of contemporary political action – as researchers and as citizens – we too may find in our arguments the tension between the 'utopian' centripetal and 'ideological' centrifugal forces at work in contemporary debates. We can visualise these tensions as creating different spaces of political action in the context of digital media, as suggested in Figure 1.

To return to Grint and Woolgar, they provide us with the argument that many claims about the 'specific' impacts of technologies are themselves socially constructed accounts of social processes that for one reason or another foreground the role of technology. Such foregrounding of technology may act to make claims about the inevitability of social change, or it may serve to reinforce the current social structure. As researchers, therefore, we need to keep an

xii Simeon Yates

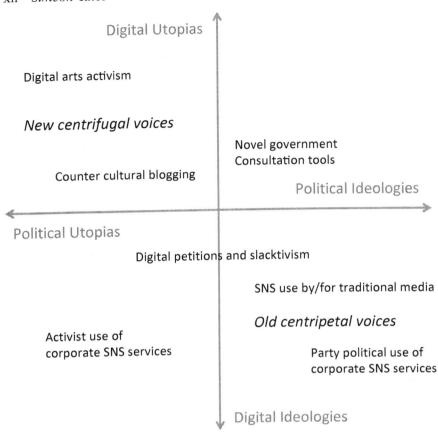

Figure 1 A model of digital and political spaces of action.

eye to how claims about the impacts of digital media on politics and political action are themselves 'ideological' and/or 'utopian' assertions about what politics or the digital should or can do. This point reinforces the need for volumes such as this that capture argument, debate, data, and examples as digital media are integrated into political life. We also need to highlight how different groups are utilising their constructions of the impact of the digital as part of their on-going political action. These three themes of: 'ideologies' and 'utopias'; technological determinisms and social constructions; and tensions between change and stasis can be found in all the studies presented in this volume.

The first part of the book addresses the participation and communication in the context of politicians and parties. In the introduction Frame points out that actual use is "explained by the different forms and logics of online activity which have developed within the political arena". He also notes that actual uses are often critiqued by scholars and commentators for failing to meet more 'utopian' models of citizen engagement or deliberative interaction.

Foreword xiii

Indeed Sharon Haleva-Amir concludes Chapter 1 by stating that: "Facebook is first and foremost a political marketing tool". Importantly the paper highlights how the 'utopian' hopes of voter interaction – underpinned by a deterministic view of technology and media effects – plays out against the realities of contemporary managed political communication. Haleva-Amir points out that this represents a "maturing" of digital political communication by Israeli MKs and their parties.

Chapters 2 and 3 look to the use of Twitter. Guido Di Fraia and Maria Carlotta Missaglia point out that despite the possibilities of direct engagement provided by Twitter, its use by politicians has become integrated into existing political communication structures. They point out: "If the platform had been used with a "social" mind set, it could have contributed to encouraging equal and bi-directional public debate that would have certainly brought citizens closer to politics and stimulated participation". Yet their research finds "a strong orientation towards mass media [t]raditional media logic is re-applied and re-adapted to the new environment; the content shows a *propagandist style* and the communication flow is *broadcast*". As a result they describe clearly how Twitter functions as a route for politicians to interact with the media and not directly with citizens in a classic two-step flow model. In Chapter 3 Mario Anastasiadis, Jessica Einspänner-Pflock and Caja Thimm point to the potential changes that Twitter brings to the political process. First, they highlight how temporary 'publics' or 'audiences' can form around hashtags. Second, they note that debate and discussion do happen on Twitter, potentially neither between candidates and citizens, nor necessarily greatly deliberative. Third, they point out that this debate is public, it is visible to many in ways that prior debate – at work, at home, in the pub, at the school gate – may not be. We have here an example of the extent, and potential limits of the 'new possibilities' set against the constraints and structures of existing political practice.

In Chapter 4 Elena Cebrián Guinovart, Tamara Vázquez Barrio and David Sarias Rodríguez again find that Twitter accounts are used as broadcast media to detail the activity of politicians and not as routes to interaction. They again note how this fails the interactive and engagement opportunity the technology (potentially) affords. Though in this case their analysis of the audience for these tweets, the followers, points to a desire by citizens to engage. The use of favourites and of posts that raise issues indicates a desire to interact with politicians. The mismatch in topics and the very limited focus on key messages and actions by the politicians give the impression of citizens being 'talked past' as their interactive activity clouds the specific and limited communication goals of the politicians or their parties. In all of these cases we can see that the 'utopian' potentials of digital media to transform interaction come into conflict with the 'ideological' needs of 'business as usual' in contemporary politics. Far from the technological determinism of some types of 'digital 'utopias' we have the heavy-handed imposition of classic political communication practices, from broadcasting two step flows and press mediation – to which Twitter adds another channel but not a transformative nor even a highly disruptive element.

This idea that use of digital media is driven not by the possibilities but by existing political communication norms is explored in Chapter 5 by Angelia Wagner. In exploring the use of social media by local rather than national politicians we find a more nuanced situation. The use of digital media is understood and deployed in terms of utility and risk, just like all media before it. The need to control communication during elections – where the risks around poor or bad communication are high – is contrasted with a more positive and open use when in office. In Chapter 6, Christelle Serée-Chaussinand argues that however new digital media forms may seem – in this case the 'selfie' – they often are, or can be seen as, building on or be tied to existing media forms and their histories. In this case Serée-Chaussinand considers the extent to which the use of 'selfies' by politicians follow on from centuries of portraiture employed by the powerful to manage the presentation of self in relation to their citizens or constituencies. Both of these chapters once again point out that context, history, political communicative goals and the need to manage communicative outcomes provide explanatory tools for understanding the form, articulation and execution everyday digital political practices. The centrifugal forces of prior political norms and processes outweigh the disruptive potential of new media forms.

Darren Lilleker in Chapter 7 continues the debate around social context. He rightly points out the rich complexity of traditional forms of political participation and points to their replication on line. Lilleker also raises questions about how we as researchers understand digital actions – from liking a photo to starting an online campaign. These clearly vary in their forms and levels of engagement and commitment but the chapter argues that what is needed here is deeper understanding of the meaningfulness and intentionality of these acts by citizens. This returns us to the central point of Grint and Woolgars' arguments against the essentialisms of technological determinist arguments and the inherent technicisms of pluralistic interpretations. We cannot treat digital media themselves as value-free and impartial actors in our political action and communications. The very technologies themselves – from the Internet itself to specific platforms such as Twitter and Facebook – have their own socio-technical histories that infuse our perceptions, inform our actions and configure us as users – as much as we seek to configure them and bend them to our wills. Lilleker's plea for researchers to take a deeper look at the social and psychological bases of the digital political actions of citizens reminds us that the focus needs to remain on the political as articulated in a complex multi-media environment.

Jaromír Mazák and Václav Štětka take up Lilleker's challenge and provide evidence that what have been termed slacktivism or clicktivism may in fact be part of broader meaningful political activity. This result provides for me a critique of the social construction of 'political engagement' as something that needs to be material and collectivist, 'on the ground' or 'in the street' to have meaning and relevance. It also critiques the manner in which digital media are socially constructed as ephemeral and transitory and therefore of lesser value to 'real' politics. For me, Arnaud Mercier in Chapter 9 continues this theme through a vivid account of the use of digital media to provide a route for voices that creatively seek to challenge contemporary ideological positions by both right and left. It provides a complex account of how social media are appropriated to provide a voice for groups who do not have access to mainstream media. In this context engaging the 'utopian' possibilities of digital media in service of their own political visions and ideals.

Lluís Anyó and Iasa Monique Ribeiro in Chapter 10 directly engage with the manner in which the 'utopian' opportunities of digital media are deployed in the context of art to articulate political 'utopian' voices. The case of digital art provides a particular context in which practitioners are seeking to configure the technologies in novel ways – unlike the more formulaic uses of corporate social media. This points out how political action may also be found in the resistance to or experimentation with digital media forms – some of which are those provided by major corporations. Caja Thimm's presentation of mini-publics and their 'polymediated' political action in Chapter 11 reminds us that contemporary politics have been on a long road to every greater 'mediatisation' over the last century. It is interesting to note that digital technologies themselves provide both 'visible' data and the tools to 'visualise' these data as networked graphs. This use of the technology to collect data, to analyse it and to provide representations of it is a recurrent methodological theme throughout the book. As argued above, digital media, their creators and their promoters are not neutral actors in the very developments under scrutiny here. The fact that we can now identify online collaborations, map and track political discourses across users, nations and digital formations provides new insights and tools for researchers. At the same time they are tools for the state to monitor and for activists to organise. Evgeniya Boklage takes this argument further through an examination of the Russian LGBT blogging community in Chapter 12. Though the medium of blogging provides both a medium for political debate and action, digital media also provide the information sources for this activism. This allows bloggers to circumvent the structures of highly regulated and controlled media sources. Once again we have an intersection of the digital 'utopia' with the 'utopian' visions of a political group providing space for a counter voice.

In the last chapter Paula Keaveney once again points out the nuanced realities of digital media use in everyday politics. By looking at the use of digital media in the practice of political lobbying Keaveney points out how the existing 'systems' of political influence are in part changed but also reinforced by new communications channels. Yet the example also points out an odd contradiction: though digital media make emailing, tweeting, liking and clicking relatively 'simple', navigating the complexities of both political engagement with representatives and the multiplicity of media routes in

xvi *Simeon Yates*

a networked society may overwhelm citizens, politicians and parties. This provides the opportunity for another group of intermediaries – in this case, organisations such as 38 degrees or change.org – to provide simple tools to support citizens in lobbying. As multiple routes to our political representatives open up, and the flow of messages increase, it begs the question of how much this can be meaningful activity on both sides. As Bolter and Grusin (2000) have underlined, the hope that the immediacy of digital media leads to greater authenticity and closeness in fact leads to the opposite, ever greater re-mediation as we and our agents (newspapers, TV channels, Facebook, Twitter, change.org …) seek to manage the mass of information we may encounter.

As noted at the start of this Foreword, volumes such as this provide important markers along the road of our engagement with digital media. The examples here provide case studies of how citizens, activists, politicians and researchers negotiate the possibilities and potentialities of digital media in the context of on-going everyday politics. Digital media have the reputation – in fact or in the public imagination – of being highly disruptive. As researchers we need to take care with such assumptions. As noted above, this argument is technological determinist. It is as much a social construction, a narrative about the impacts of technology, produced by various social actors as any 'ideological' or 'utopian' claims. The impact of digital media, its potentials and pitfalls, is therefore itself a point of political conflict and debate.

At the start of this Foreword I noted that the academic study of actual uses of the digital media has from the beginning highlighted a tension between the possibilities that digital media may bring and the ability of context, history and power to reassert existing structures and norms. The fact that this tension remains and can be found in the case studies and examples presented in this volume speaks not to a failure to resolve this through research or debate, but rather that it is inherent to the social appropriation of all novel technologies. Does this mean that I do not believe that digital media change politics? Would I argue that the possibilities implied by the combination of digital and political 'utopias' must fail (the upper left of Figure 1)? Or that 'politics as usual' will dominate and impose 'ideological' forms of both digital and political engagement (the bottom right of Figure 1)? The answer to all three questions is 'obviously not'. I believe, as the papers in this volume demonstrate, the question is not how do 'digital media' change politics, but rather: how do we understand the rich dialogic (Bakhtin) or dialectic manner in which politics in various forms interacts in actual everyday action with the digital media and technologies to hand? Returning again to Grint and Woolgar we can ask actual historical and contextual questions about the social and digital systems and histories behind contemporary practices that have been configured by and in turn configured politics.

To conclude, we are in a time of considerable social change in which digital media clearly play a role. It is incumbent upon scholars to explore, understand and document this change. In doing so they still need to be wary of seeing the technology as the determining variable. When we are faced, as we have over the last two decades, with an almost constant development of new communications technologies and media the tension between the possible and the actual becomes very visible. As Frame notes, very often, digital media in political contexts is critiqued by activists or researchers as they see it falling short of its potential to create new forms of deliberative or engaged politics. Such arguments are themselves political acts – they draw upon a specific social construction of digital media, its features, its history and its expected effects. Researchers should also keep an eye to the manners in which constructions of 'digital media' – that focus on its possibilities and potentials as well as its threats – are deployed themselves in arguments about what is and should be our contemporary politics. I have tried to use Mannheim's model of 'ideologies' and 'utopias' to point out how these socially constructed ideas of what politics and the digital 'are' or 'should be' intersect in all the chapters presented here, and in the actions of those studied. For those engaged in politics maybe the question is not what can digital media do for our politics, but rather what can we do as citizens to make use of digital media to develop our politics.

Works Cited

Bakhtin, M.M. (1981). *The Dialogic Imagination*. Austin: University of Texas Press.
Bolter, J.D., and Grusin, R. (2000). *Remediation: Understanding New Media*. Cambridge: MIT Press.
Grint, K., and Woolgar, S. (1997). *The Machine at Work: Technology, Work and Organization*. Cambridge: Polity Press.
Kiesler, S., Siegel, J., and McGuire, T.W. (1984) Social psychological aspects of computer-mediated communication. *American Psychologist*, Vol 39(10), Oct 1984, 1123–1134.
Mannheim, K. (1936) *Ideology and 'utopia*. London: Routledge.
Rheingold, H. (2000). *The Virtual Community: Homesteading on the Electronic Frontier. Revised Edition*. Cambridge: MIT Press.
Zuboff, S. (1988). *In the Age of the Smart Machine: The Future of Work and Power*. New York: Basic.

Introduction

Alex Frame

Ever since Gutenberg, the development and implementation of new media technologies has triggered accelerated economic and social change in many spheres of society. Very often, the bright sheen of novelty leads enlightened observers to proclaim the imminent demise of the previously dominant media technology, soon to be replaced by its modern successor. Yet such fears habitually turn out to be unfounded, as (a part of) society adopts the new forms of communication associated with the innovation, while the "old media" specialise in their functions and adapt their offer (Gurevitch, Coleman, & Blumler, 2009). Online forms of journalism are currently seen to threaten the existence of the printed press, yet in previous years, television was seen to be the major threat, and before it radio. In each case, these media have evolved to find new patterns of coexistence. We use each of them in different ways, our social habits also developing to reflect the changing media landscape. In this ongoing "meta-process" (Krotz, 2007) of mediatisation, or interplay between media technologies and various spheres of social life, the World Wide Web and the social networking sites (SNS) it has spawned are but the most recent media arrivals to impact society. Coming on the back of the technological developments of mass digitalisation and the Internet, the far-reaching infrastructure allowing us to distribute digital contents easily and cheaply, they appear to have changed things inexorably in many areas of social and economic life.

Politics is no exception to this ongoing trend. The mediatisation of politics long predates the Internet (Kepplinger, 2002; Nimmo & Combs, 1983; Strömbäck, 2008), as politicians adapted their communication to the needs of different media formats, notably television, and then to audience tastes for "infotainment" (Brants & Neijens, 1998). But the massive arrival of information and communication technologies (ICT) in the domain of politics has recently further impacted governance, relationships between citizens, political figures and the media, and political communication more generally, in many countries around the world (Block, 2013; Couldry & Hepp, 2013; Krotz, 2011; Thimm et al., 2014). Politicians, voters and members of civic society now commonly make use of the Internet, blogs, mainstream SNS (Facebook, YouTube, Twitter, Pinterest ...) and dedicated specialist tools (activist management platforms or specialised social networks) in relation with their political activity.

2 Alex Frame

Much of the research done into politics in the digital age has been concerned with the ways in which this development may or may not change politics for better or for worse; and studies differ as to the importance and influence they ascribe to these new tools (Couldry, 2014). Early optimistic voices saw in the Internet a new, open and accessible public sphere (Barber, 1998; Lévy, 1998; Rheingold, 1993). Yet these were countered by, and then largely gave way to, more measured views (Dahlgren, 2005; Norris, 2001), and research into the ongoing "digital divide" suggests that ICTs have not had the levelling effect some had hoped for, with age and social grade levels still influencing levels of online political activity (Yates, Kirby & Lockley, 2014). In the context of mediatisation's various purported social fallouts, such as declining trust toward politicians, packaging of politics as infotainment, increasing rates of abstention in different elections, mingling of public and private spheres and the personalisation of politics, these new media forms have been hailed by some as a further step in the wrong direction (Lits, 2009). On the level of participation, the hope that the World Wide Web would lead to massive political mobilisation notably among young people was quickly trampled by the empirical findings of Web 1.0 research (Jensen, 2013). More recent forms of SNS-based online activism have often been criticised as "slacktivism" or "clicktivism" (Morozov, 2009; Shulman, 2009), since they are seen to take the effort and hence much of the value out of political participation.

Yet the web goes on evolving. Aside from these dominantly negative aspects, some recent studies have again framed this process in more positive ways, suggesting that ICTs in a Web 2.0, post-2008-U.S.-presidential-election context can act as tools of disintermediation, allowing politicians to communicate more directly with their electorates and empowering voters by making it easier for them to have their voices heard (Dimitrova, Shehata, Strömbäck, & Nord, 2014; Effing, Hillegersberg, & Huibers, 2011; Jensen, 2013; Linders, 2012). At the same time, politicians are regularly criticised in many countries, for using SNS and other Web 2.0 tools in a non-collaborative way, preferring to broadcast information about themselves rather than interact with voters (Larsson & Kalsnes, 2014; Lawless, 2012; Mercier, 2013; Vergeer, Hermans, & Cunha, 2013), though other papers suggest that this is evolving, too (Ausserhofer & Maireder, 2013; Grant, Moon, & Busby Grant, 2010; Jackson & Lilleker, 2009). This volume will look more closely at some of the reasons why politicians might choose *not* to exploit the 'interactive possibilities' of online media and SNS to their 'full potential' in terms of entering into discussions with voters. Such behaviour can possibly be explained by several factors, including lack of time and resources, a desire to avoid having to address publicly visible hostile or aggressive discourse while striving to promote a positive image. Another possible reason suggested here is politicians' particular logics of social media use and the way they fit into their broader political activities. For many politicians, SNS have become a useful tool in order to remain "connected" and visible in the public sphere even when far from the television cameras. Functionalities such as direct messaging on Facebook or Twitter may typically provide a discreet communication channel to journalists or colleagues from one's own or other parties, while tweets can be a useful way to get information out from behind closed doors in real time (Frame & Brachotte, 2015), or to illustrate one's actions with photos. Often, politicians active on SNS tend to use them more for interactions in the political and media spheres (exchanges with other politicians or journalists, relaying or providing information for networks of activists) rather than for direct interactions with voters.

Much scientific literature also remains very cautious about the reality of "voter empowerment", while the recent book by Scullion, Gerodimos, Jackson and Lilleker (2013) provides a series of interesting insights into the complexity of power-sharing between politicians, the media and citizens, in the digital age. This question of empowerment is also frequently cited in connection with contemporary social movements or political protests, for example during the "Arab Spring", the Spanish "15-M" (or "Indignados") or the American "Occupy Wall Street" movement (though see Fuchs [ed., 2014] for a critical overview). Indeed, although the role of ICTs in these movements should not be overstated, the technological dimension certainly plays an important role in many cases, in providing a widely accessible transnational communications network that protesters can use to publicise and coordinate their political actions. In this context, Bennett and Segerberg also talk of "connective networks" (2012) in which personal capital can lead individuals to engage in political action. The authors argue that individuals are more likely to get involved in a particular action through information or calls to action which are spread on SNS, via apparently disinterested "friendship" networks, than through official communication channels or contact with unknown activists.

However, this volume is concerned not so much with protest movements or forms of alternative democracy (Dahlgren, 2013) as with **day-to-day political participation** in the age of digital media. It is not directly concerned, either, with questions such as whether or not slacktivism constitutes "meaningful" participation and whether or not it leads to a reduction of offline or overall participation (Christensen, 2011). While it necessarily touches upon the slacktivist debate, this book's central focus consists in trying to characterise and understand the logics behind different contemporary forms of what we understand as citizen participation and the way that politicians engage (or not) with this. How and to what extent do ordinary people, civic groups and politicians make use of digital tools to participate in political actions, either during or outside electoral periods, and how they **make sense of these practices** in the light of various frames of reference, both online and offline, and in various countries?

The definition of "political participation" adopted here is very broad, and covers all actions destined to support or further, directly or indirectly, the interests of a particular group or political formation in the public sphere.

4 Alex Frame

This includes such activities as overt political campaigning, signing petitions, publicly expressing views on different issues of public interest, lobbying public figures, relaying others' political comments, "liking" or "following" online a particular figure or cause, etc. The central line of argumentation in this volume is that the development of online digital media has altered the social context of everyday political participation in Western democracies and beyond, but that the digital/online component of participation can best be understood in relation to pre-existing or contemporary offline practices. New technical possibilities may trigger new forms of political action (viral tweets, flash mobs, political selfies, blogs, etc.), which in turn take on particular functions within the existing system of political participation or political communication. We believe that actors make sense of these new forms by referring both to their existing offline norms and models of political action and, increasingly, to other norms of online activity, from outside the political sphere. Indeed, if offline models commonly remained the dominant frame of reference guiding the way new media were used in the early days of the Internet (Singer, 2005), this is arguably less the case with several of the forms of citizen participation described in this book, marked by a many-to-many logic of online communication. Rather than simply opposing "pre-Internet" and "post-Internet" phases, or even "Web 1.0" and "Web 2.0" eras of political participation, we need to think about evolutions in practices, norms and representations, both online and offline, as ongoing. Mediatized forms of participation are continually evolving and this leads us to consider how particular forms of online participation and their functions might be interpreted in relation to both offline political participatory practices and other contemporary forms of online communication, whether political or not.

In this volume, scholars from several countries examine the ways in which ordinary citizens engage with politics through online tools on an everyday basis, either during election campaigns or outside these periods. Based on their observations, they bring empirical evidence to provide insights into the dominant logics and uses which seem to characterise online political activity by voters and citizens, today. Other contributions look at how digital media are used by various interest groups within society to advance their own particular political agendas, or at the ways politicians try (or not) to cope with, react to and engage with voters online, in several different countries.

A central question addressed by the contributions is the extent to which politicians, the electorate, or civic society at large might be seen as the dominant driving force behind online participatory practices. On a very general level, based on the power balance and hierarchical nature of political communication in most countries, it would appear that the public has more to gain by engaging with the politicians – or with one another in the presence, or absence, of their elected representatives – than the politicians themselves have to open up their communication or develop a more interactive style. Yet if debates are indeed taking place online, then it may also be in the interests of politicians to show they are present and participate in them, or even that they can be the instigators of these exchanges. Some politicians may claim to embrace the transparency and disintermediated real-time nature of online participation, yet to what degree can this be taken seriously and what forms of interaction can be observed? What factors might contribute to dissuade politicians from exchanging with citizens online? How do politicians employ social media as political communication tools, and to what extent does their perspective differ to that of voters and civic groups? Citizens may welcome the public forum provided by SNS, allowing them to exchange and express their political views, and yet are politicians – or even other citizens – actually listening? Does this 'armchair activism' have any more impact than when voters simply aired their views out loud, in front of their television sets? And do new media provide civic groups with more efficient channels to drum up support and have their voices heard, or are they lost in the collective clamour?

By addressing these and other questions, the different chapters in this volume all seek to characterise the ways in which different modes and forms of online political participation develop in the context of pre-existing systems of social action and political activity. In doing so, they highlight various tensions between existing norms of political communication and norms of social media communication, in different national contexts. These tensions often crystallise around such aspects as: temporality (instantaneity, brevity, real time); relationships (reciprocity, lack of hierarchy and symbolic and technical barriers, anonymity, private vs. personal vs. public); disintermediation (proximity, transparency, openness, ubiquity); sensationalism (polemics, controversy, viral communications) and humour (satire, take-offs, fakes). While many of these elements could already be associated with pre-Internet mediatisation of political communication (Kepplinger, 2002; Strömbäck, 2008), the papers presented here help us to understand the ways in which these new forms are (re)interpreted by different actors in the light of differing contexts and their particular frames of reference.

The first part of the book, "Participation and political communication: the perspective of politicians and parties", analyses the ways in which politicians themselves use online platforms for their everyday political activity. Although many politicians do interact online, they do not often seek primarily to do so with (participating) voters. The papers in this section will contend that what is sometimes denounced by scholars as a lack of maturity in social media usage, or a lack of interest in two-way communication with voters, from the politicians' side, can in fact be explained by the different forms and logics of online activity which have developed within the political arena, in relation with SNS.

Taking the example of Israeli Knesset Members, Sharon Haleva-Amir, in Chapter 1, questions the degree to which they seek to regularly interact with voters through Facebook, while identifying prevalent political usage patterns and associating each of them with a matching function in terms of

6 *Alex Frame*

political communication. Findings suggest that members of the Knesset are more likely to use Facebook for self-promotion or to exchange with existing acquaintances rather than as a platform to reinvigorate relationships between representatives and the public.

Chapters 2, 3, and 4 focus on the use of Twitter by politicians. Possibly the most "political" social media tool, in terms of its relative popularity among politicians in many countries around the world, the microblogging service can be seen to have evolved to fulfil certain key political communication functions, linked to its specific technical characteristics (Frame & Brachotte, 2015; Thimm et al. 2014). Guido Di Fraia and Maria Carlotta Missaglia (Chapter 2) consider the uses of Twitter by politicians during the 2013 National Elections in Italy, while Mario Anastasiadis, Jessica Einspänner-Pflock and Caja Thimm (Chapter 3) study politicians' interactions in ad hoc mini-publics on Twitter during the National Election campaign in Germany in the same year. In both cases, the authors set out to examine to what extent existing uses of the microblogging tool appear to be evolving as it becomes more central for political communication in each country, looking to qualify more precisely politicians' practices and relations with other users on the platform. While the Italian chapter highlights the place of Twitter as a communication tool alongside other media channels, often used for self-promotion or for direct communication with media representatives, the German study looks more closely at the media-specific operators (hashtags, @ signs, retweets, hyperlinks) and the role they play in structuring exchanges on the platform around particular topics, and the degree to which politicians participate in these exchanges.

Chapter 4 questions the extent to which the microblogging platform can be seen to invigorate democratic dialogue in Spain. By comparing the use of Twitter by the leaders of the most popular parties – PP and PSOE – during election campaigns at various levels in Spain between 2011 and 2014, Elena Cebrián Guinovart Tamara Vázquez Barrio and David Sarias Rodríguez examine the ways in which these Spanish politicians react to requests from electors. They analyse the characteristics and the quality of the interactions observed, and highlight different strategies employed by the politicians when faced with voters' attempts to engage them in debates.

In Chapter 5, Angelia Wagner concentrates on the use or non-use of various forms of ICT by candidates in Canadian municipal elections, interviewing the candidates themselves in order to confront their practices and their declared representations of the potential of ICT in political communication. Because of the largely non-partisan nature of these local elections, the author argues, they provide key insights into the perceived importance of ICT for political engagement independently of party politics and digital policies. Candidates surveyed were asked to discuss what they perceived to be the relative importance of ICT tools, next to traditional forms of political communication. The interviews and observations both tend to show that practices vary depending on a variety of factors, including the size of

Introduction 7

the electorate, type of Internet services available, knowledge about digital media, and differing attitudes towards traditional methods of political communication.

In Chapter 6, Christelle Serée-Chaussinand looks literally at the self-images politicians in different countries project through social media platforms in the form of political "selfies". She discusses the logics and semiotics of this new mode of online visual self-presentation, its place in communication strategies, and links with pre-existing norms and traditions of offline political portraiture. She explores questions of identity and political communication, analysing the impact of the way selfies are composed and the visual perspective adopted, but also the way they circulate in a given political context, and how this may modify, redistribute or reinforce perceptions of existing power relations between political representatives and electors.

The second part of the book, dedicated to "Emerging forms of digital media-based political participation by voters and civic activists", shifts the focus away from politicians, candidates or political movements themselves to voters and civic activists and the forms of participation which they try to develop in the context described in Part One. Darren Lilleker's chapter introduces a series of reflections and questions which seek to define different forms of digital political participation. While pointing out the continuity between the forms and purposes of political participation in both online and offline environments, the chapter suggests that distinctions can often – but not always – be made in terms of the intentionality of such participation, highlighting the need to question users themselves about the motivations and origins of undertaking behaviours, so better understanding the psychology of online political participation.

In Chapter 8, Jaromír Mazák and Václav Štětka do just that, analysing the results of a representative survey of voters during the 2013 Parliamentary Elections in the Czech Republic, looking into both their online and offline political participation. They thus seek to test and challenge the "slacktivism" hypothesis (Morozov, 2009) in this particular electoral context. The results of their analysis suggest that concerns about slacktivism or clicktivism might be exaggerated, as there are indications of a positive relationship between online political expression and more traditional participatory behaviour, including voting in elections.

Arnaud Mercier focuses on non-institutional forms of participation on Twitter, during two French election campaigns: the presidential elections in 2012 and the local elections in 2014. In Chapter 9, he highlights the ways in which the micro-blogging platform is used by citizens creatively and virally, to share, comment on and deform political messages, and to criticise and undermine the legitimacy of individual politicians, in an electronic counterpublic sphere. Focusing on the specifics of "protest participation" in the French context, he makes the case for a "social media turn" in political communication, whereby citizens manipulate, recontextualise and take control of political discourse to use it against the politicians themselves. Chapter 10

8 Alex Frame

further analyses the role of emerging creative practises online, and in particular the collaborative nature of forms of online artistic contestation. Focusing on the tensions between art and culture, Lluís Anyó and Iasa Monique Ribeiro take examples from Spain and Brazil to illustrate and analyse the ways in which artistic contestation too has taken the digital turn and highlight the particular participatory dynamics associated with social media.

In Chapter 11, Caja Thimm seeks to conceptualise the relationship between the mediatization of politics and ongoing societal change, by focusing specifically on the role played by mini-publics (Goodin & Dryzek, 2006) in forming a digital public sphere. The author argues that mini-publics play a key role in structuring political participation online, and that they have become essential to understanding the meta-process of mediatization in the political sphere.

Evgeniya Boklage brings together mini-publics and contestation in Chapter 12, through her study of a Russian LGBT blogging community whose existence constitutes a "counterpublic sphere" in the face of a blanket ban in Russia on positive representation of non-heterosexual identities and relationships in the media and elsewhere. The author underlines the political dimension of everyday citizen news blogging in this particular context, whereby contributors seek to use the relative freedom of the Internet to co-construct an identity and a voice which is practically unheard in mainstream media.

Finally, in Chapter 13, Paula Keaveney focuses on another practice which is not particularly visible either to academics or voters, and yet which constitutes direct political participation on the part of the pressure groups which employ it. She analyses forms of online lobbying in an electoral context, examining the methods used and thinking behind this activity which has long existed in politics, and which has now been adapted to the digital sphere. In doing so, she asks whether online lobbying carries the same weight as its offline counterpart, in terms both of the perceived commitment of lobbyists and the possible impact on the candidates lobbied.

Works Cited

Ausserhofer, Julian, and Maireder, Axel. 2013. "National Politics on Twitter." *Information, Communication & Society* 16 (3): 291–314.

Barber, Benjamin R. 1998. *A Place for Us: How to Make Society Civil and Democracy Strong*. New York: Hill and Wang.

Bennett, W. Lance, and Segerberg, Alexandra. 2012. "The Logic of Connective Action." *Information, Communication & Society* 15 (5): 739–68.

Block, Elena. 2013. "A Culturalist Approach to the Concept of the Mediatization of Politics: The Age of 'Media Hegemony.'" *Communication Theory* 23 (3): 259–78.

Brants, Kees, and Neijens, Peter. 1998. "The Infotainment of Politics." *Political Communication* 15 (2): 149–64.

Christensen, Henrik Serup. 2011. "Political Activities on the Internet: Slacktivism or Political Participation by Other Means?" *First Monday* 16 (2). Retrieved from

Introduction 9

http://firstmonday.org/ojs/index.php/fm/article/view/3336. Accessed May 20, 2015.

Couldry, Nick. 2015. "The Myth of 'us': Digital Networks, Political Change and the Production of Collectivity". *Information, Communication & Society* 18 (6): 608–26.

Couldry, Nick, and Hepp, Andreas. 2013. "Conceptualizing Mediatization: Contexts, Traditions, Arguments". *Communication Theory* 23 (3): 191–202.

Dahlgren, Peter. 2005. "The Internet, Public Spheres, and Political Communication: Dispersion and Deliberation". *Political Communication* 22 (2): 147–62.

Dahlgren, Peter. 2013. *The Political Web: Media, Participation and Alternative Democracy*. Houndmills, Basingstoke, Hampshire; New York: Palgrave Macmillan.

Dimitrova, Daniela V., Shehata, Adam, Strömbäck, Jesper, and Nord, Lars W. 2014. "The Effects of Digital Media on Political Knowledge and Participation in Election Campaigns Evidence From Panel Data". *Communication Research* 41 (1): 95–118.

Effing, Robin, van Hillegersberg, Jos, and Huibers, Theo. 2011. "Social Media and Political Participation: Are Facebook, Twitter and YouTube Democratizing Our Political Systems"? In *Electronic Participation*, edited by Efthimios Tambouris, Ann Macintosh, and Hans de Bruijn, 25–35. Lecture Notes in Computer Science 6847. Berlin: Springer.

Frame, Alex, and Brachotte, Gilles. 2015. "Le Tweet Stratégique: Use of Twitter as a PR Tool by French Politicians". *Public Relations Review*, Digital Publics, 41 (2): 278–87.

Fuchs, Christian, ed. 2014. *Social Media, Politics and the State: Protests, Revolutions, Riots, Crime and Policing in the Age of Facebook, Twitter and YouTube*. London: Routledge.

Grant, Will J., Moon, Brenda, and Busby Grant, Janie. 2010. "Digital Dialogue? Australian Politicians' Use of the Social Network Tool Twitter". *Australian Journal of Political Science* 45 (4): 579–604.

Gurevitch, Michael, Coleman, Stephen, and Blumler, Jay G. 2009. "Political Communication – Old and New Media Relationships". *The ANNALS of the American Academy of Political and Social Science* 625 (1): 164–81.

Jackson, Nigel A., and Lilleker, Darren G. 2009. "Building an Architecture of Participation? Political Parties and Web 2.0 in Britain". *Journal of Information Technology & Politics* 6 (3-4): 232–50.

Jensen, Jakob Linaa. 2013. "Political Participation Online: The Replacement and the Mobilisation Hypotheses Revisited". *Scandinavian Political Studies* 36 (4): 347–64.

Kepplinger, Hans Mathias. 2002. "Mediatization of Politics: Theory and Data". *Journal of Communication* 52 (4): 972–86.

Krotz, Friedrich. 2007. "The Meta-Process of 'mediatization' as a Conceptual Frame". *Global Media and Communication* 3 (3): 256–60.

Krotz, Friedrich. 2011. "Media as Societal Structure and a Situational Frame for Communicative Action: A Definition of Concepts". In *Critical Perspectives on the European Mediasphere*, edited by Ilija Tomanić Trivundža, Nico Carpentier, Hannu Nieminen, Pille Pruulmann-Vengerfeldt, Richard Kilborn, Ebba Sundin, and Tobias Olsson, 27–40. Ljubljana: Hermina Krajnc.

Larsson, Anders O., and Kalsnes, Bente. 2014. "'Of Course We Are on Facebook': Use and Non-Use of Social Media among Swedish and Norwegian Politicians". *European Journal of Communication* 29 (6): 663–67.

Lawless, Jennifer L. 2012. "Twitter and Facebook: New Ways for Members of Congress to Send the Same Old Messages"? In *iPolitics: Citizens, Elections, and Governing in the New Media Era*, edited by Richard Logan Fox and Jennifer Ramos, 206–32. New York: Cambridge University Press.

Lévy, Pierre. 1998. *Qu'est-Ce Que Le Virtuel?* Paris: La Découverte.

Linders, Dennis. 2012. "From E-Government to We-Government: Defining a Typology for Citizen Coproduction in the Age of Social Media". *Government Information Quarterly*, Social Media in Government - Selections from the 12th Annual International Conference on Digital Government Research (dg.o2011), 29 (4): 446–54.

Lits, Marc. 2009. "La médiatisation du politique ou le passage d'un espace public délibératif à un espace public symbolique narratif". *A contrario* 12 (2): 85–100.

Mercier, Arnaud. 2013. "Avènement Du Twiléspectateur et Hashtags Contestataires". In *Présidentielle 2012 : Une Communication Politique Bien Singulière*, edited by Philippe J. Maarek, 165–200. Paris: L'Harmattan.

Morozov, Evgeny. 2009. "The Brave New World of Slacktivism". *Foreign Policy Blogs*. May 19. http://neteffect.foreignpolicy.com/posts/2009/05/19/the_brave_new_world_of_slacktivism. Accessed May 20, 2015.

Nimmo, Dan D., and Combs, James E. 1983. *Mediated Political Realities*. Longman.

Norris, Pippa. 2001. *Digital Divide: Civic Engagement, Information Poverty, and the Internet Worldwide*. Cambridge University Press.

Rheingold, Howard. 1993. *The Virtual Community: Homesteading on the Electronic Frontier*. Reading, Mass: Perseus Books.

Scullion, Richard, Gerodimos, Roman, Jackson, Daniel, and Lilleker, Darren. 2013. *The Media, Political Participation and Empowerment*. New York: Routledge.

Shulman, Stuart W. 2009. "The Case Against Mass E-Mails: Perverse Incentives and Low Quality Public Participation in U.S. Federal Rulemaking". *Policy & Internet* 1 (1): 23–53.

Singer, Jane B. 2005. "The Political J-Blogger 'Normalizing' a New Media Form to Fit Old Norms and Practices". *Journalism* 6 (2): 173–98.

Strömbäck, Jesper. 2008. "Four Phases of Mediatization: An Analysis of the Mediatization of Politics". *The International Journal of Press/Politics* 13 (3): 228–46.

Thimm, Caja, Dang-Anh, Mark, and Einspänner, Jessica. 2014. "Mediatized Politics – Structures and Strategies of Discursive Participation and Online Deliberation on Twitter". In *Mediatized Worlds: Culture and Society in a Media Age*, edited by Andreas Hepp and Friedrich Krotz. London: Palgrave Macmillan.

Vergeer, Maurice, Hermans, Liesbeth, and Cunha, Carlos. 2013. "Web Campaigning in the 2009 European Parliament Elections: A Cross-National Comparative Analysis". *New Media & Society*, 15 (1), 128–148.

Yates, Simeon, Kirby, John, and Lockley, Eleanor. 2014. *Supporting digital engagement: final report to Sheffield City Council*. Project Report. Institute of Cultural Capital, Liverpool. (Unpublished).

Part I

Participation and Political Communication

The Perspectives of Politicians and Parties

1 Talking to Themselves

A Classification of *Facebook*'s Political Usages and Representatives' Roles Among Israeli Members of Knesset

Sharon Haleva-Amir

Introduction

Social media platforms such as Facebook, Twitter and YouTube are currently the main online platforms parliamentarians use to communicate and connect with their constituents, alongside traditional media and Party events. The mainstream view on politicians' usage of the Internet and mainly of social media is that the widespread use of the Internet for networking has the potential of fostering democracy and enhancing the connections between representatives and constituents; but as politicians are not using it to its full potential, they fail to induce engagement, but instead replicate their offline communication practices into the virtual sphere (e.g., Stromer-Galley 2000; Ward and Lusoli 2005; Jackson and Lilleker 2009b; Jackson and Lilleker 2011; Vergeer, Hermans and Sams 2013; Strandberg 2013; Stromer-Galley 2014).

This chapter is based on a study of the use of online platforms by Members of Knesset (Israeli parliament, henceforth MKs) for political communication purposes. The empirical research lasted two years (July 2009 – July 2011) using a combination of in-depth interviews, partly structured questionnaires and web content analysis. *Inter alia* I studied MKs activity on Facebook in order to identify activity formats and to characterize prevalent usages. Based on the assumption that representatives' parliamentary roles as well as their political communication forms are changing due to social media, establishing a typology of political usages of Facebook will enable us to identify the way MKs currently occupy their roles as representatives and whether they use their online platform to stimulate citizens engagement and increase participation. To the author's knowledge, this is the first study of its kind conducted in Israel. In addition to its novelty, the typology created in this study may subsequently prove applicable to parliamentarians worldwide.

1.1 Politicians and Social Media

The Internet has created an opportunity to restructure communication between parliament members (MPs) and their constituents (Zittel 2003) as web technologies change the very nature of communication (Castells 2000).

14 Sharon Haleva-Amir

Nevertheless, it seems that MPs continued to focus largely on promoting themselves by reporting their in-house efforts (Williamson 2009a). Furthermore, politicians in different countries use the web to produce electorally advantageous impressions (Stanyer 2008), rather than for engaging with the public (Jackson 2003; Vegyte, Malinauskiene and Petrauskas 2008). For those who expected that the web's unique interactive characteristics would reduce the gap between politicians and citizens, this approach was rather disappointing (Vergeer, Hermans and Sams 2013). But then came social media and the Web 2.0 era.

While Web 1.0 period was characterized by websites predominantly providing static content and delivering one-sided, top-down messages, Web 2.0 is characterized by social platforms which enable users to share content items and converse more easily. Some commentators (e.g., Lilleker and Jackson 2009; Vergeer, Hermans and Sams 2013; Tenscher 2013; Klinger 2013) hoped that this shift of web generations would fundamentally change the way MPs communicate with their constituents, as conversations facilitated by social platforms were more horizontal than vertical.

"By inhabiting the same online spaces as their constituents on a day-to-day basis, MPs will interact with them in much more normal conditions – when the MP is not the privileged voice of authority, but merely one member of a conversation among many. In doing so, perhaps they will get a much more realistic idea of what their constituents actually think" (Colvile 2008; Virkar 2007). This hope has not really been fulfilled as research shows that politicians' use of Web 2.0 applications resembles their use of websites during the web 1.0 phase; they still focus on delivering messages and promoting themselves and not on engaging with their constituents (Vergeer, Hermans and Sams 2013; Tunez and Sixto 2011; Jackson and Lilleker 2009a).

Nevertheless, use of social media among parliamentarians is constantly on the rise. In 2009 The Hansard Society had already identified British MPs as increasingly adopting social media, including Facebook (Williamson 2009b). This is also the case for New Zealand MPs (Busby and Bellamy 2011), United States congressmen and senators (Facebook 2010) Israeli MKs (Haleva-Amir 2014) and legislators in other western democracies.

1.2 Representatives' Roles and Correlating Web Tools

Literature has recognized five main roles that representatives play: delegate, trustee, partisan, constituency service and promotion of self (Lilleker and Jackson 2009; Jackson and Lilleker 2009a). It should be mentioned that these roles are not exclusive: most representatives switch roles according to the circumstances. Each of these roles can be supported by specific digital usages.

1 The notion of delegation was developed during the sixteenth and seventeenth centuries by philosophers such as John Locke. A delegate

representative receives a mandate from his voters. He serves as an agent of particular interests, and his duty is to act in accord with these interests and not on his own discretion. To enable this, an MP acting as a delegate should identify the views of his constituents and act accordingly. Identifying constituents' views can be facilitated by using online forums, polls and questionnaires as well as emails (Lilleker and Jackson 2009, 3).

2 The model of the representative as a trustee was classically articulated by Edmund Burke in the eighteenth century. Burke opposed the idea of 'mandate' or 'instructions' from the parliamentarian's constituents dictating how he should vote or what line he should take on any particular issue. Citing Burke, "Your representative owes you, not his industry only, but his judgment; and he betrays, instead of serving you, if he sacrifices it to your opinion" (Arblaster 2002). In other words, a trustee-model MP may hear his constituents' opinions and take them into consideration, but his decision must be independent and based on his best judgment. Referring to web tools, some believe the web burdens the trustee in making independent decisions as he is exposed to his constituents' opinions over the internet (Ferber, Foltz and Pugliese 2007), while others believe the trustee can use the internet to share and promote his views (Lilleker and Jackson 2009, 3).

3 The partisan role, presented in the nineteenth century, places the party to which the parliamentarian belongs as his main priority. Parties control the selection processes and are, therefore, responsible for the political candidates' careers; MPs find themselves obliged to vote according to party stands on different issues. Lilleker and Jackson argue that a partisan MP would use Web 2.0 applications while promoting his "party's image, policy and activity ... whilst also eschewing any move towards acting as a delegate, as voting decisions are more likely to be dominated by the party line" (Lilleker and Jackson 2009, 4).

4 The fourth model of constituency service prioritizes constituents. It is perceived by British MPs as their most important role (Power 1998; Rush 2001). Within this role, MPs try to communicate with constituents and address both individual and constituency problems. Lilleker and Jackson (2009) assert that Web 2.0 platforms usage can also enhance a sense of community and pertinence.

5 Political scientists have recently added a new role: promotion of self (Lilleker and Jackson 2009; Vergeer, Hermans and Sams 2013). This role exists only in the web (it is also referred to as e-Representation) and accompanies one of the other four roles mentioned above. This role corresponds with the current trend of personal politics as well as permanent campaigning (Blumenthal 1982; Rahat and Sheafer 2007; Stanyer 2008; Williamson 2009a); and it aims at presenting the MP in the most positive manner. Web 2.0 platforms such as social networks enable MPs to present themselves as human beings and not as placards,

16 Sharon Haleva-Amir

allowing them to share family photos, personal experiences, preferences of music and TV shows and so on. This personal and informal presentation of self can draw constituents nearer while decreasing estrangement and may result in increased political involvement on the part of the citizenry.

1.3 Politicians and Facebook – the Israeli Angle[1]

MKs begun using social networks for political purposes way back in 2007. MKs' presence on SNS allowed them to become acquainted with youngsters who are usually detached from politics, do not consume news through traditional media outlets, and spend many hours in online social activities (Lenhart et al. 2007). A recent LSE study discussing possible ways of increasing and extending youth participation suggests that youth are in favor of developing Facebook debates with political candidates as a possible way to increase youth participation in democratic life. The study details youth modes of participation over social platforms and mainly on Facebook. These include receiving political information, signing petitions and commenting on political issues (LSE Enterprise 2013).

In an editorial, the *Yalla Kadima* website (the portal for Kadima Party supporters and field activists) highlighted the advantages of joining social networks.

> To all other Kadima MKs who are still having doubts. ... Joining a social network is better than [my emphasis – SHA] establishing a website ... the social network enables the elected representative to be in an active and exciting Internet core ... In an SNS such as Facebook, elected representatives need not make an effort to bring users nearer. Facebook's accessibility is high and its usage patterns are homogeneous. Moreover, it has a unique, uniting language which enables everybody to speak to one another eye to eye.
>
> (Yalla Kadima 2007)

Many MKs adopted this recommendation and joined Facebook, creating both personal profiles (the application for private people, designed to create a network of friendships) and politician pages (the application specifically designed for politicians and used to create a network of supporters). The number of MKs active on Facebook in January 2009 was more than twice the number of MKs who had an active website. Sixty-one MKs (51 per cent) had a personal profile, a politician page or both. As of September 2010, political activity on Facebook had expanded further: 84 MKs (70 per cent) had a Facebook account.[2] Many MKs also appeared on a local Israeli SNS – The Marker Café. One of the crucial factors that contributed to this proliferation of online activity was the general instruction to members of the Knesset by its general manager, Dan Landau, in March 2010, to establish a formal profile on Facebook. This instruction's objective was to encourage the creation of direct and straightforward channels of communication between representatives and citizens (Channel 2 News 2010).

Some MKs harnessed the advantages of social networking to their benefit and used the public sphere to trumpet their opinions – by publishing posts and referring to other content items in their own websites, by prompting discussions; by responding to questions and comments, by having long, direct dialogues with users, and by motivating young people to become socially engaged and politically active. However, most MKs used their profile wall (designed for public messaging) as an online billboard. As of July 2011 (endpoint of this study), 86 per cent of MKs (103 out of 120) had a personal profile, political page or both on Facebook (Haleva-Amir 2014).

1.4 Methodology

As a qualitative researcher following the grounded theory paradigm, I have stayed in the field during research period (July 2009 – July 2011) and tracked MKs' political activity over the web: mainly their websites, blogs and social network sites. As part of the research I compiled a list of all (as opposed to a sample of) profiles and political pages of the 103 MKs active on Facebook (which constitute 86 per cent of Knesset Members). Using Facebook Interests Lists, I created a list of "18th Knesset MKs". Choosing this list on Facebook's sidebar facilitated a designated newsfeed compiled only of recent posts and activities from people included on the list.[3] I did not store the data but rather kept constant track of this feed. This had enabled me to identify usage formats as well as thematic categories and develop a typology of political usages of Facebook. While doing so, I have collected specific examples of each of the categories.

The analysis was based on web content analysis broadly interpreted, though classification and theme analysis can also be seen as traditional web – content analysis. Susan Herring defines web-content analysis as "the analysis of web content, broadly construed, using various (traditional and non-traditional) techniques" (Herring 2010, 235). A qualitative researcher often has to create his own scheme based on the specific 'field' studied. Adopting the grounded theory approach to categorisation while staying in the "field", I had developed the scheme and classified the posts. The categories mostly exclude one another and do not overlap.

1.5 Findings

Activity Formats

Findings show that MKs preferred the Personal Use format (personal profile) to the Designated Political Page Pattern (formal page).

Eighty-two out of 103 (80 per cent) MKs who had a Facebook account operated a personal profile; 61 per cent (63 MKs) operated some kind of

18 Sharon Haleva-Amir

formal page: politician page (63 MKs), public figure page (6 MKs), community page (4 MKs), government official page (2MKs) and even organization page (2MKs). These formats do not exclude one another; they can accumulate if MKs combine personal profiles and formal pages. About 47 per cent of MKs had operated a few personal profiles / formal pages according to their own preferences and needs, in various combinations.

Consequently, most MKs' personal profiles reached the top limit of 5,000 friends; had they used a formal page they would have had no maximal limitation. Furthermore, using personal profiles MKs "collect friends" while using the formal pages format there is no need for the mutual process of users sending friend requests and MKs approving them. One can join a page simply by clicking the Like button to become a follower.

Facebook's Political Usages Typology

Prevalent Facebook political usages by MKs were classified into seven categories:

1 Status updates that state political positions. MKs often use their walls to describe and detail their positions on political issues. Sometimes statuses are accompanied by a link to an online article on the issue or to a longer post they wrote using Facebook Notes.
2 Referring to current matters. MKs refer to matters of the day in a global or local context (the killing of Osama Bin-Laden, the royal wedding of Prince William, Duke of Cambridge, and Kate Middleton, Maccabi Tel Aviv basketball team advancing to the Euroleague Final Four in Barcelona, and so on).
3 Media references. MKs post on their wall links to journalistic items concerning them, refer their supporters to upcoming television and radio interviews and upload links to audio and video files of prior media appearances.
4 Reports of their in-parliament and out-of-parliament activities. MKs often update their followers on their ongoing activities in parliamentary committees, during Knesset plenum sittings, local tours, formal delegations and so on.
5 Raising issues to create discussion and encourage engagement. Only a few MKs use the platform to induce discussion of current matters to engage people in political and social involvement as well as to sense the public opinion in a direct manner. Generally, even those MKs who do initiate topics do not take an active part in the subsequent discussions.
6 Photo albums. MKs often upload photos from public, formal and informal events they attend as part of their duties. Mostly these pictures are arranged in separate albums and accompanied by captions. It is important to note that some of the photos are uploaded and tagged by different users (other MKs or non-politicians).[4]

7 Personal photos and notes, personal and holiday greetings. This kind of activity is the most intimate as it enables a more direct connection. The personal note is expressed using personal photos (e.g., with family and friends), personal status updates, greetings and comments to specific friends written on their walls as well as holiday greetings. By doing so, politicians may seem to create a bond that constituents feel is stronger.

It should be noted that the relative frequency of each category is not steady but rather varies under the circumstances. For example, before the holidays most of the posts will include greetings and bear a festive nature; while a major Israeli political event (such as PM Benjamin Netanyahu's speech in front of the UN's general assembly) will affect most MKs who will refer to it in their posts and so on.

1.6 Discussion and Conclusions

Multiple profiles and pages might cause confusion if some of the pages or profiles visible on Facebook are not active and others do not offer matching and consistent feeds. This situation could mislead users who follow the channel, which is not active. In addition, users' approaches may not be handled, as this is not the main Facebook page and the MK is not aware of these appeals at all. While staying in the field I noticed only a few instances in which an alerted user or a parliamentary assistant had addressed the appellant and forwarded him to the appropriate page; while in most cases the requests will be left neglected and unattended. These unaddressed users' applications on MKs' Facebook walls might harm their image as they are likely to be perceived as unresponsive and cause a decrease in trust and political participation, instead of strengthening the ties between politicians and citizens.

Moving to the issue of representative roles, three main roles were identified to which the above mentioned categories can be assigned: (1) the trustee role; (2) the partisan role and (3) the presentation of self e-role. The most dominant role of these three is the presentation of self role as it can be assigned to five categories while the trustee role and the partisan role can be each assigned only to one of the seven categories as elaborated below:[5]

1 The trustee role can be assigned to the category of parliamentary and off-parliamentary activities reports. These reports enable MKs to acknowledge their constituents by showing their ongoing activities and thus displaying accountability.
2 The partisan role can be assigned to the category of stating political positions through statuses updates. Stating their political and social stands tie MKs to their political home, i.e., their parties.
3 The representative as a political persona (promotion of self) can be assigned to the next categories: references to current events, media

references, raising issues to create discussion and photo albums and personal activity. These usages enable MKs to represent themselves optimally while creating a positive public image. An important reservation regarding the use of the Facebook platform to raise discussion issues is that this activity supports the appearance of public availability though it is only a strategic move which has nothing to do with a real intent to engage the public.

The discussions initiated by MKs who do not continue to actively engage strongly illustrate how communication is still mainly one-sided. The ongoing discussion is not really a dialogue between citizens and politicians but rather between citizens themselves.

While conducting my study in the field I found that MKs on Facebook tend to interact more with people and party members they know from "the real world" than with constituents they have not yet met in person. This finding was clearly demonstrated through the last-mentioned category of personal activity, as from time to time MKs write to specific people on their walls or in a thread and call them by their nicknames. They use a familiar tone as if they were among old friends. The reason for this is that as mentioned above, the usage of personal profiles involves an approval of friend requests by the account administrator while formal pages do not require the approval of page administrator in order to follow its activity. Therefore, personal profiles will be first and foremost populated by users which the politician knows in person. As a result, this habit is more prevalent on personal profiles, which exhibit a more familiar nature, than on formal pages.

The research findings of Vergeer, Hermans and Sams (2013) suggest that the more people follow the politician the less likely there is to be reciprocal following. As politicians become more popular on social media, their social media accounts become less social. This goes to show that politician–constituent reciprocity is probably facilitated only at a small scale and, of course, is easier when the politician happens to know his 'friends'/'followers'. As long as real-life relationships are being replicated on the web, the ideal of enhancing representative–constituent ties will not be fulfilled.

Research findings suggest that the main representative role among MKs is the promotion of self. The significance of this is that MKs use Facebook as a mere media channel: a channel through which they can present themselves and promote their agendas while neglecting to communicate with their constituents.

An interesting study suggests that since political parties and their representatives are increasingly using more interactive features online and making their communication more individual, political involvement among citizens could increase, which would foster a stronger democracy (Kruikemeier et al. 2013). On the other hand, politicians' networks were characterized as predominantly aimed at informing citizens and not at being informed by citizens or at communication (Vergeer, Hermans and Sams 2013, 21). My research findings reflect both trends: the trend of increasing individualized usage of social web tools as well as the trend of 'information rather than communication' activity format.

These findings imply, in reference to the Lilleker and Jackson study (2009), that despite the notion that social media will enable a closer bond between politicians and citizens and will have a great impact on representation and participation by encouraging citizens to become politically involved, it seems that Israeli parliamentarians still use social media the old fashioned way, mainly as a one-sided hierarchical platform. Therefore, notwithstanding the high rate of presence of Israeli MKs on Facebook, politics is still as usual, at least where Israel is concerned. As a result, the broadened unmediated communication between constituents and elected representatives via Web 2.0's social media has not been demonstrated yet.

The Current State of Affairs

Three and a half years have gone by since the endpoint of this study: almost an eternity in Internet terms. A lot has changed, and yet nothing has changed in the realm of Israeli personal politics on Facebook. On the one hand, political activity formats have gone through a shift and nowadays the main activity format is the political page rather than the personal profile. On the other hand, politicians' attention to users and approachability has not grown.

As of December 2014, 108 MKs (90 per cent) were active on Facebook. Only twenty-nine MKs (27 per cent) operate a personal page while eighty MKs (74 per cent) operate politician pages and eleven (10 per cent) public figure pages. Twenty-two of them (20 per cent) operate more than one page/profile. This shift indicates a move toward professionalized web activity. This trend of growing levels of professionalization is compatible with the literature (Gibson and Rommele 2009; Lisi 2013; Stromback 2007; Vergeer, Hermans and Sams 2013; Tenscher 2013; Larsson 2015).

The mere presence of MKs on Facebook generates political participation as it induces people to follow them, express their views, share political statuses and conduct discussions on political issues with other users. If we take the number of likes for MKs' political pages as some kind of indication of political participation then the figures look promising. For example, here are the numbers of likes for each of the six largest parties in the twentieth Knesset leaders, as of April 4, 2015: PM Benjamin Netanyahu (Likud) – 1,287,915 likes; Isaac Herzog (Labor party) – 95,648 likes; Ayman Odeh (Arabic Joint List) – 19,063 likes; Yair Lapid (Yesh Atid) – 378,773 likes; Moshe Kahalon (Kulanu) – 92,284 likes; Naftali Bennett (HaBayit HaYehudi) – 54,524 likes. As encouraging as it may seem, as this perspective was not studied yet, it calls for a future research.

While this study's findings have demonstrated the politicians' personalized, informal attitude, possibly aimed at bridging the gap between them and their public, the switch to a designated political pages activity format illustrates growing maturity in political web activity. Politicians have now been using web tools long enough to assimilate their nature; they seem to consider web activity to be a routine political chore and therefore turn to pages tailored for politicians and outsource their administration to professionals. This shift has not been accompanied by a higher degree of availability to the public: the politicians' personal attitude is less apparent and posts are much more informative and remote. In my opinion, this shift is just further proof of the fact that, for the vast majority of politicians, Facebook is first and foremost a political marketing tool.

Notes

1. This paragraph is based on my previous research, elaborated in Haleva-Amir, Sharon. 2013. "MKs Usage of Personal Internet Tools, 2009: On the Verge of a New Decade", *World Political Science Review*, 9(1): 219–261.
2. Benjamin Netanyahu's *Facebook* profile was removed from the web only to be replaced by a formal *'The Prime Minister of Israel'* account, which is equivalent to the formal *'White House'* profile. Ironically, it weakened his social web presence, because this profile does not try to interest or engage the users. It just delivers information. Ehud Keinan, "The Prime Minister is Joining YouTube and Twitter", *Ynet*, August 30, 2010, Internet section (Heb), http://www.ynet.co.il/articles/1,7340,L-3946278,00.html; Gal Mor, "Office of the Prime Minister of Israel on Facebook: What Netanyahu Does Not Tell Us", *Holes in the Net*, August 31, 2010 (Heb).
3. Facebook Help Center: Interests Lists https://www.facebook.com/help/440058336033758/.
4. Obiter dictum – An issue which requires consideration involves commercial tagging when one or more of the MK 'friends' tag him in photos for commercial purposes.
5. It is important to note that most usage categories can be assigned to several representative roles. The classification made is the most suitable in my own view but one may disagree with it.

Works Cited

Arblaster, Anthony. 2002. *Democracy*. Buckingham: Open University Press.
Blumenthal, Sidney. 1982. *The Permanent Campaigning*. New York: Simon & Schuster.
Busby, Christine and Bellamy, Paul. 2011. "New Zealand Parliamentarians and Online Social Media ." *New Zealand Parliament's Parliamentary Library*. Accessed March 22, 2015. http://www.parliament.nz/en-nz/parl-support/research-papers/00PLSocRP11021/new-zealand-parliamentarians-and-online-social-media.
Castells, Manuel. 2000. The Rise of the Network Society: The Information Age: Economy, Society & Culture Vol. I. Cambridge, MA; Oxford, UK: Blackwell Press.
Channel 2 News, "Knesset Members were Instructed to Join Facebook; MK Mozes: 'What is this?'" (Heb), *Globes*, Hi-Tech, Communication and Internet section, March 11, 2010. http://www.globes.co.il/news/article.aspx?did=1000545872&fromMador=594&fromErechMusafHP.

Talking to Themselves 23

Colvile, Robert. 2008. "How MPs can Use the Internet to Become More Relevant", *Conservative Home*. Accessed March 22, 2015. http://www.conservativehome.com/platform/2008/02/robert-colvil-3.html.

Facebook. 2010. "Snapshot: The day after Election Day", *Government and Politics on Facebook*. Accessed March 26, 2015. https://www.facebook.com/note.php?note_id=448930025881.

Ferber, Paul, Foltz, Franz, and Pugliese, Rudy. 2007. "Cyber democracy and Online Politics; A New Model of Interactivity". *Bulletin of Science, Technology & Society*, 27(5): 391–400.

Gibson, Rachel K., and Rommele, Andrea. 2009. "Measuring the Professionalization of Political Campaigning". *Party Politics*, 15(3): 265–293.

Haleva-Amir, Sharon. 2013. "MKs Usage of Personal Internet Tools, 2009: On the Verge of a New Decade". *World Political Science Review*, 9(1): 219–261.

Haleva-Amir, Sharon. 2014. "Personal Web Applications in the service of Knesset Members: Personal Israeli Politics in the Digital Era". (Heb) PhD Diss., University of Haifa.

Herring, Susan C. 2010. "Web Content Analysis: Exploring the Paradigm". In *International Handbook of Internet Research*, edited by Jeremy Hunsinger, Lisbeth Klastrup and Matthew Allen. Heidelberg, London, New York: Springer.

Jackson, Nigel A. 2003. "MPs and Web Technologies: An Untapped Opportunity?" *Journal of Public Affairs*, 3(2): 124–137.

Jackson, Nigel A., and Lilleker, Darren G. 2009a. "MPs and E-representation: Me, MySpace and I". *British Politics* 4: 236–264.

Jackson, Nigel A., and Lilleker, Darren G. 2009b. "Building an Architecture of Participation? Political Parties and Web 2.0 in Britain". *Journal of Information Technology and Politics*, 6(3–4): 232–250.

Jackson, Nigel A., and Lilleker, Darren G. 2011. "Microblogging, Constituency Service and Impression Management: UK MPs and the Use of Twitter". *The Journal of Legislative Studies*, 17(1): 86–105.

Keinan, Ehud. 2010. "The Prime Minister is Joining YouTube and Twitter" (Heb), *Ynet*, Internet section, August 30, 2010. Accessed March 29, 2015., http://www.ynet.co.il/articles/1,7340,L-3946278,00.html.

Klinger, Ulrike. 2013. "Mastering the Art of Social Media: Swiss Parties, the 2011 National Election and Digital Challenges". *Information, Communication & Society*, 16(5): 717–736.

Kruikemeier, Sanne, van Noort, Guda, Vilegenthart, Rens, and de Vreese, Claes H. 2013. "Getting Closer: The Effects of Personalized and Interactive Online Political Communication". *European Journal of Communication*, 28(1): 53–66.

Larsson, Anders Olof. 2015. "The EU Parliament on Twitter – Assessing the Permanent Online Practices of Parliamentarians". *Journal of Information Technology and Politics*, 12(1): 1–18.

Lenhart, Amanda, Madden, Mary, Smith, Aaron, and McGill, Alexandra. 2007. "Teens and Social Media", *Pew Internet & American Life Project*. Accessed March 26, 2015. http://www.pewinternet.org/Reports/2007/Teens-and-Social-Media.aspx.

Lilleker, Darren G., and Jackson, Nigel A. 2009. "Interacting and Representing: Can Web 2.0 Enhance the Roles of an MP?" paper presented at the *ECPR workshop: Parliaments, Parties and Politicians in Cyberspace*. Lisbon, April.

Lisi, Marco. 2013. "The Professionalization of Campaigns in Recent Democracies: The Portuguese Case". *European Journal of Communication*, 28(3): 259–276.

London School of Economics. 2013. *Youth Participation in Democratic Life*. EACEA 2010/03. London: LSE Enterprise. Accessed March 30, 2015. http://www.lse.ac.uk/businessAndConsultancy/LSEEnterprise/pdf/YouthParticipationDemocraticLife.pdf.

Mor, Gal. "Office of the Prime Minister of Israel on Facebook: What Netanyahu Does Not Tell Us" (Heb), *Holes in the Net*, August 31, 2010.

Power, Greg. 1998. Representatives of the People? The Constituency Role of MPs. London: Fabian Society.

Rahat, Gideon, and Sheafer, Tamir. 2007. "The Personalization(s) of Politics: Israel, 1949–2003". *Political Communication*, 24(1): 65–80.

Rush, Michael. 2001. The Role of the Member of Parliament Since 1868: From Gentlemen to Players. Oxford: Oxford University Press.

Stanyer, James. 2008. "Elected Representatives, Online Self Presentation and the Personal Vote: Party, Personality and Web-styles in the United States and United Kingdom". *Information, Communication and Society*, 11(3): 414–432.

Strandberg, Kim. 2013. "A Social Media Revolution or just a Case of History Repeating Itself? The Use of Social Media in the 2011 Finnish Parliamentary Elections". *New Media & Society*, 15(8): 1329–1347.

Stromback, Jesper. 2007. "Political Marketing and Professionalized Campaigning: A Conceptual Analysis". *Journal of Political Marketing*, 6(2–3): 49–67.

Stromer-Galley, Jennifer. 2000. "On-line Interaction and Why Candidates Avoid it". *Journal of Communication*, 50(4): 111–132.

Stromer-Galley, Jennifer. 2014. *Presidential Campaigning in the Internet Age*. New York: Oxford University Press.

Tenscher, Jens. 2013. "First and Second Order Campaigning: Evidence from Germany". *European Journal of Communication*, 28(3): 241–258.

Tunez, Miguel, and Sixto, Jose. 2011. "Social Networks, Politics and Commitment 2.0: Spanish MPs on Facebook". Revista Latina de Comunicacion Social, 66: 210–246. Accessed March 22, 2015. http://www.revistalatinacs.org/11/art/930_Santiago/09_TunezEN.html.

Vegyte, Neringa, Malinauskiene, Egle, and Petrauskas, Rimantas. 2008. "E-Participation in Lithuanian Representative Power". Paper presented at the *6th International Eastern European e-Gov Days: Results and Trends*, Prague, April 23–25.

Vergeer, Maurice, Hermans, Liesbeth, and Sams, Steven. 2013. "Online Social Networks and Micro – Blogging in Political Campaigning: The Exploration of a New Campaign Tool and a New Campaign Style". *Party Politics* 19(3):477–501.

Virkar, Shefali. 2007. "Top Trumps or Trivial Pursuit? Political Engagement in the Age of Web 2.0", Paper presented at the *Eighth Annual Conference of the Association of Internet Researchers* (AOIR8) Vancouver, Canada, October 17–20.

Ward, Stephen, and Lusoli, Wainer. 2005. "'From Weird to Wired': MPs, the Internet and Representative Politics in the UK". *The Journal of Legislative Studies*, 11(1): 57–81.

Williamson, Andy. 2009a. MPs Online: Connecting with Constituents: A Study in to how MPs Use Digital Media to Communicate with their Constituents. London: Hansard Society.

Williamson, Andy. 2009b. *MPs on Facebook*: Digital Papers Series 1. London: Hansard Society.

Yalla Kadima (editorial). 2007. "Even MK Yoel Hasson Has a Facebook Profile". (Heb). *Yalla Kadima*.

Zittel, Thomas. 2003. "Political Representation in the Networked Society: The Americanization of European Systems of Responsible Party Government?" *Journal of Legislative Studies*, 9(3): 32–53.

2 Two Step Flow Twitter Communication in 2013 Italian Political Election

A Missed Opportunity for Citizen Participation

Guido Di Fraia and Maria Carlotta Missaglia

Introduction

In 2013, Italian political communication changed. During the national elections, many politicians adopted or increased their use of social media, focusing particularly on Twitter. Twitter was the main protagonist of the new communication environment (Bentivegna, 2014) and the most used platform by politicians and journalists. In today's society, Twitter has become a fundamental part of institutional communication and it plays a central role within politicians' image building.

In the early years of social media adoption, the main hope was in their power to allow citizens to participate more actively, allowing direct dialogue between politicians and voters. The invention of these new communication channels created a new way to bridge the ever-growing gap between political parties and citizens that had developed over the last two decades (Dalton, 2000; della Porta 2002; Mazzoleni and Sfardini, 2009). This gap was characterised by disaffection and disillusion towards political behaviour that was becoming increasingly self-referential and focused on power play, often with personal ends, rather than cooperative public planning. Internet, new social media and the new communication paradigm linked with the advent of "Web 2.0"[1] represented new opportunities to listen to and involve citizens in advisory and decisional processes (Trippi, 2005). These factors were seen also as able to stimulate citizens' desire to participate in political debate, if used in such a way as to provide a communicative, inclusive and relationship-oriented space. Nevertheless, national and international literature on the topic and case histories have demonstrated that these communication channels, when used by politicians, still tend to rely on traditional communicative models commonly used in traditional media, that present a significant disadvantage compared to the involvement and engagement opportunities that characterise social media (Graham et al., 2013; Cosenza, 2013; Marchetti, 2014; Larsson and Hallvard, 2012; Graham et al., 2014).

The goal of this paper is to determine if Twitter generated more direct communication and dialogue between Italian politicians and citizens during the 2013 Italian general elections.

A quantitative/qualitative study was conducted in order to test this hypothesis. Its aim was to reconstruct a communication model based on Twitter use by Italian politicians, notably by defining the following elements:

1 *"What"* politicians were talking about on Twitter. What was the message content, and how was it distributed between political and policy issues?
2 *"Who"* were the politicians that talked to through Twitter, and consequently which accounts were "addressed" in the messages?
3 *"How"* did they communicate using this new tool? Which communicative styles did they adopt, and what kind of relationship (**equal** or **asymmetrical**) did they create with citizens?

To pursue these research goals, the main analysis method used was content analysis (Antenore, 2012; Bentivegna, 2014; Tipaldo, 2014), specifically, content analysis as a survey (Losito, 1993). Through this method, contents (video, texts, images) are analysed and questioned using a standardised survey.

The research was carried out at the Communication and New Technologies Institute at IULM University in Milan. Over 5,600 tweets were analysed, taken from forty-one politicians selected through a two-stage sampling process (*cf. infra* for details). All tweets and replies sent from the politicians' accounts (by themselves or their staff) were included in the study, since they were considered to form part of the politicians' communication strategy.

2.1 Twitter and Political Communication: International Research

Some of the first studies focused on political communication and the use of Twitter date back to 2009. At that time the social network had been quite widely adopted in some parts of Europe and the United States. Nevertheless, the platform was almost unknown in Italy. The studies, conducted using quantitative and qualitative methodologies, can be divided into three major categories:

1 **Custom and habit research**: focused on new media spread and how it was adopted.
2 **Predictive research**: used to find a correlation between independent variables and social media adoption to develop predictive models about politicians' use of social media.
3 **Content-based research**: studies based on content analysis methodology, investigating textual content produced by politicians on social media.

Jackson and Lilleker (2011) in Great Britian, and Lassen and Brown (2010) in the United States did research on custom and habit. Interesting adoption data was represented by the fact that in the U.S., Twitter popularity was higher within the Republican party. On average, members of this party are usually older and more conservative compared to the Democrat party. English research, on the other hand, showed the complete opposite. It demonstrated a higher percentage of early adopters among progressive and leftist parties (Goldbeck et al., 2010; Lassen and Brown, 2010). Chi and Yang (2011) demonstrated that politicians with high digital media familiarity were most frequently early adopters of the Twitter platform. Particularly, they discovered that politicians with a Facebook (FB) profile tended to have opened a Twitter page about six months earlier than those without a Facebook presence (*ibid.*). Results of these different studies could seem antithetical. Actually, they confirm that digital media adoption is not only linked to one variable but rather is a complex process. Many variables have to be considered to build a fruitful study about adoption habits, including: size of the party, economic resources and party's relationship with traditional media.

Scholars have also focused their attention on different uses of Twitter by politicians. Using content analysis techniques, Goldbeck et al. (2010) recognise six different functions applicable to tweets generated by politicians: 1. *Direct Communication* (direct tweets to specific users); 2. *Personal Message*; 3. *Information*; 4. *Questing Action*; 5. *Activities*; 6. *Fundraising*. Graham et al. (2013) focused on politicians' behaviour on Twitter. Their study aimed to understand if MPs were aware of the connected representation opportunities of Twitter. They underlined how Labour candidates used the medium to open more direct dialogue with voters, while Conservative candidates used it more as a traditional tool. They highlighted these behaviours through topic analysis: principal topics were political campaigns and party affairs. Larsson and Hallvard (2012) continued this theme in research about the 2010 Swedish election campaign. They tried to understand what political Twitter use was composed of. The Swedish context makes this study particularly interesting. Sweden has a strong democracy, a high rate of Internet penetration and a high level of freedom of speech (Carlsson and Facht, 2010). Nevertheless, the results show that major politicians used Twitter in *uni-directional* ways, focusing less on the conversational potential. Research on English-speaking countries demonstrates that politicians seem poorly oriented to use Twitter to generate an effective relationship with voters and activate a dialogue on political issues with citizens. Di Bonito (2013) developed comparative research between the Catalan elections of 2010 and 2012. She showed that despite the fact that the number of tweets had tripled in 2012, the typology of tweets was almost the same in both elections. The majority of tweets focused on important campaign events. The main result was that Catalan politicians used Twitter to distribute information rather than to build a

28 Guido Di Fraia and Maria Carlotta Missaglia

direct dialogue. All of this research reported Twitter use as being similar to the *broadcasting model*, typical of mass media communication.

2.2 Twitter and Political Communication: Italian Research Environment

Since 2009, numerous studies have focused on Italian political communication and its evolution through social media. However, despite the number of studies conducted on this topic, the variety of approaches makes it difficult to compile the results. For this reason, our analysis is exclusively focused on studies concerning political logic and Twitter use, the underlying communication model and the effects this type of communication had on citizen participation in politics.

The first study of this type was carried out by Antenore in 2012. In this research, the scholar studied political communication through Twitter during the 2012 national election campaign. Analysing the type of post based on relative content, he demonstrated that only 11 per cent of politician's tweets in the analysed period aimed to stimulate citizen participation in politics, while the majority of tweets (49 per cent) were informative or served to publicise traditional media presence.

Cosenza (2013), in a qualitative study with a semiotic approach, revealed that the main political leaders, throughout the course of the 2013 electoral campaign, principally used Twitter with two communicative models: the *one to many* model and the *one to one* model.

Bentivegna (2014) conducted a similar study using a quantitative approach. In his analysis relative to the 2013 election, he identified two main models of Twitter communication: the *broadcast communicational* model, and the *conversational* model. The first type resulted as being the most used, which suggests a top-down use of Twitter; also, the hashtags created during the analysed period confirmed this kind of usage: 36.5 per cent of them were about politicians, 29.5 per cent were focused on the campaign and 18.6 per cent referred to mainstream media. Hashtags often coincide with politicians' profile names, demonstrating the focus on creating strong presence within the Twitter-sphere, rather than generating relationships with citizens and stimulating political participation.

Bentivegna, in another study wholly focused on Beppe Grillo[2] and his social media communication for the 2012 electoral campaign, found what appeared in many ways to be a reproduction of typical media broadcasting logic, presenting a traditional political agenda in a more contemporary, POP-oriented (Mazzoleni and Sfardini, 2009) form.

Another study investigating Twitter political communication models was conducted by Vaccari and Valeriani (2013), who focused their research more on followers than on politicians. Trying to understand in what ways tweets were broadcast through social networks, they identified the role of the *Power Follower*. Power Followers are users with at least 1,000 followers or who have tweeted at least 1,000 times. The net of Power Followers identifies a preferential channel on Twitter for indirect communication. This kind of communication permits politicians to have their online messages spread by many users, even if they are not directly following politicians' profiles. On the other hand, scholars underline that, often, power followers and well-known personalities of the web and media system coincide. What seems to emerge from these results is a reproduction of more "classic" models, typical of traditional media, within the political communication sphere on social media: the "two-step flow of communication".

To study the efficiency of political communication through Twitter, aimed at engaging citizens and encouraging increased political participation, Bentivegna and Tesconi (2014) collected all the tweets containing the hashtag #Elezioni2013. Based on this data, 47,086 users were identified as citizens; scholars analysed the tweets and the hashtag of a consistent subsample of them. Hashtag analysis highlighted that only one third of users were really and steadily interested in politics and often talked about it on Twitter. For the remaining part of the sample, citizens seemed occasionally involved in political discourse and, for most of them, it could be considered as a collateral topic.

Cassetta and Cobianchi (2013) analysed the Lombardy 2013 regional electoral campaign with a content analysis of tweets and hashtags about elections or candidates. Counting and analyzing the tweets produced by politicians and citizens, the study highlights an interesting result about what mainly activates online citizen debate. It demonstrated that citizens were more engaged when tweets were about skirmishes rather than when tweets were about policies, even in a local campaign. The language used was direct and aggressive, being more focused on jokes rather than debates. This is a classic demonstration of the "traditional" Italian political environment. Moreover, in tweets by local politicians, no references were made to political planning or political issues. Consequently, Twitter was not used to express the party's beliefs or to drive their campaigns.

Overall, the studies mentioned well represent the developing communicative environment in the Twitter-sphere. If we look particularly at citizen participation and disintermediation practices, we can highlight how both phenomena adopt normalised practices. Citizens participate more in conversations connected to politics when they are about "politainment" or pop politics topics that they are used to (Mazzoleni e Sfardini, 2009). In terms of disintermediation practice, it can be stated that after a brief initial period where social networks were used to bypass party logic barriers and traditional media, as demonstrated in Vergani's 5 Star Movement study in 2011, the situation quickly developed into predominant broadcasting use connected to the traditional elite. The one-to-many practice and political marketing logic reigned over the citizen participation opportunities that could have been exploited.

2.3 Social Media in Italian Political Communication

In the first decade after the millennium, with the birth of Web 2.0, a new communication model started to develop. From there, it continued to evolve and transform how global societies communicated (Castells, 2008; Jenkins, 2006; Boccia Artieri, 2012; Kramp et al., 2014). This new model, characterised by a permanent state of interconnection that allowed people to live in a *multiple-life* dimension (Boccia Artieri, 2012), corresponds to what Castells (2009) called the era of *"mass self-communication"*, in which mediated communication is *"self-generated"* content, *"self-directed"* emission, and *"self-selected"* reception. Among the fundamental characteristics of the 2.0 paradigm was citizen ability to participate in global communication processes, directly and on an even playing field, where they could be intermediaries in the communication and consumption process. Another characteristic of this period is the increased confidence of *peer-to-peer relationships* (Di Fraia, 2012; Loader, 2011) and willingness to participate in the processes of media content production (prosumer and user generated content UGC). In today's society, social media have made possible the rise of phenomena such as participatory news production and citizen journalism (Allan & Thorsen, 2009; Outing, 2005; Lewis et al., 2010), something that prior to this was reserved to professional journalists and politicians. (Shirky, 2008; Splendore, 2013).

The effect of these phenomena and how stimulating this new media is to encourage active citizen participation in politics is a highly debated topic. Indeed, some scholars adopted a more critical approach to social media (Fuchs, 2014), and others are skeptical about their potential to help the process of democratization (Morozov 2011, 2014; Hindman 2009; Willhelm, 2000). Nevertheless, it is important to consider that this new technological environment made of social software, social network sites (Twitter, Facebook, Pinterest, Instagram) and communication apps, brings many innovative elements to the way people communicate, find information and participate.

Political communication is connected with the majority of the factors changed by the new communication environment. Political communication is directly connected to three fundamental elements: citizens, politicians and the media (della Porta, 2002) so we can ask ourselves: "To what extent has the new paradigm been able to change online political practice?" Research on this topic should also take into account the specifics of different national environments.

In Italy, for example, this new environment, characterised by the development of Web 2.0, gave rise to a "fourth period" of political communication. Mazzoleni (2004), re-adapting the Blumler and Kavanagh (1999) theory to an Italian context, defined three principal political communication eras. The first, from the end of the first World War to the 1960s, was a period of strong ties between citizens and politicians. The second, from the 1960s to the 1990s, is characterised by personalisation politics (Anania, 2012). The third, from the 1990s to the establishment of Web 2.0, is characterised by the mediatization of political processes (Lundby, 2009) and the process defined as "going public" (Kernell, 1997). Starting from this theory we can add a "fourth era" of political communication (Di Fraia and Missaglia, 2013), or the age of "media hegemony" (Bloch, 2013). For the first time, social media could open possibilities for politicians to communicate overtly with citizens and voters without the mediation of a journalistic system or party affiliation (Cillizza, 2013). At a time when there is a deeply rooted disaffection in politics (Flickinger and Studlar, 2007; Mazzoleni and Sfardini, 2009; Fontana and Mieli, 2014) digital media seem to offer new opportunities to revive citizens' political interest. This situation coincides with a renewed need for transparency toward voters that is well represented by the electoral success of the Five Star Movement (M5S) during the 2013 elections (Bentivegna, 2013; Biorcio, 2013). A tweet collected during the research summarised these feelings well, a mix of disaffection and hope for change: "Suit-wearing politicians cannot understand those who wear hoodies".[3]

In Italy, social media adoption was slower than in other European countries. However, in the last five years, this situation changed dramatically. In 2014, more than 60 per cent of Italian families had Internet access (ISTAT, 2014). This growth coincided with a higher social media adoption rate. In January 2014 more than 26,000,000 Italians were on Facebook (Cosenza, 2014). Even if, in Italy, Twitter is a smaller-scale phenomenon, from the 10th December 2011 its use increased markedly. In 2013 there were 9.5 million Twitter users (Della Dora, 2013).

2.4 The Research

Consequently, the 2013 political election can be considered as the first *"Italian Social Election";* however, even if it is possible to identify this election as the starting point of a late Italian Twitter (R)Evolution in political communication, it should not be taken for granted that Italian politicians are really interested in the *"social"* use of the tool. The goal of the research was to highlight whether (and how much) politicians' communication was finalized to open dialogue and induce participation or if it was directed to maintain the *communication status quo.*

To understand their approach and use of Twitter, the study focused its attention on the analysis of the politicians' communication model developed on Twitter. In order to analyse it, the research investigated a sample of Italian political candidates' Twitter activities at two different intervals. The first was defined as the *"campaign period".* This started from 25 January 2013 and ended on the 26 February, 2013. The second period was called the *"post-election"* period and it was from 27 February, 2013 to 27 April, 2013. During this particular phase, Italy didn't have a government or a president of the Republic. Party lists chosen for the research were: The Democratic Party (PD), The People of Freedom (PDL), The Future and Freedom

32   Guido Di Fraia and Maria Carlotta Missaglia

(FLI), The Left Ecology Freedom (SEL), The Civic Choice-Monti, Act to Stop the Decline (FiD), The Five Star Movement (M5S), The CasaPound Italy (CPI), The Italian Civil Revolution (ICR) and The Union of the Centre (UDC). These lists represented the general Italian political situation but also included emerging movements with strong populist ideas and a new way to approach politics, such as M5S, FiD and CasaPound. Forty-one candidates were selected by applying the following criteria: for each selected party, the leader and three representatives were selected. The representatives included in the sample were the ones present on the highest number of different regional lists presented by their party.

Descriptive Results

The final sample was composed of thirty-three politicians (only active profiles were considered for the study). From the sample 5,621 tweets were collected and investigated. A strong heterogeneity within the total number of tweets generated by different candidates was one of the first quantitative figures noticed. Candidates presented a maximum of 1,230 tweets and a minimum of five in the first period and a maximum of 335 and a minimum of zero in the second. During the first period, the average number of tweets for each candidate was about 109 (median=forty-nine) and thirty for the second (median=thirty). Differences among the tweets generated during campaign and those created within the following period was another interesting piece of macro-data. Evidence shows a decrease of 3,592 tweets (one-month campaign period) to 2,020 tweets (two-month post-election period). The reduction was about 44 per cent. This data suggests a "strategic" use of the tool. The use of Twitter appears to be focused on obtaining higher visibility and better reputation during the campaign. This hypothesis is strengthened by the politicians' behavior. Some of them opened their account during the pre-campaign period, while others stopped using the micro-blog immediately after Election Day. In fact, about nine politicians, including the Senator and ex-Prime Minister Mario Monti, ceased tweeting or drastically reduced their Twitter use (Mario Monti tweeted 273 times during the campaign and only three times over the following period). According to the results, no politicians adopted a joint strategies during the campaign period. It was evident that there was no coordination between members of the same party. In fact, data analysis based on the "party affiliation" variable did not generate any statistically significant difference. The use of Twitter as a *personal medium* allowed candidates to bypass the traditional logic of mediation carried out by parties between themselves, the media and citizens.

The qualitative part of the study employed content analysis techniques applied to the three main questions previously identified: who politicians were talking to, about what, how they used Twitter. For each politician, the tweet sampling pattern was built as follows: if there were less than fifty tweets, all of them were examined; if there were more than fifty, one tweet out of three (k=3) was analysed.

Content Analysis

In order to understand what politicians were talking about, content analysis was applied to detect the presence of policy or politics issues within tweets. One of the most important pieces of data collected was the reduced presence of policy issues. Over the two phases, only 40 per cent of tweets presented "policy relevant" subjects. This situation was typical of the various parties without any differentiation based on political beliefs. Particularly, 31 percent of tweets presented the economy as the most quoted topic, followed by welfare (3 percent), work (2 per cent) and justice (2 per cent). The percentages did not significantly change over the periods. Coherently with results that emerged from other Italian studies, this one also suggests that political communication on Twitter is in line with communication styles used for all the other media. It confirms how within the Italian "3P System" – "Policy, Political and Personal Issues" – the Policy area is under-represented within political discourse. Prevalent discussions were about disputes between parties and well-known politicians in the media spotlight.

As part of the sample content analysis, hashtags (#) were naturally included as they identify conversation themes on Twitter. Out of a total of 1,899 hashtags collected, only 156 (about 8 per cent) were connected to policy issues, 4 per cent referred to *television programmes* or *other media*, 6 per cent to institutional issues, 10 per cent to relevant places for the election campaign and about 63 per cent (about 1,189 hashtags) to political candidates themselves. Among them, Berlusconi's communicational anomaly emerged. On his account (@berlusconi2013), activated during the campaign, the large majority of messages produced presented personal hashtags (#berlusconi, #consilvio). During the period studied, they represented about 37 per cent of the total hashtags. An interesting case is connected with Romano Prodi (PD) hashtag: #noprodi. It was found in more than sixty messages generated in the post-election period. Many politicians, who were against the ex-prime minister's election as president of the Italian Republic, adopted it in order to lobby for his candidacy to fail.

This evidence confirms that politicians tended to use the micro blog in a self-centered way, typical of general Italian political communication. In this way they exclude citizens from an active communication process and participation in political discourse.

To answer to the second research question an analysis based on tweet recipients was conducted. It emerged that politicians themselves were the protagonists of around a quarter of tweets (24.9 per cent); followed by *"we"* referred to their own *political party* (which represents 15.6 percent of the sampled tweets) and *"their/them"* used to talk about *political opponents*

(15 per cent). Fini is the lead example of this, by talking about himself in 82 per cent of his own tweets, followed by Galletti 66 per cent, De Maria 51 per cent, Letta 48 per cent and Franceschini 40 per cent. Giannino and Boldrini are two exceptions. They also used Twitter to talk about the economic situation (8 per cent of Giannino's tweets) and the political situation (7 per cent of Boldrini's tweets) respectively and to give direct, useful information to (potentially active) citizens.

Nevertheless, in the majority of cases there is no demonstration of interest in building stronger relationships with citizens or in making them an active part of a dialogue about political problems. In fact, politicians focused most of their tweets on themselves.

The research highlights the usage of the term *"them"* (as opponents) as one of the main subjects tweeted by the PDL politicians (Brunetta 19 per cent, Berlusconi 20 per cent and Alfano 29 per cent) to reach the highest numbers among those gathered on the whole sample (with the exception of Di Stefano who used "them" in 27 per cent of his tweets). On the PD side the numbers are different with Franceschini at 6 per cent and Bersani plus Letta at 8 per cent. The analysed tweets use the comparison between *I-We* on one hand, and *Them* on the other, which relate to the underlying aims. In the case of the PDL representatives they are, in fact, mainly aimed at tarnishing the opponents' reputation and credibility (30 per cent of Alfano's tweets have this purpose, as well as 26% per cent of Berlusconi's and Brunetta's). Fini's main goal on Twitter seems to be his own personal branding (70 per cent of his tweets were aimed at this), while only Boldrini mainly used Twitter to inform her potential voters (49 per cent of her tweets were for that purpose).

Moreover, the study highlighted how one of the main themes of the Italian political Twittersphere was *"opponent mistakes"* or *"opponent critique"*, in accordance with electoral campaign strategy carried out on other media.

Finally, to answer the third and last research question, the form and style of politicians' tweets were investigated applying Jakobson's functions of language model (Jakobson, 1963). During the campaign and the post-campaign phases a great prevalence of tweets with *referential* functions emerged, specifically 50 per cent for the first period and 40 per cent for the second. This function is associated with tweets that provide information about candidates' TV shows or electoral rally participations, or that indicate articles or links connected with their personal blogs. This kind of detected practice showed that the usage was mainly unidirectional and top-down, with focus on the politicians' agenda to build their personal press review. The *emotive* function was the second-most used during the two periods. In the first period the percentage produced was 30 per cent and 40 per cent over the second. This result enables us to build two different hypotheses. The considerable weight of emotive tweets can be depicted as a pertinent use of the medium. Politicians can exploit it to communicate in a non-mediated way with citizens, showing their subjectivity and personal experiences with openness and authenticity. On the other hand, use of the emotive function can be interpreted as additional evidence of personalization politics reproduced through Twitter. It consists of a self-centered and self-reflective communicational logic. This contrasts completely with another logic which embraces the opportunities offered by Twitter to create active audiences and direct communication with voters. Considering the entire context, this last interpretation seems to be the more correct. *Phatic* tweets were generated during the campaign period only. Their percentage was extremely small compared to what was expected. This type was detected within only 7 per cent of tweets. This rate, which was reduced to zero in the post-election phase, shows a limited interest in building direct communication. In both periods, *conative* functions within the analysed tweets were very low and were used to stimulate participation in political events. *poetic* (4,4 per cent) and *meta-linguistic* functions (0,02 per cent) were used the least.

Using the same scheme, *most retweeted tweets* were analysed. These returned interesting insights about virtual conversations occurring between candidates and citizens. Among these retweets, *emotive* ones were prevalent (they account for 47 per cent of most retweeted messages, compared to 35 per cent of the total examined tweets). This result shows that passionate elements easily generate engagement and viral effect. Most commonly, retweeted messages expressed a direct and emotional critique towards politicians (mainly regarding Berlusconi, Grillo and Bersani). This fact demonstrates that voter-followers' interest on Twitter was focused on leaders and personal or political issues.

To sum up, the logic of *pop politics*, which characterizes a political communication style based on *infotainment, soft news* and *politainment* (Mazzoleni and Sfardini, 2009), typical of mass media, seemed to characterize the 140-character Twitter content too. Even M5S did this, despite being defined as a possible alternative to traditional parties and the predominant role of leaders in relationship dynamics between politicians and followers. Although M5S describes itself as a political movement and not as a party, founded on principles of horizontal and equal relationships among its members, findings and figures show that most retweeted tweets were exclusively those of the leader Beppe Grillo, while other candidates' tweets generated very little interest.

The research is still in progress and it is part of a bigger project including a part about the 2014 European elections in Italy. Further publications will be focused on this last topic and narrative analysis.[4]

2.5 Conclusion: the "Two-Step-Flow" of Twitter Communication

The aim of our research was to investigate the adoption processes of Twitter by Italian politicians and reconstruct the communicative model and underlying practices adopted. To reach this goal, our research attempted to identify "who politicians were talking to", the "content" of their tweets and what "style of communication" they used. In 2013, Twitter was a fundamental tool, and it was used in many different and sometimes contradictory ways. Over the electoral period, candidates became aware of the power of Twitter within political communication. Particularly, they began to consider it more important than before because of a penetration rate increase within *social/ political* and *news* elite. New politicians' awareness was demonstrated by their significant use of the tool, particularly during the *pre-election period* (*or campaign period*). Former Prime Minister, Mario Monti and Pier Silvio Berlusconi, for example, opened their accounts during the electoral campaign. Nevertheless, this data indicates a mainly *strategic and propagandistic* use of the tool as was demonstrated by the strong decrease of tweets after Election Day.

Awareness among politicians of the importance of being on Twitter was not directly connected with an open style of dialogue or direct implication of citizens to participate. Moreover, according to Cassetta and Cobianchi (2013), citizens are more active when politicians talk about familiar topics dealt with in political entertainment programs. Results emerging from the research demonstrate that despite using Twitter, Italian politicians continued to talk mainly to other politicians or the media. This could have been fostered by the peculiar Italian political system and, in particular, by the electoral law, derogatively referred to as *"porcellum"* by very the politician who proposed it! The law is based on a proportional system with blocked lists. Citizens cannot choose which individual candidate to vote for because voting for a political party automatically includes all candidates associated with that party, selected by the party secretaries (Bentivegna, 2012). For this reason, candidates have no interest in communicating with citizens to have more votes; they are interested, rather, in communicating with party leaders to be put on the shortlist.

Even if the medium provided conversational, listening and informative opportunities toward citizens and vice versa, Italian politicians did not take advantage of these. The analysis conducted using Jakobson's function scheme made it possible to highlight a main *"referential function"* for tweets. According to Jakobson (1963), this function is that of giving information, to talk about the addresser of the message (tweet) and describe his/her action. Adapted to the political dimension, this is the typical function of traditional political campaigns, not suitable to stimulate dialogue with or feedback from the audience. Applying Ederoclite and Punziano's (2013) definition, it was also possible to frame *content type of communication*. Policy dimension was hardly mentioned, while political and personal language were the most frequent. This evidence underlines similar logics that connect mainstream media and Twitter. In the period of *pop politics* (Mazzoleni and Sfardini, 2009), media tended to focus more on this kind of news and information. On Twitter, politicians arranged their communication in the same way. Even *emotional tweets* were mainly used to argue with, attack or belittle opponents. Berlusconi, Bersani and Grillo, leaders of their parties or movements, used these tweets to be re-tweeted and get attention from mass media. In this way, leaders like Grillo, who claimed that he did not want to be part of the media system, sought attention on mainstream media through social media. This hypothesis was also confirmed by the *hashtag content analysis*: mainstream media is often present within tweets. In this way politicians can create direct dialogue with mainstream media rather than citizens influencing the media agenda and the agenda-setting process.

More formally, the result of our work shows that the communicative model mainly used by politicians is that represented in Figure 2.1:

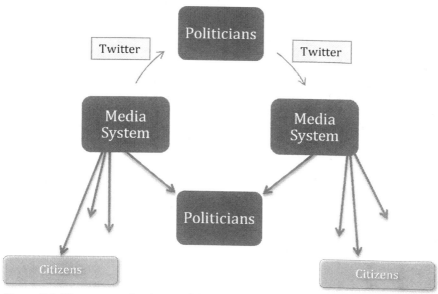

Figure 2.1 The communication model adopted by Italian politicians on Twitter during the 2013 General Election.

This result is coherent with the results from previous Italian research. For example, Bentivegna (2014) underlines how the *broadcast/one-to-many* model of communication was the one mainly adopted by politicians for their strategies and Cosenza (2013) has similar results even if she adopted a different methodological approach. Moreover, our results confirm this communicational habit: politicians mainly communicate with media, especially mainstream media, in order to obtain consensus rather than dialogue.

All these elements suggest that what is happening in Italian political communication is *normalized use of Twitter* (Margolis and Resnik, 2000) with a strong orientation towards mass media. Traditional media logic is re-applied and re-adapted to the new environment; the content shows a *propagandist style* and the communication flow is *broadcast*. In detail, it is possible to say that the most commonly used communication model for Italian politicians within Twitter is similar to *the two-step-flow communication theory* (Lazarsfeld and Katz, 1955): politicians used Twitter to interact with the media system, while the mass media system is the intermediary between politicians and citizens.

These results combined highlight a missed opportunity in the Italian political communication system. Citizens demonstrate strong disaffection and disappointment towards politics and see it as a power tool for personal gain, after a long period of government leadership that was stable, although characterised by scandal. This perception certainly contributed to a distancing and disinterest in political participation, similar to situations in many Western countries. The popularity of social media and in particular the use of Twitter (mainly starting from 2013) could have given Italian politicians many opportunities to re-install direct dialogue with citizens and electorates. If the platform had been used with a "social" mindset, it could have contributed to encouraging equal and bi-directional public debate that would have certainly brought citizens closer to politics and stimulated participation. However, this didn't happen, and almost all Italian politicians used Twitter purely for propaganda, bending the communication logic back toward a broadcasting style, typical of traditional media. Politicians sheltered themselves from new equal relationship opportunities that social media could have offered in exchange for maintaining their deeply-rooted status quo. This status, in fact, depends on low participation and disinterested citizens. The Italian political system missed an important opportunity to re-install citizen participation and ways of doing politics.

Notes

1. The term Web 2.0 was coined during a conference in 2004 by Tim O'Reilly. With this term he wanted to underline a passage from a static web (1.0) to a dynamic one (2.0) characterised by an elevated level of interaction between the web and its users. A common trait of this form of web is the centrality of the users. O'Reilly (2005) defines Web 2.0 services as an "architecture of participation" where the web is principally considered as a platform where users can produce, modify or share content in a steady flux of transformation.
2. Bepper Grillo, a former comedian, is the leader of a new Italian political movement called Movement 5 Stars.
3. Facebook Users status on September 21, 2012.
4. In a new part of the study, 3,000 tweets were analysed, out of about 9,000 tweets produced by forty-five politicians in the month before the European parliamentary elections. Preliminary results pertaining to Jakobson's functions confirm the trend observed during the 2013 national campaign. The *referential* function was the most used (53 per cent), followed by the *emotive* function (22 per cent) and then the *phatic* function (14 per cent). The Actor category shows that 34 per cent of tweets included *I/Me* as a principal actor. Only 13 per cent referred to their *membership party* while 10 per cent has *Them* (political enemies) as protagonists.

Works Cited

Allan, Stuart, and Thorsen, Einar. 2009. *Citizen journalism: Global perspectives.* New York: Peter Lang.

Anania, Francesca. 2012. *Potere politico e mass media. Da Giolitti a Berlusconi.* Roma: Carocci editore.

Antenore, Marzia. 2012. "Soundbite Politics. I parlamentari su Twitter". In *Parlamento 2.0. Strategie di comunicazione politica in internet,* edited by Bentivengna Sara. Milano: Franco Angeli.

Bentivegna, Sara. 2012. *Parlamento 2.0, strategia di comunicazione politica in internet.* Milano: Franco Angeli.

Bentivegna, Sara. Ed. 2014. *La politica in 140 caratteri. Twitter e spazio pubblico.* Milano: Franco Angeli.

Bentivegna, Sara. 2013. "il «boom» di Grillo nella twittersfera. Parlare di politica in 140 caratteri". *Comunicazione politica,* 1: 85–108.

Bentivegna, Sara, and Tesconi, Maurizio. 2014. "Discutere di politica nella twitersfera:vero amore o passione passeggera?". In *La politica in 140 caratteri. Twitter e spazio pubblico,* edited by Bentivengna Sara. Milano: Franco Angeli.

Biorcio, Roberto. 2013. "Le tre ragioni del successo del MoVimento 5 Stelle".*Comunicazione politica,* 1: 43–62.

Block, Elena. 2013. "A Culturalist Approach to the Concept of the Mediatization of Politics: The Age of "Media Hegemony"". *Communication Theory,* 23 (3): 259–278.

Blumler, Jay G., and Kavanagh, Dennis. 1999. "The third age of political communication: Influences and features". *Political communication,* 16 (3): 209–230.

Boccia Artieri, Giovanni. 2012. *Stati di connessione: pubblici, cittadini e consumatori nella (social) network society.* Milano: Franco Angeli.

Carlsson, Ulla, and Facht, Ulrika. 2010. "Medie-Sverige: statistik och analys. 2010". *NORDICOM-Sverige.*

Cassetta, Ludovica, and Cobianchi, Vittorio. 2013 "Una brava persona" Esplorazione del lessico dei tweet sulla campagna elettorale lombarda del 2013". *Comunicazione politica* 3: 373–392.

Castells, Manuel. 2008. "The new public sphere: Global civil society, communication networks, and global governance". *The ANNALS of the American Academy of Political and Social Science* 616 (1): 78–93.

Castells, Manuel. 2009. *Communication power.* Oxford/New York: Oxford University Press.

Chi, Feng, and Yang, Nathan. 2011. "Twitter Adoption in Congress." *Review of Network Economics,* 10 (1): 1–44.

Cosenza, Giovanna. 2013. "I politici italiani su Twitter, fra esagerazioni, pasticci e qualche buon risultato". *Comunicazione politica,* 3: 299–318.

Cosenza, Vincenzo. 2014. *I 10 anni di Facebook visti dall'Italia: Statistiche e Trend,* in Vincos Blog, http://vincos.it/2014/01/27/i-10-anni-di-facebook-visti-italia-statistiche-social-network/.

Cillizza, Chris. "How Twitter has changed politics—and political journalism". *The Washington Post,* November 7, 2013. Accessed March 21, 2015. http://www.washingtonpost.com/blogs/the-fix/wp/2013/11/07/how-twitter-has-changed-politics-and-political-journalism/.

Dalton, Russell J. 2000. "The decline of party identification". In: *Parties without partisans: political change in advanced industrial democracies,* edited by Russell J. Dalton and Martin P. Wattenberg, Oxford: Oxford University Press, 19–36.

Della Dora, Luca. 2013. *The latest 3 years of Twitter: 3.4 milioni di utenti attivi in Italia*, in We are social, http://wearesocial.it/blog/2013/12/latest-3-years-twitter-34-milioni-di-utenti-attivi-italia/.

Di Bonito, Ilaria. "New media, old attitude? The use of Twitter during the Catalan campaign of 2010 and 2012". Paper presented at the New Trend in Political Communication. Evidence, theories, implications, opportunities, ECREA, Milan, 2013.

Di Fraia, Guido. 2012. *Social media marketing: manuale di comunicazione aziendale 2.0*. Milano: Hoepli.

Di Fraia, Guido, and Missaglia, Maria C. 2014. "The Use of Twitter In 2013 Italian Political Election". In *Social Media in Politics*, edited by Bogdan Pătruţ and Monica Pătruţ. Springer International Publishing.

Ederoclite, Tommaso, and Punziano, Gabriella. 2013. "Le Applicazioni Quanti-Qualitative nella Ricerca Politica". In *Content analysis tra comunicazione e politica*, edited by Enrica Amaturo and Gabriella Punziano. Milano: Ledizioni.

Flickinger, Richard S., and Studlar, Donley T. 2007. "One Europe, many electorates? Models of turnout in European Parliament elections after 2004". *Comparative Political Studies*, 40 (4): 383–404.

Fontana, Andrea, and Mieli, Ester. 2014. *Siamo tutti storyteller. Dalla fiction americana alla politica*. Roma: Giuliano Perrone Editore.

Fuchs, Christian. 2014. *Social media: A critical introduction*. London: Sage.

Goldbeck, Jennifer, Grimes, Justin. M, and Rogers, Anthony. 2010. "Twitter Use by the U.S. Congress". *Journal of the American Society for Information Science and Technology*, 61 (8): 1612–1621.

Graham, Todd, Broersma, Marcel, and Hazelhoff, Karin. 2013. "Closing the gap? Twitter as an instrument for connected representation". In *The Media, Political Participation and Empowerment*, edited by Richard Scullion, Roman Gerodimos, Daniel Jackson and Darren G. Lilleker. London: Routledge.

Graham, Todd, Jackson, Dan, and Broersma, Marcel. 2014. "New Platform, Old Habits? Candidates' Use of Twitter during the 2010 British and Dutch General Election Campaigns". *New Media & Society*, August. doi:10.1177/1461444814546728.

Hindman, Matthew, 2009. *The myth of digital democracy*. Princeton: Princeton University Press.

ISTAT. 2014. "Cittadini e NuoveTecnologie". Accessed March 21, 2015. http://www.istat.it/it/archivio/143073.

Jakobson, Roman. 1963. *Essais de linguistique générale*. Paris: Minuit.

Jackson, Nigel A., and Lilleker, Darren G. 2011. "Microblogging, Constituency Service and Impression Management: UK MPs and the use of Twitter". *The Journal of Legislative Studies*, 17 (1): 86–105.

Jenkins, Henry. 2006. *Convergence Culture: Where old and new media collide*, New York: NYU Press.

Kernell, Samuel. 1997. *Going public: new strategies of presidential leadership*.

Kramp, Leif, et al. (eds.) 2014. *Media Practice and Everyday Agency in Europe*. Bremen: edition Lumière.

Larsson, Anders O., and Moe, Hallvard. 2012. "Studying political microblogging: Twitter users in the 2010 Swedish election campaign". *New Media & Society*, 14 (5): 729–747.

Lassen, David S., and Brown, Adam R. 2010. "Twitter: The Electoral Connection?" *Social Science Computer Review*, 28 (4): 1–18.

Lazarsfeld, Paul F., and Katz, Elihu. 1955. *Personal influence: the part played by people in the flow of mass communications*. Illinois: Glencoe.

Lewis, Seth C., Kaufhold, Kelly, and Lasorsa, Dominic L. 2010. "Thinking about citizen journalism: The philosophical and practical challenges of user-generated content for community newspaper". *Journalism Practice*, 4 (2): 163–179.

Loader, Brian D., and Mercea, Dan. 2011. "Networking democracy? Social media innovations and participatory politics". *Information, Communication & Society* 14 (6): 757–769.

Losito, Gianni, 1993. *L'analisi del contenuto nella ricerca sociale*. Milano: Franco Angeli Lundby Knut, ed. 2009. *Mediatization: concept, changes, consequences*. Brussels: Peter Lang.

Marchetti, Rita. 2014. "Alla ricerca degli influencer, ovvero gli eredi dei leader d'opinione". In *La politica in 140 caratteri. Twitter e spazio pubblico*, edited by Bentivengna Sara. Milano: Franco Angeli.

Margolis, Michael, and Resnick, David. 2000. *Politics as Usual: the Cyberspace 'Revolution'*. London: Routledge.

Mazzoleni, Gianpietro, and Sfardini, Anna. 2009. *Politica Pop. Da "Porta a Porta" a "L'isola dei famosi"*. Bologna: Il Mulino.

Mazzoleni, Gianpietro. 2004. *La comunicazione politica*. Bologna: Il Mulino.

Morozov, Evgeny. 2014. *Internet non salverà il mondo*. Milano: Edizioni Mondadori.

Morozov, Evgeny. 2011. *The Net Delusion: How not to liberate the world*. London: Penguin UK.

O'Reilly, Tim. 2005. "What is Web 2.0?". *www.oreillynet*, http://www.oreillynet.com/pub/a/oreilly/tim/news/2005/09/30/what-is-web-20.html, accessed 15 April 2015.

Outing, Steve. 2005. "The 11 Layers of Citizen Journalism". *Poynter Online*, http://www.poynter.org/content/content_view.asp?id=83126, accessed 14 April 2015.

della Porta, Donatella. 2002. *Introduzione alla scienza politica*. Bologna: il Mulino.

Shirky, Clay. 2008. *Here comes everybody: The power of organizing without organizations*. New York: Penguin.

Splendore, Sergio. 2013. "La produzione dell'informazione online e l'uso della partecipazione implicita". *Comunicazione politica*, 13 (3): 341–360.

Tipaldo, Giuseppe. 2014. *L'analisi del contenuto e i mass media. Oggetti, metodi e strumenti*. Bologna: Il Mulino.

Trippi, Joe. 2005. *The Revolution Will Not Be Televised: Democracy, the Internet, and the Overthrow of Everything*. New York: Regan Books.

Vaccari, Cristian, and Valeriani, Augusto. "Follow the leader! dynamics and patterns of activity among the followers of the main italian political leaders during the 2013 general election campaign". Paper presented at the New Trend in Political Communication. Evidence, theories, implications, opportunities, ECREA, Milan, 2013.

Vergani, Matteo. 2011. "Internet e partecipazione politica, Uno studio comparato tra V-Day e No B-Day". *Comunicazione politica*, 12 (2): 197–222.

Wilhelm, Anthony G. 2000. *Democracy in the Digital Age: Challenges to Political Life in Cyberspace*. London: Routledge.

3 Ad Hoc Mini-Publics on Twitter
Citizen Participation or Political Communication? Examples from the German National Election 2013

Jessica Einspänner-Pflock, Mario Anastasiadis and Caja Thimm

3.1 Introduction and Theoretical Background: Discursive Participation in Twitter Mini- Publics

By drawing on empirical Twitter data, this present chapter aims to assess the extent to which the microblogging platform can be seen to offer a digital public sphere for political discursive participation. It is assumed that especially during election times citizens try to engage in political discussions on Twitter (either by actively contributing or passively reading along), which are linked to wider public discourse. Twitter's technological structure enables accounts (people, organisations, institutions) to be highly interconnected, and themes, opinions and ideas to circulate rapidly. It is believed that Twitter thus offers a conducive environment for discursive participation and deliberation processes.

Tweets sent by citizens, journalists and politicians during the German National Election 2013 will be analysed, in order to examine digital discourse on Twitter during election times, the various groups of actors which are constituted and the role they play within certain discursive contexts. Those 'contexts' are conceptualised as *mini-publics*: publicly visible and publicly accessible online spaces that evolve around topics or individuals on social media platforms over a period of time and are characterised by "self-formation and self-selection" (see Chapter 11 in this volume). In the present study the concept of online mini-publics will be substantiated especially with respect to *ad hoc publics*, a particular type of mini-publics, which form and persist only for a specific period of time. Unless specified differently, the concept of ad hoc (mini-)publics are only used within the framework of the microblogging platform Twitter.

Analysing Twitter Ad Hoc Publics

On Twitter, everyone can participate in exchanges on a certain topic by actively contributing (tweeting, retweeting, favoriting, replying) or passively following the thread by reading along. Ad hoc publics characterised by a short duration and high intensity often become established *just because* users seize the opportunity to participate in an unrestrained setting for discussion.

The feature of Twitter's structural openness has led to the assumption that the microblogging platform bears the potential to enhance deliberation among the interacting individuals (Kim and Woo 2012, Bor 2013, Thimm, Dang-Anh, and Einspänner 2014). However, while critics claim that there is no room for reasonable political discourse within 140 characters, the extent of one tweet (Fuchs 2013), Twitter must not be regarded as a substitute for traditional public spheres (online or offline). Twitter should rather be seen as a new digital environment among others that holds the potential to play an important role in individuals' media repertoires. Twitter publics build spaces for interaction with an open outcome, which can but does not necessarily meet the normative conditions for deliberation. In addition, whereas other (offline-focused) approaches addressing the idea of bottom-up deliberation (Chambers 2009, Lafont 2015) exclude certain actor constellations (i.e., "campaign debates" or "citizen-to-elite-communication", Delli Carpini, Cook, and Jacobs 2004), it is considered that discussions among Twitter publics are always open to all individuals belonging to various actor groups (e.g., among politicians, journalists or a specific interest group). Even if single mini-publics on Twitter might appear exclusive with respect to the active participants involved ("ingroup-communication"), discourses in the public space of Twitter can be easily followed by others and thus also foster processes of interaction, discussion, and deliberation.

The basic structural openness of Twitter publics is closely related to the immediacy and rapid growth that particularly characterise topic-centred ad hoc formations. In comparison to other media environments where "stories must be written, edited, published and commentary pages must be set up" (Bruns and Burgess 2011), the creation of a topic-centred ad hoc public on Twitter, for example via hashtags, is easily initiated. Hashtags function as clickable keywords, which semantically and lexically refer to the respective thematic issue (exemptions might be acronyms or neologisms). By searching for specific hashtags Twitter users can detect, follow and engage in discussions on the platform. They can also create their own thematic contexts by creating a hashtag and tweeting it to the digital public. However, not every "hashtag community" (Bruns and Burgess 2011) is an ad hoc public. Mostly, ad hoc publics arise around sudden events or major breaking news. Examples are the nuclear accident in Japan or the terror attacks in Oslo in 2011, which gave rise to ad hoc publics on Twitter around the respective hashtags #Fukushima and #Oslobomb (Bruns 2012). Ad hoc publics can also form around known or announced hashtags, which is often the case with live TV events (#ESC for the Eurovision contest or #TellEurope as a name for the EU Election TV debate) or big sports events (#olympia, #superbowl).

Yet other discourses – although having a similar structure like the described hashtag communities – are not regarded as ad hoc publics, as they are prolonged and already last over several days, weeks or even months. For example the discourses around the German #s21 construction project (see Thimm in this volume) or #BER (the hashtag referring to the new Berlin airport) form extended discourses that might be the result of an ad hoc discourse but can no longer be regarded as such, as the event in question is not recent (any more).

For the analysis and description of ad hoc publics in Twitter, the *functional operator model* (see also Thimm et al. 2012, 2014) provides an adequate framework (see Figure 3.1). The model distinguishes four levels of Twitter communication: (1) the operator level, (2) the text level, (3) the action level, and (4) the functional level. The operator level consists of the four specific semiotic signs @, RT, # and http://, which are used to perform communicative action on Twitter. By combining these *operators* with text (second level), like an account name, a URL, or a random phrase, the text referred to not only gets marked and becomes clickable, but the user also performs action in the Twitter universe (third level). This is accomplished either by the mechanisms of the media logic provided (and programmed) by Twitter (i.e., the fact that the combination of certain signifiers and text becomes hyperlinked within Twitter) or the specific dynamically changing appropriation techniques of the Twitter users. The functional level (fourth level) can be seen as the analytic level for interpreting the respective operator-text-action-combination and constructing its meaning.

By using the *@-operator*, Twitter users directly address and/or mention other users within a tweet (@-symbol + Username). This reflects on the public Twitter timeline and allows other users to find the accounts involved and possibly to extend their own personal Twitter network. The *retweet function* enables users to re-send other users' tweets, which is not only a way of citing or distributing the thoughts of others but is also seen as an acknowledgement for the originator. The *#-operator* is used to highlight keywords and to semantically mark tweets. The combination of the #-sign and a character string turns them into a *hashtag*. On Twitter, hashtags are essential signifiers and enable organisation and contextualisation of discourses. Finally, *hyperlinks* (strings headed by http://) allow users to substantiate arguments by implementing external content, such as photos, videos or URLs. Hyperlinks enable a connection to online content outside the "Twitter universe" and provide additional information.

The functional operator model offers the opportunity to evaluate the structures of discursive participation in mini-publics on Twitter. By integrating the model into a mixed method design of quantitative and qualitative tweet analyses it becomes easier to assess the formation and establishment of mini-publics and especially ad hoc publics. The inherent network structure of automatically linked content and user accounts enhances the connectivity between individuals and thus the spontaneous and quick development of the shared communicative space (Bruns and Burgess 2011, Maireder and Schlögl 2014).

In addition, the functional operator model provides a framework for a quantitative assessment of users' *tweeting styles*. The amount of operators employed by a Twitter user over a certain period of time can serve as a basis for interpreting his or her preferred way of tweeting. Tweeting styles can

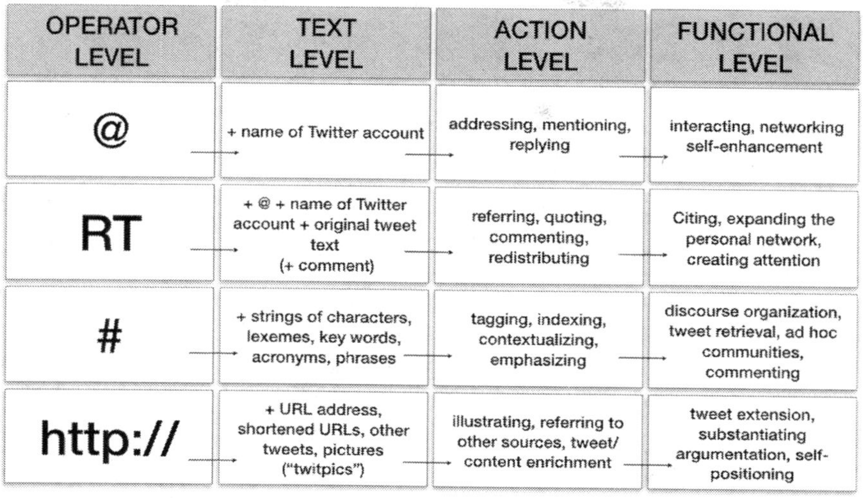

OPERATOR LEVEL	TEXT LEVEL	ACTION LEVEL	FUNCTIONAL LEVEL
@	+ name of Twitter account	addressing, mentioning, replying	interacting, networking self-enhancement
RT	+ @ + name of Twitter account + original tweet text (+ comment)	referring, quoting, commenting, redistributing	Citing, expanding the personal network, creating attention
#	+ strings of characters, lexemes, key words, acronyms, phrases	tagging, indexing, contextualizing, emphasizing	discourse organization, tweet retrieval, ad hoc communities, commenting
http://	+ URL address, shortened URLs, other tweets, pictures ("twitpics")	illustrating, referring to other sources, tweet/ content enrichment	tweet extension, substantiating argumentation, self-positioning

Figure 3.1 The functional operator model: analytic levels of Twitter communication. (Modelled after Thimm et al. 2012, 2014.)

be located on a continuum between two major categories: on the one hand the *personal-interactive tweeting style* is defined by a more frequent usage of @- and RT-operators compared to the http://-operator usage; and on the other hand the *topical-informative tweeting style* is characterised by a higher usage of hyperlinks compared to the usage of @- and RT operators (Thimm, Dang-Anh, and Einspänner 2012). It is assumed that the @- and RT-operators mainly serve as markers for interaction within one's personal follower network on Twitter whereas the hyperlink is supposed to contain additional information which helps to make more precise the meaning of a tweet. The tweeting style of a person may range between the two categories and thus be interpreted as either personal-interactive or topical-informative – or even balanced. Apart from the two main styles, the distribution of hashtags within a user's tweeting profile can be important, especially with respect to their discursive function. In this regard, a user who employs many hashtags can be seen as more participative and as providing more discursive connecting points than someone with a comparably lower usage of the hashtag operator.

3.2 Discursive Participation in Twitter Mini-Publics During the German National Election 2013

Although Germany is still lagging behind other countries regarding the number of Twitter users, the microblogging service has become more and more important as a tool for distributing news and group networking in Germany (van Eimeren and Frees 2014). For political parties and candidates, the role of Twitter as a strategic communication tool gained particular momentum during the 2013 election campaign. Ninty-five percent of the 631 elected

46 *Jessica Einspänner-Pflock, Mario Anastasiadis and Caja Thimm*

candidates own social media accounts, and about half of them have a Twitter account (cf. www.pluragraph.de).

The German National Election on 22 September 2013 has received wide attention on social media. Twitter itself even called for political participation by sending emails to its users and inviting them to use certain hashtags such as #gehwählen ("get out the vote") or #btw13 (acronym for "Bundestagswahl 2013"–"National election 2013"). Twitter hence became an active player during the election by providing statistics such as charts with numbers of tweets sent by the political parties or individual candidates. In fact, the discussions that happened on Twitter during the election campaign drew attention to upcoming topics and thus even influenced the offline media agenda (Nuernbergk 2013). Although the quality of political communication on Facebook and Twitter can partially be questioned, more than one third of the voters stated in various surveys that social media would influence the electoral outcome (Kempf/ Güllner 2013).

Research Questions and Method

Our empirical analysis of Twitter communication during the National Elections in Germany is led by the assumption that discursive participation in (ad hoc) mini-publics on Twitter can be evaluated by isolating certain hashtags and by looking at the usage styles of politicians. Therefore we analyse how these selected hashtags have been employed by Twitter users during the electoral period, in terms of their semantic and structural context. In addition, we look at the different actors making up Twitter mini-publics. By focusing on selected discourses we examine the way politicians contributed to these Twitter publics during the campaign. Do they engage in an exchange with citizens or rather take part merely in in-group discourse (among themselves) and thus establish their own mini-publics? How can their tweeting styles and discussion patterns be analysed and interpreted in terms of their inclusive or participatory potential?

The database consists of over 1.3 million tweets collected in the period of three weeks before and one week after Election Day (September 22, 2013). For the tweet collection, the streaming and search APIs of Twitter were used to compile the data set. The corpus contains tweets sent by selected politicians (electoral candidates of all parties and all incumbent members of the Cabinet with a Twitter profile), by the major party accounts (such as @cdu_news, @spdde, @FDP_Fraktion etc.), various media accounts (e.g., @weltonline, @tazgezwitscher, @zeitonline etc.), and citizens addressing the respective candidates. In addition, for the concrete purpose of detecting ad hoc publics, different event-related hashtags have been collected: some of those hashtags were pre-selected on the basis of former data collections in electoral contexts (such as #wahl "election" or #tvduell); others were continuously added during the data collection as a result of a constant monitoring process.

For the addressed areas of research, the method of computer-assisted content analysis of tweets was applied. The analysis process combined quantitative as well as qualitative proportions on selected samples. With the help of QDA Miner analysis software (v.4.1) the collected tweets, the content and the operator usage were indexed and interpreted with regard to the following categories (for more on qualitative tweet analyses with computer software, see Einspänner/Dang-Anh/Thimm 2014):

- Topics and hashtags (quantitative sorting, frequency analysis, and qualitative analysis regarding their semantic contexts)
- Quantitative operator usage of selected users in order to assess the interactive or informative potential of their tweets ("tweeting styles")
- Combined operator and content analysis of participants' tweets in selected discussion threads in order to delineate their interactional and argumentative patterns

Hashtag-Centred Ad Hoc Publics

Before examining individual Twitter users' (politicians') tweeting styles and analysing their operator usage, we first focus on the specificities of hashtag-centred ad hoc publics. For illustration, the mini-publics from the present data set, related to certain hashtags, can be categorized as "event related" or related to "second screen communication".

a) Event Related

Intensive usage of certain hashtags on Twitter during a certain point in time might be an indicator for the formation of an ad hoc public around the respective issue. Apart from the structural function of hashtags as topical anchors, hashtags are also used in order to comment, criticize, ironize or satirise topics of public interest (Dang-Anh/Einspänner/Thimm 2013). Not only but especially during election campaigns, it can be observed that topical-centred (ad hoc) publics emerge as users "invent" hashtags related to current political events.

Most attention is drawn to particularly amusing or interesting word creations (also neologisms), which have the potential for "virality". From the hashtags in the present data set considered relevant during the 2013 election (measured by frequency rate), the hashtag #Stinkefinger ("stinkfinger", a term used for describing the insulting hand gesture with a raised middle finger) can serve as an example for campaign related ad hoc publics: this hashtag (collected in over 3.100 tweets, cf.Figure 3.2) referred to a photo of the top candidate of the Social Democrats Peer Steinbrück, which was published in a well-known newspaper magazine ("Süddeutsche Magazin"). In answer to the question: "'Peerlusconi', 'problem-peer' and so on: you don't have to worry about a shortage of nice nicknames, do you?", Steinbrück simply raises his middle finger (see http://tinyurl.com/pzounuo). After the

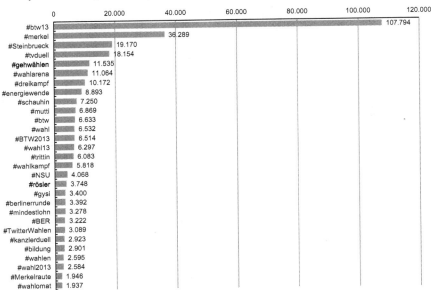

Figure 3.2 Top 20 hashtags from tweets collected during the German National Election.

publication, Twitter users started discussing the "stinkfinger-gate" by using the hashtag #Stinkefinger. Moreover, they created photomontages of the respective picture (i.e., Streinbrück showing his middle finger to the Pope, to Barack Obama or to the president of the German Bundestag),[1] which also helped the topic becoming viral and added to the ad hoc public. This issue received numerous comments in the online and offline media.

A comparison of tweets and discourses around various hashtags related to the two top candidates (Angela Merkel from the Christian Democrats and Peer Steinbrück from the Social Democrats) shows that, while the hashtag #Merkel (36,289 tweets) was mostly associated with political issues, tweets with #Steinbrueck (19,170 tweets) often referred to him as persona (see also Wladarsch, Neuberger, Brockmann and Stieglitz 2014, 467). "Stinkfinger-gate" is one example of this sort of personalisation.

b) Second Screen Communication

The practice of using Twitter on a "second screen" while following a television programme is becoming a widespread phenomenon (Buschow, Schneider, and Ueberheide 2014, Giglietto and Selva 2014). Twitter users often communicate on the microblogging platform in order to comment on the TV programme they are watching. In order to participate in the discussion on a particular TV programme, users tag their tweets with a hashtag related to the programme's name, for example the acronym #SATC for the TV sitcom "Sex and the City".

The formation of Twitter users discussing a particular TV event can be regarded as an ad hoc mini-public as individuals spontaneously come together around a clearly defined issue (the TV programme) and form a small public for a defined period of time (usually the time of the broadcast). If the discussion lasts longer than the broadcast, the ad hoc mini-public might further stabilise and develop into an event-related mini-public (at least as long as it is linked to the specific hashtag).

During election times almost "foreseeable" ad hoc publics on Twitter constitute around the TV debates among the top candidates. In the German National Election 2013 two hashtags were of importance which mark the second screen communication referring to the TV debates: #tvduell and #wahlarena. The former referred to the TV debate between chancellor Angela Merkel and her challenger Peer Steinbrück. That day, 18,154 tweets containing #tvduell were collected, while on the day of the TV debate (1 September 2013) this hashtag was used in approximately 3,000 tweets during the broadcast and in over 9,000 tweets on the day after the debate. This finding indicates the relevance of Twitter as a medium for follow-up communication and points to a certain stabilisation of the ad hoc public. Similar assumptions can be made for the hashtag #wahlarena that relates to a TV show in which citizens can ask questions to the candidates. On the day of the show with Angela Merkel (September 9, 2013) 4,867 tweets were collected during the event, 2,925 tweets two days later during the show with Peer Steinbrück. About 8,000 tweets containing the hashtag #wahlarena were sent before and after the timeframe of the live events.

When analysing Twitter users' participation in these ad hoc publics *during* the political TV events, one finding is particularly interesting: a lot of users used the hashtags #TVduell or #wahlarena as tags besides other election related hashtags. For example, on September 11th user @Dunya_Balu tweeted: "I can't help being more and more in favour of Steinbrück, the longer the campaign goes on! #wahlarena #btw13" ("Ich komme ja nicht umher, je länger Wahlkampf ist, Steinbrück immer besser zu finden! #wahlarena #btw13"). In this tweet, the user admits that her opinion about Peer Steinbrück becomes increasingly positive – apparently due to the candidate's presentation in the TV show "wahlarena" (marked by the respective hashtag). The Twitter user indicates that she is watching the show "wahlarena" and thus presents herself as being politically interested. By using #btw13 additionally, the tweet gets clustered in the broader context of the National Election 2013.

3.3 Analysing Discussion Patterns in Twitter Ad Hoc Publics: Politicians' Tweeting Styles

By extending Thimm's definition of ad hoc mini-publics as "reactions to incidents of all kinds" (cf. Chapter 11 in this volume) it is assumed that ad hoc publics on Twitter may also form around discussions, which are not necessarily marked by hashtags but by the network coherence created by the usage of @-operators between the participants. By analysing the tweeting styles of selected politicians we will discuss in what respect politicians' use of Twitter might play a role in the creation of (ad hoc) mini-publics.

50 Jessica Einspänner-Pflock, Mario Anastasiadis and Caja Thimm

Among the most active tweeting politicians during the German national election 2013 are eight members of the Green Party ("Bündnis 90/Die Grünen"), eight members of the Social Democrats ("SPD"), seven members of the Left wing party ("Die Linke"), four members of the Free Democrats ("FDP") and three members of the Christian Democrats ("CDU") (cf. Table 3.1).

Table 3.1 Top 30 of the most active members of the German parliament on Twitter during the 2013 election

Politician	Account	Political Party	Tweets Sent	Tweets Received	Retweeted by others	Overall Twitter activity
Renate Künast	@RenateKuenast	B90/Die Grünen	542	1354	1459	3355
Oliver Luksic	@OlliLuksic	FDP	516	223	518	1257
Eva Högl	@EvaHoegl	SPD	435	719	690	1844
Ulrich Kelber	@UlrichKelber	SPD	418	1037	1293	2748
Steffi Lemke	@SteffiLemke	B90/Die Grünen	349	846	1424	2619
Peter Altmaier	@peteraltmaier	CDU	316	4510	2834	7660
Monika Lazar	@monikalazar	B90/Die Grünen	315	NA	408	723
Patrick Kurth	@Patrick_Kurth	FDP	266	473	525	1264
Elke Ferner	@Elke_Ferner	SPD	242	137	374	753
Volker Wissing	@Wissing	FDP	229	398	621	1248
Petra Sitte	@Petra_Sitte_MdB	Die Linke	182	138	210	530
Burkhard Lischka	@LischkaB	SPD	178	130	240	548
Tabea Rößner	@TabeaRoessner	B90/Die Grünen	163	172	309	644
Jan Mücke	@jan_muecke	FDP	141	NA	177	318
Bärbel Höhn	@BaerbelHoehn	B90/Die Grünen	136	337	354	827
Peer Steinbrück	@peersteinbrueck	SPD	131	13814	11525	25470
Sabine Leidig	@SabineLeidig	Die Linke	126	129	370	625
Diana Golze	@GolzeMdB	Die Linke	106	22	75	203
Katja Kipping	@katjakipping	Die Linke	106	590	1327	2023
Gabriel Sigmar	@sigmargabriel	SPD	82	3194	2779	6055
Manfred Grund	@manfred_grund	CDU	71	51	67	189

Politician	Account	Political Party	Tweets Sent	Tweets Received	Retweeted by others	Overall Twitter activity
Dr. Harald Terpe	@terpeundteam	B90/Die Grünen	70	33	53	156
Florian Pronold	@FlorianPronold	SPD	67	149	163	379
Carsten Schneider	@schneidercar	SPD	61	102	108	271
Heike Brehmer	@HeikeBrehmerMdB	CDU	59	44	23	126
Gregor Gysi	@GregorGysi	Die Linke	56	3353	4083	7492
Jan van Aken	@jan_vanaken	Die Linke	50	110	354	514
Sahra Wagenknecht	@SWagenknecht	Die Linke	46	745	549	1340
Kerstin Andreae	@kerstinandreae	B90/Die Grünen	39	191	236	466
Luise Amtsberg	@Luise_Amtsberg	B90/Die Grünen	25	66	40	131

Two politicians, Peter Altmaier (Christian Democrats CDU) and Renate Künast (the Greens), have been chosen to illustrate the candidates' tweeting styles during the 2013 election campaign. Renate Künast, top candidate for the Greens in Berlin, sent the most tweets during the evaluation period (542 tweets – more than nineteen tweets per day). Peter Altmaier, the Federal Minister of the Environment, is the candidate who received the most tweets during the evaluation period (4,510 tweets) apart from the major parties' top candidates like Peer Steinbrück from the Social Democrats (Angela Merkel from the Christian Democrats doesn't have a Twitter account). This makes Altmaier's tweets an interesting issue for analysis, especially with regards to question of how interactive and dialogical this politician acts on Twitter. The two politicians' Twitter operator usage will be analysed on the one hand in order to find out if their primary tweeting style is more informative or rather interactive and dialogical. On the other hand, a qualitative tweet analysis will shed light on the politicians' ways to structure arguments and participate in the digital public discourse.

(a) the Tweeting Style of Peter Altmaier, Cdu (@Peteraltmaier) During the 2013 Election Campaign

Apart from the top candidate of the Social Democrats Peer Steinbrück (with over 13,800 tweets received, see Table 3.1) no other politician has been mentioned or directly addressed on Twitter as often as Peter Altmaier, the Federal Minister of the Environment (member of the Christian

Democrats, almost 50,000 Twitter followers at the time of the election). He gets addressed or mentioned by other Twitter users in 4,510 tweets (see Table 3.1). The operator analysis of Altmaier's Twitter usage shows a very distinctive usage of operators that can be interpreted as *personal-interactive* (see Figure 3.3).

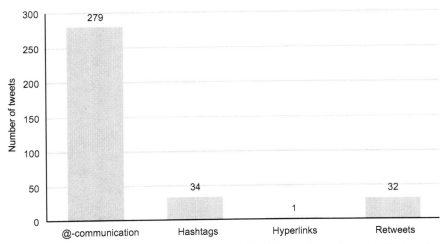

Figure 3.3 Illustration of the operator usage of politician Peter Altmaier during the 2013 election campaign (evaluation period: 1–29 September 2013).

The personal-interactive Twitter style is defined by a more frequent usage of @- and RT-operators compared to the http://-operator usage, especially as the hyperlink has a more informative function in Twitter. In contrast to that, the topical-informative Twitter style is characterised by a higher usage of hyperlinks compared to the usage of @- and RT operators. Altmaier uses more @-operators (in 78 per cent of his tweets) than hyperlinks, which he only uses in one single tweet (this is a link to a post on the online news site spiegel.de, which discusses the controversial middle finger photo by Peer Steinbrück). Due to the fact that Altmaier uses an @- or RT-operator in almost every tweet he sent, his way of tweeting can be described as interactive. However, it must be considered that Altmaier is not able to react to all the requests and comments that reach him via Twitter: With 4,510 tweets in twenty-nine days there are 155 tweets on average addressing him per day. Due to the fact that the politician himself is tweeting as @peteraltmaier (he claims that in a tweet from May 23 2013, 6:21 p.m.) it therefore must be assumed that he only responds to those tweets which are most recent or which he holds to be relevant. The analysis of his interaction with other Twitter users sheds light on the group of people (politicians, citizens, journalists) with whom he interacts most frequently. Here we find that Altmaier mainly addresses other politicians or party accounts which he does in over one-third of all tweets. It is striking that tweets addressing political opponents remain unanswered in many cases. For example, Altmaier mentions the chairman of the Social Democrats Sigmar Gabriel (@sigmargabriel) in eleven tweets and the top candidate of the Greens Jürgen Trittin (@JTrittin) in nine tweets; however, he hardly receives any response from these two politicians in return. During the entire evaluation period, Altmaier receives not a single Tweet from the account @sigmargabriel; @JTrittin answers him twice (see Table 3.2).

Table 3.2 Peter Altmaier's actor specific usage of the @-operator

@-communication to	Number	Tweets	% Tweets
Politicians & parties	144	112	35,4%
Journalists & media	27	25	7,9%
Citizens, bloggers & activists	185	179	56,6%

Another example that gives more detailed information on Altmaier's tweeting style is a dialogue between the politician and a well-known German journalist and publisher of the 'Frankfurter Allgemeine Zeitung FAZ' Frank Schirrmacher (@fr_schirrmacher, more than 35,000 followers). The conversation (cf. Table 3.3 and Figure 3.4) took place in the week after the National Election (on September 27, 2013). At this point in time, it was clear that the only possible coalition partners for the Christian Democrats (lead by Angela Merkel) could be either the Social Democrats or the Green

Table 3.3 Twitter dialogue between the politician Peter Altmaier (CDU) and the journalist Frank Schirrmacher[2]

Schirrmacher: *@peteraltmaier tweets to @jTrittin in order to make @sigmargabriel read it. Twitter as some kind of Sothebys for political auctions*

Altmaier: *@fr_schirrmacher @jTrittin @sigmargabriel Sothebys is time-honored and cares for the balance of demand and supply*

Schirrmacher: *@peteraltmaier @jTrittin @sigmargabriel Right. But it is also a space for raising prices.*

Altmaier: *@fr_schirrmacher @jTrittin @sigmargabriel I see, this is something completely new. We need to have the courage to look at the intersections*

Schirrmacher: *@peteraltmaier @jTrittin @sigmargabriel I am only asking if you are auctioneer and bidder in one person. No reason to be upset.*

Altmaier: *@fr_schirrmacher @jTrittin @sigmargabriel I am super cheerful. Shall we enter new ground? Or shall we consolidate?*

Schirrmacher: *@peteraltmaier @jTrittin @sigmargabriel You say! We are not all bidding, we are only writing the auction report.*

Altmaier: *@fr_schirrmacher @jTrittin @sigmargabriel OK. I will say it: When time has come. I have a dream, but sometimes I wake up.*

Chrissie: *The old politicians @fr_schirrmacher @peteraltmaier @jTrittin @ sigmargabriel copy the Pirate's way of communicating* ☺

Schirrmacher: *@peteraltmaier @jTrittin @sigmargabriel Careful with the meta data. Someone could find out the price you would go along with.*

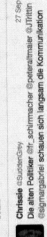

Figure 3.4 Twitter dialogue between the politician Peter Altmaier (CDU) and the journalist Frank Schirrmacher (original text).

Party. The conversation is initiated by Schirrmacher's ambiguous and ironic comment on Altmaier's tweeting style as "a kind of Sotheby's for political auctions". The metaphor of Twitter being an auction house is obviously meant as an allusion to the politician's strategy to communicate on Twitter with fellow politicians: the journalist claims that Altmaier directly addresses certain politicians on Twitter (by using the @-operator) in order to make other (opposing) politicians actually read these messages.

Schirrmacher's remark that Altmaier is trying to put the Social Democrats (personified by their chairman Sigmar Gabriel, @sigmargabriel) under pressure in terms of coalition concessions while simultaneously addressing the member of the Green Party Jürgen Trittin (@jTrittin), is playfully accepted by Altmaier and continued through an argumentative expansion on the metaphor of the "auction house", originally introduced by Schirrmacher. At the end of the dialogue, in which Sigmar Gabriel as well as Jürgen Trittin don't get involved actively but are addressed through @-mentions and @-addresses, Twitter user Chrissie (@SuddenGrey, actors group 'citizens') intervenes. However, her comment gets no visible reaction on Twitter by the addressed politicians.

The depicted conversation can serve as an example for other dialogues in the present data set. They point to a certain tendency showing that the politician rather uses Twitter as a tool for discussions with other politicians or "equal actors" (journalists), but rarely interacts with other "ordinary" users. It appears that politicians (as well as journalists) use Twitter as a *public stage* on which they *perform* their arguments. As those conversations emerge spontaneously and are not necessarily held in order to include a wider public, they can be seen as *in-group ad hoc publics*. They resemble an open conversation everyone *might* take part in (as they happen on the public Twitter stage) but take actually place between a defined group of people. Especially during election times, it can be assumed that those in-group ad hoc publics between authorities function as a self-presentation strategy. Politicians know that their Twitter communication is followed and judged by their voters, the media, and fellow politicians.

(b) the Tweeting Style of Renate Künast, the Green Party (@Renatekuenast) During the 2013 Election Campaign

Renate Künast from the Greens was also very active on Twitter in the time around the election in 2013. During the period of data collection she sent a total of 542 tweets. Similar to Peter Altmaier, Künast frequently uses the main Twitter operators, whereby she uses more hyperlinks in her tweets than Altmaier (see Figure 3.5).

By inserting hyperlinks in tweets an external source is integrated, which is then used to refer to other websites, providing background information, news, photos or videos. Compared to Altmaier, Künast uses the retweet function about three times more often. Retweeting can be understood as digital affirmation with which the retweeting user considers the specific

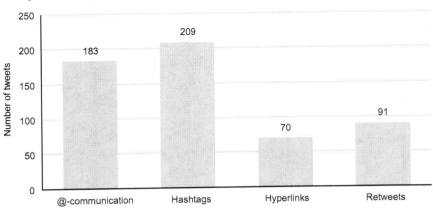

Figure 3.5 Renate Künast's Twitter style.

tweet important and interesting enough to be worth redistributing to their own followers. This function is vital to create and extend visibility in the politics-media ecosystem (Vaccari & Valeriani 2013). In addition, the author of the original tweet gets notified about the retweet. One example indicates that Renate Künast seems to be well aware of this communication process: she retweets a tweet by journalist Frank Schirrmacher, which deals with the possibility of addressing targeted voters selectively by using big data: "RT @fr_schirrmacher: How big data are invalidating the electoral secret: we know who you vote for http://t.co/di7X6mYqUD #faz" ("RT @ fr_schirrmacher: Wie Big Data das Wahlgeheimnis aushebelt: Wir wissen, wen du wählen wirst http://t.co/di7X6mYqUD #faz"). The strategy with which Künast addresses potential constituents on purpose substantiates the assumption that politicians who use Twitter in a professional way are well aware of their potential influence beyond their own followers.

Regarding her Twitter activity during the evaluation period, Renate Künast is particularly active during specific political events, i.e., the TV debate between Angela Merkel and Peer Steinbrück. Künast's participation is characterised by a high usage of topic-related hashtags (she uses more than five times as many hashtags as Peter Altmaier). For example, she comments on Steinbrück's statements in the TV debate by summarizing the most important aspects of his candidacy: "Steinbrück: affordable housing, education for my children. The daily life of the people. Exactly! #tvduell" ("Steinbrück: bezahlbarer Wohnraum, Bildung meiner Kinder. Der Alltag der Menschen. Genau! #tvduell").

Particularly during times of elections, politicians are subject to critical and polemic tweets (see Chapter 9 in this volume). In 2013, Renate Künast was often personally addressed on Twitter when users expressed their disrespect towards her party. In one tweet, a voter addresses Künast by telling her that he would not vote for the Greens but for the new party AfD ("Alternative for Germany", Euro-sceptical party): "@RenateKuenast @Die_Gruenen Well, of course! Anything but Die Grünen! Tomorrow AfD!!!!" ("@RenateKuenast @Die_Gruenen Aber sicher doch! Nur nicht die Grünen! Morgen AfD!!!!"). On the other hand, when the electoral debacle of the Greens became apparent, Twitter users also sent messages of solidarity and regret to Künast as a representative for her party: "@RenateKuenast focus on your areas of expertise! I am disappointed. Lost so much popularity in such a short time" ("@RenateKuenast besinnt euch auf euere kompetenzfelder! Was bin ich enttäuscht. In so kurzer Zeit soviel Zuspruch verlieren").

The analysis of the Twitter communication of Altmaier and Künast highlights the role of Twitter as a public stage for politicians during election campaigns. Both candidates use Twitter less to publicly address their (prospective) voters but more particularly to engage with colleagues as well as political opponents openly. Twitter allows both for political controversy, which can be used to distinguish oneself, and for digital appeasement, which manifests itself in an extreme form of intra-party support. This "heterarchical" in-group talk among politicians points to Twitter's function as political stage instead of a platform for interaction between politicians and citizens.

3.4 Conclusion

This chapter emphasises two central aspects of Twitter as a digital space for political communication and discourse. On the one hand we find that during election campaigns citizens as well as politicians and journalists actively participate in digital public discourse on Twitter and foster the formation of ad hoc (mini-)publics. Here, they negotiate and try to explain political issues by using hashtags or taking a rather satirical standpoint. In addition, it was shown that Twitter has become a relevant discussion platform for people while watching political events on TV (second screen type of use). Especially during TV debates the politicians' statements are commented and discussed on Twitter within the respective topic-centred mini-publics. The specific media logic of Twitter creates a highly interconnected network of themes and people by supporting the technical distribution of ideas and opinions among its users.

On the other hand, communication happening on Twitter can be regarded as an integral part of the digital public sphere that can serve as a conducive environment for deliberation processes. Although Twitter in this respect is mainly used by politicians for interacting with each other and less as a means for dialogue between citizens and politicians, political discussions are performed publicly, can be observed and potentially contributed to by everyone.

All in all these findings underline the growing relevance of Twitter as a public discursive space, which allows for the creation of deliberative mini-publics. However, digital discursive participation always has to be seen against the background of a broader context, which needs to integrate the

58 Jessica Einspänner-Pflock, Mario Anastasiadis and Caja Thimm

technological *and* social circumstances. Therefore, for future research the focus should lie upon Twitter as one component within wider online and offline media repertoires.

Notes

1. See http://jensipresident.tumblr.com for an illustration. Page accessed on 15/05/2015.
2. Additional remark: neither the mentioned @jTrittin nor @sigmargabriel actively took part in this conversation.

Works Cited

Albrecht, Steffen. 2006. "Whose voice is heard in online deliberation? A study of participation and representation in political debates on the Internet". *Information, Communication & Society* 9 (1): 37–41.

Bor, Stephanie E. 2013. *Democratic Deliberation on Social Network Sites: A Study of Digital Deliberative Discourse in the 2012 Election*. Dissertation. The University of Utah. Accessed March 24, 2015. http://content.lib.utah.edu/utils/getfile/collection/etd3/id/2191/filename/2193.pdf.

Bruns, Axel. 2012. "Ad hoc innovation by users of social networks: The case of Twitter". *ZSI Discussion Paper 16*. Accessed March 26, 2015. http://eprints.qut.edu.au/49824/3/2012002284.pdf.

Bruns, Axel, and Burgess, Jean. 2011. "The use of Twitter hashtags in the formation of ad hoc publics" (paper presented at the 6th European Consortium for Political Research General Conference, 25 - 27 August 2011, University of Iceland, Reykjavik). Accessed 13 March 2015. http://eprints.qut.edu.au/46515/.

Buschow, Christopher, Schneider, Beate, and Ueberheide, Simon. 2014. "Tweeting television: Exploring communication activities on Twitter while watching TV". *Communications* 39 (2): 129–149.

Chambers, Simone. 2009. "Rhetoric and the Public Sphere: Has Deliberative Democracy Abandoned Mass Democracy?" *Political Theory* 37 (3): 323–350.

Dang-Anh, Mark, Einspänner, Jessica, and Thimm, Caja. 2013. "Kontextualisierung durch Hashtags. Die Mediatisierung des politischen Sprachgebrauchs im Internet". In *Öffentliche Wörter. Analysen zum öffentlich-medialen Sprachgebrauch. Perspektiven Germanistischer* Linguistik, edited by Hajo Diekmannshenke and Thomas Niehr, 137–159. Stuttgart: Ibidem.

Delli Carpini, Michael X., Cook, Fay L., and Jacobs, Lawrence R. 2004. "Public Deliberations, Discursive Participation and Citizen Engagement: A Review of the Empirical Literature". *Annual Review of Political Science*, 7 (1): 315–344.

Eimeren van, Birgit and Frees, Beate. 2014. "79 Prozent der Deutschen online – Zuwachs bei mobiler Internetnutzung und Bewegtbild". *Media Perspektiven* 7–8/2014: 378–396.

Einspänner, Jessica, Dang-Anh, Mark, and Thimm, Caja. 2014. "Computer-assisted content analysis of Twitter data". In *Twitter and Society,* edited by Katrin Weller, Axel Bruns, Jean Burgess, Merja Mahrt, and Cornelius Puschmann, 97–108. New York, NY: Peter Lang.

Fuchs, Christian. 2013. *Social Media. A Critical Introduction.* Los Angeles: Sage.

Giglietto, Fabio and Selva, Donatella. 2014. "Second Screen and Participation: A Content Analysis on a Full Season Dataset of Tweets". *Journal of Communication* 64 (2): 260–277.

Kempf, Dieter, and Güllner, Manfred. 2013. "Demokratie 3.0 – Bedeutung des Internets für den Wahlkampf". Accessed March 13, 2015. http://www.bitkom.org/files/documents/BITKOM_PK_Bedeutung_des_Internets_im_Bundestagswahlkampf_07_05_2013.pdf.

Kim, Minjeong, and Woo, Han. 2012. "Measuring Twitter-based political participation and deliberation in the South Korean context by using social network and Triple Helix indicators". *Scientometrics* 2012 (90): 121–140.

Lafont, Cristina. 2015. "Deliberation, Participation, and Democratic Legitimacy: Should Deliberative Mini-publics Shape Public Policy?" *The Journal of Political Philosophy* 23 (1): 40–63.

Maireder, Axel, and Schlögl, Stephan. 2014. "24 Hours of an #outcry: The Networked Publics of a Socio-Political Debate". *European Journal of Communication,* Sept. 2014, 1–16.

Nuernbergk, Christian. 2013. "Twitternde Bundestagsabgeordnete: Aktivität, Inhalte, Interaktion". Accessed 13 March 2015. http://www.hamburger-wahlbeobachter.de/2013/09/twitternde-bundestagsabgeordnete.html.

Thimm, Caja, Einspänner, Jessica, and Dang-Anh, Mark. 2012. "Twitter als Wahlkampfmedium: Modellierung und Analyse politischer Social-Media-Nutzung". *Publizistik* 57 (3): 293–313.

Thimm, Caja, Dang-Anh, Mark, and Einspänner, Jessica. 2014. "Mediatized Politics – Structures and Strategies of Discursive Participation and Online Deliberation on Twitter". In *Mediatized Worlds: Culture and Society in a Media Age,* edited by Friedrich Krotz and Andreas Hepp, 253–269. London: Palgrave Macmillian.

Vaccari, Christian, and Valeriani, Augusto. 2013. "Follow the leader! Direct and indirect flows of political communication during the 2013 Italian general election campaign". *New Media & Society.*

Wladarsch, Jennifer, Neuberger, Christoph, Brockmann, Tobias, and Stieglitz, Stefan. 2014. "Der Bundestagswahlkampf 2013 in den Social Media". *Media Perspektiven 9/2014,* 456–474.

4 Is Twitter Invigorating Spanish Democracy?

A Study of Political Interaction through the Accounts of The Prime Minister and The Leader of the Main Opposition Party

Elena Cebrián Guinovart, Tamara Vázquez Barrio and David Sarias Rodríguez

Introduction

Twitter erupted into Spanish politics during the 2011 national elections. At that time, this social networks' capacity to generate political mobilisation and even ideological transformation was already the object of intense debates stimulated by the presence of the new media within the Arab Spring, the Movimiento 15-M in Spain and Occupy Wall Street in the United States (Ferreras, 2011; Menéndez, 2011; Martínez, 2011; Romero, 2011) as well as by the extensively publicised use of the social media by Barak Obama's 2008 presidential campaign (Talbot, 2008; Manlow, Weiser and Friedman, 2009). Moreover, that same year Parmelee and Bichard found that users of the San Francisco-based micro-blogging service Twitter in the United States perceived it as a means to re-define political participation and to re-configure the established patterns of interaction between political representatives and their constituents. According to these authors, Twitter forces upon candidates the expectations of bi-directionality espoused by electors, compelling political hopefuls to redefine accordingly their thematic agenda. Simultaneously, the limitation of 140 characters imposed by Twitter also obliges politicians to clarify their message. Finally, Parmelee and Bichard also pinpoint the enhanced explicative power added by links included within tweets, the multiplied outreach power brought by users' capacity to forward politicians' messages through retweets and the positive side-effects, from the viewpoint of political participation, of politicians who use Twitter to increase both political support for their proposals and economic contributions for their campaigns (Parmelee and Bichard, 2011).

Although Twitter's potential to revitalise political participation in Spain has been evaluated since the earliest published examinations of the phenomenon, it has been so as part of broader analyses, rather than as the central object of study. Thus, a professional briefing published halfway through the 2011 campaign and focused on strategic communication observed that Twitter had become the social network of choice for most

Spanish political leaders and pointed out the potential of the micro-blogging platform to foster deliberative democracy, given that it (apparently) handed control of the thematic agenda to users through messages and hashtags (Observatorio Político 2.0/ Ketchum Pleon, 2011). A first academic assessment of Twitter was presented by two authors of this chapter in a paper delivered shortly after the end of the 2011 campaign. This work examined the electoral use of Twitter through a comparative analysis of the official accounts of the leaders of the two main Spanish political parties: the Popular party's Mariano Rajoy and the Socialist party's Alfredo Pérez Rubalcaba. The resulting conclusions demonstrated significant differences in the handling of Twitter by both politicians, but also noted a shared failure to use the opportunities for enhanced participation that it afforded. (Cebrián and Vázquez, 2013).

Two other papers presented in 2012 which examined the themes that appeared in the tweets published in the accounts of Mariano Rajoy and Alfredo Pérez Rubalcaba during the legislative campaign of 2011 also confirmed that "political participation" was slightly higher in the latter's account. Mariano Rajoy's account, on the other hand, served as a mere venue to advertise the candidate's other campaign activities and miserably failed to foster dialogue about citizen's concerns (García Ortega y Zugasti, 2012). Rubalcaba's account, however, was employed to talk to the citizenry and to mobilise the electorate, even if in a limited fashion circumscribed to pre-established electoral aims and intended as a reinforcement to the themes developed within the traditional campaign (Zurutuza, 2012).

The possibilities for enhanced political participation offered by Twitter were still underused during the Spanish regional elections of 2012. Another essay by Elena Cebrián and Tamara Vázquez examining the use of Twitter by the candidates of the four main parties running in the Basque regional elections demonstrated again that fostering political participation does not seem to be a priority for politicians using Twitter. Given the scarcity and poor quality of conversations and the predominant frequency of series of comments unconnected with each other as well as the original tweet and dealing with issues of little political relevance, it could be concluded that dialogue between elected and electors was non-existent. The opportunities for greater political dialogue afforded by hypertextuality were not used either: hyperlinks were rarely employed to expand the information provided by the available 140 characters of a tweet and, when used at all, these links were intended to reinforce the electoral message rather than to expand and clarify it. (Cebrián Guinovart, Vázquez Barrio and Olabarrieta Vallejo, 2013).

Luis Deltell has sought to clarify the political effects of Twitter in two essays that examine both the quantity and quality of political activity on this platform. The first article analyses the relationship between the degree of activity taking place in social networks and final voting outcomes. This essay efficiently debunks the widespread assumption that social networks are more efficient for small or newly appeared parties. Deltell examines

62 *Elena Cebrián Guinovart et al.*

here the strategy with which the green party eQuo approached the 2011 campaign and concludes that although the party made a technically flawless use of social networks, it failed to achieve its electoral aims. The fact that Deltell's work allows him to affirm in eQuo's case "most votes were gained in the places and neighborhoods where the party followed the most traditional campaigning methods such as speech-making, mass rallies, billboards and entertainment activities" invites a less optimistic evaluation of the impact of social networks upon voting patterns among minority groups (Deltell, 2012).

Deltell's second study focuses on the role of Twitter during the Andalusian regional elections of 2012 and, through a comparison between the frequency and characteristics of the use of Twitter and electoral returns, concludes that activity patterns in the micro-blogging platform may be useful to predict electoral results for well-established, main parties (Deltel, Claes and Osteso, 2013). Another author, Pablo Barberá, has also contributed to a greater understanding of the correlation between activity on Twitter and political participation. Firstly, Barberá questions whether the citizens most active on Twitter are actually representative of the public at large, for political users of Twitter tend to be "mostly men, living in urban areas, and with strong ideological preferences", to which it must also be added that "the followers of political parties are more active in political discussions than the rest" (Barberá and Rivero, 2014). Secondly, Barberá interprets the different ways in which retweets are employed by users from different ideological backgrounds as indicative of different forms of understanding political participation. In the Spanish case, conservative users re-tweet at a considerably higher rate than their progressive counterparts, and Barberá concludes that "this kind of behaviour suggests that the political discussion among rightwing voters is more hierarchical and more structured" (Barberá and Rivero, 2014). Lastly, Barberá also emphasises the role of ideological affinity within patterns of political participation noting how, in the case of the U.S. presidential campaign of 2012 "public exchanges on Twitter take place predominantly among users with similar viewpoints".

Overall, the works mentioned above tend to coincide in their assessment of the low quality of participation in Spanish political life through Twitter, although it must also be considered that all these analyses assess the issue from the viewpoint of political participation during electoral campaigns – that is, at precisely the juncture where it may be considered natural that forms of political persuasion aimed at gaining votes displace conventional, presumably more reflexive, forms of political debate. Moreover, as pointed out earlier, all these studies treat political participation as a secondary matter within evaluations focused elsewhere in the political process. In contrast, the present chapter aims at furthering research about political participation through Twitter in Spain according to an alternative framework focusing on the basic characteristics of political participation itself and doing so in a non-electoral context so as to ascertain whether day-to-day political activity

Is Twitter Invigorating Spanish Democracy?   63

through Twitter allows for enhanced participation, and whether it helps to invigorate the quality of democratic political debate.

4.1 Methodology

This study focuses on the official Twitter accounts of the leaders of the two national parties with the highest parliamentary representation: those of the prime minister and president of the Popular Party, Mariano Rajoy – @marianorajoy – and of Alfredo Pérez Rubalcaba – @rubalcaba – the then-leader of the The Spanish Socialist Workers' Party PSOE, the main opposition party. More specifically, this chapter is based on an examination of 625 tweets published on both accounts on a sample of days randomly selected from the first half of 2014: January 6 and 14, February 15 and 23, March 19 and 25, April 23, May 1 and 31 and June 6 and 30. The total number of tweets is divided between the sixty-seven authored by the politicians and the 558 comments on these authored by members of the public. Each category is analysed separately so as to gauge the quality of participation. In the case of tweets written by the politicians, we have evaluated the type of message, *authorship, intention, theme*, the *type of interaction* it elicited and whether it includes a hashtag, a mention or a hyperlink.

Politicians' messages were also classified according to the proportion of tweets and retweets posted by the political leader himself or members of his team. Retweets are considered as a form of expansion of the political discourse that, from the viewpoint of participation, could imply an invitation to dialogue. The type of author of both tweets and retweets has also been taken into account to establish this typology. In the case of tweets we distinguish between tweets whose author was the politician himself – identifiable because politicians use a particular signature – or by a member of his team, in which case no signature is used. From the viewpoint of political participation, the proportion of messages authored by the politician is taken as proportional to his availability for direct engagement with the public whereas the proportion of tweets authored by his campaign team is taken to represent the degree of bureaucratisation of his political Twitter style. Retweets by politicians are categorised according to fourteen different types of authors established by Pérez, Berná and Arroyas (Pérez Díaz, Berná Sicilia, and Arroyas Langa, 2013). We have categorised authors of these retweets according to the degree of openness they indicate to dialogue and to the themes to which such dialogue is directed. Thus re-tweeted authors that are categorised as *Traditional Cyber- media, Native Cyber- media, Journalist,* and *Opinion Leader* imply openness to dialogue towards current affairs issues. Four other categories – *Politician, Political Party, Political Institution,* and *Grassroots Political Activist* – imply a willingness to engage in ideological discussion. Two other types of authors re-tweeted labeled *Financial or Economic Entities* and *Social Movements or NGO* imply a will to debate social affairs. Finally, authors categorized as *Citizen* imply a disposition for

64   Elena Cebrián Guinovart et al.

dialogue with members of the general public. A last category called *Other* includes all other types of author which are not covered by the above.

There are nine possibilities under the category of *Intention*. Thus, *Visibility of Politicians*; *Live Tweeting of a Political Act* and *Advertising Achievements* are considered as low-quality intentions from the viewpoint of political participation, because they are oriented toward the politician's self-promotion. Three more categories under the labels *Ideological Discourse*, *Proposal* and *Critical/Defensive Message* are considerably more promising from the viewpoint of political participation as they imply some kind of ideological positioning likely to elicit valuable political exchanges. A further category called *Human Side* has been associated with the personalisation of politics and therefore has also been considered a form of low-quality participation. Finally, all tweets with aims not listed above have been classified as *Other*.

Tweets are categorised according to the typology employed by the Spanish government-run public opinion research organism, Centro de Investigaciones Sociológicas (CIS), although the CIS's twenty categories are in turn split in two different macro-types from the viewpoint of political participation. The first category includes sixteen themes associated with different types of political engagement or political activity, which may elicit high value political interaction: *National, International and Regional Politics, Economy, Employment, Population, Environment, Housing, Health, Justice, Science and Technology, Education, Social Problems, Media, Culture, Sports* and *Ideology*. The second category includes two themes – *Political Activity* and *Political Leader* – associated with political 'theatralisation', in the sense of political activities aimed at promoting the politician's activities but devoid of meaningful political content, and which, therefore, are likely to lead to low-quality political participation.

The appearance of hashtags and mentions in politicians' messages and their types has been assessed as reflecting the politician's willingness to engage either in a general debate with the public at large in the case of hashtags, or in a specific exchange with a given Twitter user in the case of mentions. Links are understood to represent an invitation by the politician to go beyond the 140-character limit imposed by the Twitter format and, therefore, as an attempt to enrich the political discourse employing other resources.

Last but not least, the success of politicians' tweets and the interaction they generate has been assessed through the number of retweets and favorites gained by the politicians' accounts as both are considered as low-level forms of interaction. In those cases in which messages provoke further reactions these have been divided into two categories: *conversation* when politicians reply to citizens' responses and *comments* when members of the public do answer to messages, but politicians fail to reply. In this last instance, when citizens do react but politicians fail to respond, cases that generate dialogue between electors even without politicians' participation have also been categorised independently. In this framework *conversations* represent examples of qualitatively valuable political interaction and *comments* as instances in which the public expresses an interest in interacting with politicians that goes unattended.

The 558 comments to the politicians' tweets have been assessed to ascertain the aspirations for interaction directed to politicians by members of the public. The categories employed in this case are *authorship, theme, intention* and *quality. Authorship* and *theme* reproduce the same parameters applied in the analysis of the original tweets. Those comments in which there is a clear *intention* have been categorised as *favourable, unfavourable, neutral* or as a *question*, when information was requested from the politician. The quality of the tweets written by the public has been assessed according to two variables: *consistency* with the theme of the original tweet posted by the politician, and *relevance* in the sense of raising or addressing a politically significant issue.

The resulting conclusions of this analysis are organised under two sub-sections related to both the characteristics and the quality of the political participation that emerges from the sample examined. The first subsection evaluates whether the "Twitterstyles" of @marianorajoy and @rubalcaba actually contributes to fostering political participation. The second sub-section identifies the general characteristics of the comments posted on each account by members of the public from two different perspectives: the first approaches the usage of retweets and favourites; the second analysis evaluates the contents of the *comments*. Retweets and favourites have been considered as basic forms of interaction that imply some evaluation and interaction with the political content uploaded by the politicians but only after a mechanical, highly impersonal fashion. *Comments*, however, require a greater degree of commitment and deliberative effort. *Comments* also allow for assessment of the users' attitude and of whether users' direct the capacity for interaction provided by Twitter toward an enhanced form of political participation.

4.2 Politicians' Behaviour: "Twitterstyle" and Participation

This section examines how politicians employ Twitter, what we may call their "twitterstyle", so as to ascertain whether and to what degree these styles foster political participation. A first difference that emerges from comparing the Mariano Rajoy and Pérez Rubalcaba Twitter accounts is that the prime minister uploads twice as many messages as Pérez Rubalcaba – forty-five tweets in @marianorajoy against twenty-two in @rubalcaba – and also receives twice as many *comments* – 385 against Rubalcaba's 173.

In the case of @marianorajoy the number of tweets and of retweets are roughly the same – twenty-three original messages against twenty-two retweets – whereas in @rubalcaba's case the number of retweets is almost double the number of original messages – a mere eight original messages against fourteen retweets. The source of the retweeted messages provides

66   *Elena Cebrián Guinovart et al.*

a first inkling of the politician's (dis)interest in promoting genuine political participation among the general public: of the six possible authorships mentioned in the methodological introduction, @rubalcaba employs only one and @marianorajoy six. Rubalcaba invariably retweets messages produced by his own party whereas @marianorajoy indulges in such behaviour only once. However, although the prime minister's account retweets other sources, those most frequently used are accounts of political institutions linked with the government such as the Congress of Deputies, Moncloa (the office of the Spanish Prime Minister), the Ministry of Defence and the office of the deputy prime minister. Although the specific sources used by each account are indeed at variance, their aims and strategy are identical: both accounts retweet – exclusively in the case of @rubalcaba and predominantly in the case of @marianorajoy – from sources that reinforce pre-established political identities. In the sample analysed, retweets are not used either to foster debate or to invigorate citizen participation in the political debate.

The data about the intentionality of tweets uploaded to both accounts (Table 4.1) also confirms that the aim of these tweets appears to be to reinforce the politician's standing.

Table 4.1 Intentionality of the tweets posted at the politicians' profile

	@marianorajoy		@rubalcaba	
	Frequency	%	*Frequency*	%
Visibility of politicians	30	66,7	5	22,7
Live tweeting a political act	10	22,2	11	50,0
Advertising achievements	0	0,0	0	0,0
Ideological discourse	0	0,0	1	4,5
Proposal	0	0,0	0	0,0
Criticism	0	0,0	3	13,6
Defensive message	0	0,0	0	0,0
Expression of gratitude	0	0,0	0	0,0
Human side	0	0,0	2	9,1
Other	5	11,1	0	0,0
Total	45	100	22	100

In both cases, even if in reverse proportion, most messages either describe the politician's activities or merely reproduce statements pronounced during the course of those activities. Thus, nine out of ten messages uploaded by @marianorajoy and seven out of ten messages published by @rubalcaba deal with announcing events attended by the politician. Tweets that may be interpreted as aiming to foster greater political dialogue – that is, as falling under the categories of *ideological discourse, proposal* and *criticism* – can only be found in @rubalcaba, and even then only exceptionally: they make up two out ten published messages.

There is considerable variation between the themes predominantly used in each account. Thus, @marianorajoy focuses on trying to communicate the activities of the prime minister and the achievements of his government, whereas @rubalcaba opts for criticizing the government according to already established main party lines of opposition.

Table 4.2 Politicians' tweets by theme

	@marianorajoy		@rubalcaba	
	Frequency	*%*	*Frequency*	*%*
National Politics	4	8,9	2	9,1
International Politics	3	6,7	0	0,0
Regional Politics	0	0	0	0,0
Economy	9	20	0	0,0
Employment	0	0	1	4,5
Population	0	0	1	4,5
Environment	0	0	0	0,0
Housing	0	0	0	0,0
Health	2	4,4	1	4,5
Justice	0	0	6	27,3
Science and Technology	0	0	0	0,0
Education	0	0	0	0,0
Social Problems	0	0	1	4,5
Media	0	0	0	0,0
Culture	1	2,2	5	22,7
Sports	0	0	0	0,0
Ideology	0	0	0	0,0
Political Activity	23	51,1	2	9,1
Political Leader	0	0	1	4,5
Other	3	6,7	2	9,1
Total	45	100	22	100

The range of themes dealt with by @rubalcaba is broader than those addressed by @marianorajoy: the leader of the opposition covers ten out of nineteen selected themes while the prime minister only deals with seven. Furthermore, the prime minister's account focuses on political theatralisation rather than on meaningful political engagement: well over half of the messages uploaded in this account deal with the prime minister's schedule of public appearances. The remaining half focuses on *national* and *international politics*. Political gimmickry is much less present in @rubalcaba, where messages falling under the categories of *political activity* and *political leader* only represent 14 per cent of the total. The leader of the opposition's tweets deal mostly with relevant political issues, notably – one in four

68   *Elena Cebrián Guinovart et al.*

tweets – with questions associated with the heading *justice*. Within these matters, Rubalcaba focuses on the judicial proceedings then dealing with corruption cases and on the debate surrounding the modification of the legal framework regulating abortion. The second most frequently used theme by Rubalcaba is *culture*, particularly the debate about the adequate VAT percentile applied to cultural activities, which is used as a means to criticise the government. The leader of the opposition also uploads tweets, although rarely, about *national politics, employment, population* and *social problems*.

A first thematic analysis shows that the most-tweeted issues in both accounts are those that provide greater visibility to the politicians, their activities and interests. Themes that may elicit political or ideological debate and that may foster citizen participation in the political process are generally neglected on both Twitter accounts. This conclusion is reinforced even further by a comparison between the themes preferred by the politicians and those chosen by the public in its commentaries as seen under subheading 14.2.

Hashtags can be found in approximately half of the messages uploaded by the politicians' accounts: in twenty-three messages out of @marianorajoy's forty-five and in ten of the twenty-two uploaded by @rubalcaba. As noted in the methodological introduction, the appearance of hashtags is sometimes taken to indicate the intent to introduce a debate which is taking place elsewhere than on the politician's account. Yet the cases included within the sample examined either do not support this assumption or show that this tool is not used to introduce qualitatively relevant political debates. Although in both accounts hashtags are present in about half the messages, the debates they seem to be directed toward – if, indeed, these are debates at all – are invariably related to either the candidate himself or the party, rather than toward substantive political or ideological issues.

Table 4.3 Hashtags uploaded by @marianorajoy and @rubalcaba

@marianorajoy			@rubalcaba		
	Frequency	*%*		*Frequency*	*%*
Without Hashtag	23	51,1	Without Hashtag	12	54,5
#CdE30	7	15,6	#aborto	2	9,1
#Cmin	4	8,9	#AbortoLegal	2	9,1
#SesióndeControl	4	8,9	#Congreso	4	18,2
#Libano	3	6,7	#TúMuevesEuropa	2	9,1
#PresidenteSuárez	2	4,4	**Total Tweets**	22	–
#España	1	2,2			
#EUCO	1	2,2			
#Insulza	1	2,2			
#Rajoy	1	2,2			
Total Tweets	45	–			

The most frequently used hashtag in @marianorajoy refers to an economic-related event attended by the prime minister; the two next most frequently mentioned ones regard a cabinet meeting and a weekly parliamentary question-time session. These are in turn followed, although at a considerable distance, by more hashtags dealing with the prime minister and his activities, as in the case of hashtags from the EU council's press and from general secretary of the Organisation of American States José Manuel Insulza, whom Rajoy met during his official visit to the United States.

Although hashtags are slightly less frequent in @rubalcaba, these are all devoted to the politician's activities and to party affairs: the most frequent, #Congreso, is a general, non-partisan hashtag, but Rubalcaba employs it to tweet about his own parliamentary interventions. Also present is #TúMuevesEuropa, the Socialist party hashtag for the European parliamentary elections. The two remaining hashtags which appear in this account, #aborto and #AbortoLegal, are those employed by the PSOE to oppose the Popular Party-proposed law to regulate abortion.

In the case of *mentions* there are some qualitative differences between @rubalcaba and @marianorajoy but, again, the communication strategy of both accounts is identical. In the first place, *mentions* more frequent in @rubalcaba, where they appear in six out of ten messages or thirteen of the twenty-two whereas @marianorajoy's case only two out of ten (nine of the forty-five messages) employ this resource. Secondly, the list of mentions included in Table 4.4 shows how both accounts employ this resource to reinforce the image and the visibility of the politician and of his political party, but never to foster greater participation from the public in the political debate.

Table 4.4 Mentions uploaded in @marianorajoy and @rubalcaba

@marianorajoy			@rubalcaba		
	Frequency	*%*		*Frequency*	*%*
Without Mention	37	82	Without Mention	9	41
@CdEconomia	3	7	@ElenaValenciano	10	45
@MalosseHenri	2	5	@psoe	3	14
@matteorenzi	1	2	@abarceloh25	1	4
@Ppopular	1	2	Total	23	–
@cancerinfantil	1	2			
Total	45	100			

The Socialist-party-lead candidate to the European elections – Elena Valenciano – is mentioned in about half of the tweets uploaded by @rubalcaba, followed by Àngels Barceló, the anchorwoman of a leading radio program attended by Rubalcaba. @marianorajoy, on his part, mentions an economic meeting in which he partakes, two international politicians whom he meets and his own party. Non-political *mentions* include politically bland support for an NGO, which is promoting a day supporting efforts to fight childhood cancer. In conclusion, of the two basic functions of *mentions* on Twitter – to interact with other users and to promote one's own published content – only the second is used in the examined accounts: to invigorate democratic dialogue, foster interaction and promote political debates are, quite simply, not discernible objectives of either @rubalcaba, or @marianorajoy.

With regards to the most frequently used *links* @marianorajoy exhibits twice as many as his opponent, as shown in Figure 4.1 but the aims with which *links* are used in both accounts also seem to be quite different. Most links in @marianorajoy direct readers towards events in which Rajoy is participating and towards the web page of the office of the prime minister, where more information about the same and similar issues may be found. Rajoy never directs his followers towards other social networks. In sharp contrast, these are the preferred targets of the links uploaded by @rubalcaba. The leader of the opposition also directs his own followers towards, in this order, his party's web page and self-promoting videos. The other social network linked to Rubalcaba's account is Facebook (free of the character limit imposed by Twitter), where he publishes expanded opinions and comments: it appears that Rubalcaba's use of Facebook is considerably more intense than his use of Twitter.

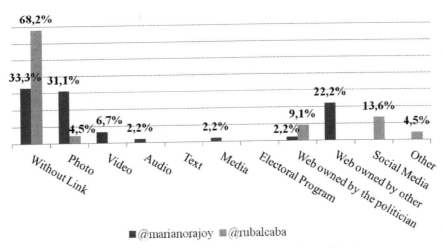

Figure 4.1 Type of links uploaded in @marianorajoy and @rubalcaba.

4.3 Political Participation through Retweets, Favourites and Comments

The following pages examine user participation – understanding a user as any person who interacts with the politicians' account regardless of whether the said person is or not a follower as well – through the presence of *retweets*, *favourites* and *comments*. *Retweets* and *favourites* are considered, as indicated in the introduction, as indicating a basic level of participation, in the sense that their production is undemanding. *Comments* are considered as indicating higher user engagement inasmuch as they are a form of user-generated content.

As shown in Table 4.5 retweets are the form of participation most frequently employed in both accounts. @marianorajoy uploads twenty-three original messages, which are retweeted twice as many times as they are marked deemed favourites and thrice as many times as they are commented upon. In @rubalcaba's case, the number of retweets is triple the number of favourites and double the number of *comments*.

Table 4.5 Total amount of retweets, favourites and comments

	Tweets	Retweets	Media	Favourites	Media	Comments	Media
@marianorajoy	23	1243	54,0	686	29,8	385	16,7
@rubalcaba	8	428	53,5	145	18,1	173	21,6

The fact that *comments* are the second-most-frequent form of participation in @rubalcaba seems to support the findings of Barberá regarding ideological differences in Twitter usage during the national elections of 2011 (Barberá and Rivero, 2014): the pattern of participation in an ideologically conservative account such as @marianorajoy appears to be more hierarchically structured and to predominantly materialise in the form of echoing the leadership's messages through retweets.

The next level of analysis examines the 558 comments uploaded on both accounts and it is aimed at establishing a framework of interpretation for the political interaction that these imply. We examined *authorship, intentionality*, the *themes* covered and the political *quality* of their contents as well as the relationship of these comments with the original tweets.

The account of the Prime Minister receives a larger number of *comments* than those elicited by the leader of the opposition. As pointed out in section 14.1, of the 558 *comments* included in the sample, 385 appear in @marianorajoy and 173 in @rubalcaba. However, *comments* in Rubalcaba's account carry more weight as a form of political participation, because this is the second most frequently used form of interaction as shown in Table 4.5.

Although there is a range of fourteen possible authors, *comments* to both accounts are almost exclusively written by common citizens: in the case of @rubalcaba all of the 173 comments are written by individual members of the public, in the case of @marianorajoy this is so in nine out of ten cases – 350 out of 385. Most authors who are not private citizens are politicians affiliated to the prime minister's party.

Two per cent of the *comments* uploaded in @marianorajoy – up to seven of the total – fall under the category of *other* authors. These are profiles which, appearing to be those of individual citizens turned out to be quite

72　*Elena Cebrián Guinovart et al.*

impersonal in their general contents and very scarce activity, which was also almost exclusively dedicated to criticise the government and its representatives. These accounts are assumed to follow a political strategy rather than an individual's initiative.

The range of *themes* of the *comments* uploaded in @marianorajoy and @rubalcaba is shown in Table 4.6. In this occasion, in quantitative terms, there is no significant difference between the range of themes treated in each account. Twelve themes appear in the *comments* uploaded in @marianorajoy whereas those found in @rubalcaba fall under thirteen different categories.

Table 4.6 *Comments* by theme

	@marianorajoy		@rubalcaba	
	Frequency	*%*	*Frequency*	*%*
National Politics	88	22,9	68	39,3
International Politics	17	4,4	1	0,6
Regional Politics	2	0,5	1	0,6
Economy	67	17,4	26	15,0
Employment	12	3,1	3	1,7
Population	0	0	4	2,3
Environment	1	0,3	0	0
Housing	0	0	0	0
Health	3	0,8	2	1,2
Justice	0	0	1	0,6
Science and Technology	0	0	0	0
Education	1	0,3	2	1,2
Social Problems	39	10,1	19	11,0
Media	0	0	0	0
Culture	0	0	36	20,8
Sports	0	0	0	0
Ideology	0	0	0	0
Political Activity	7	1,8	0	0
Political Leader	100	26,0	3	1,7
Electoral Campaign	0	0	0	0
Other	48	12,5	7	4,0
Total	385	100	173	100

The qualitative difference between the themes dealt with in each account is, however, quite significant. A quarter of the *comments* in the prime minister's account are about himself – under the category *political leader* – and another 25% deal with the arrangements of the Spanish political system. From within the remaining half of the total, the most frequently treated themes are *economy* and *social problems*. In @rubalcaba's case the largest category of *comments* (39%) deals with the Spanish political system, the second most frequently discussed issue (21%) is *culture* followed by *economy* and *social problems* – both with a sizeable presence.

It is worthwhile examining in detail the notable difference between *comments* regarding the political leader in both accounts which represent 26 per cent of all *comments* in Mariano Rajoy's account and only 1.7 per cent in Rubalcaba's. It is also important to emphasise that these *comments* are predominantly negative and, therefore, actually damage the image of the Prime Minister. This difference can have two potential causes. One is related to the differences in the range of themes touched upon by the original tweets uploaded by the politicians' accounts. As seen under section 14.1 (*supra*), most of @marianorajoy's tweets attempt to promote the prime minister's image and to inform about the prime minister's activities, hence offering more opportunities for followers to criticise these same issues. An alternative, or complementary, explanation would be that the prime minister's figure endures greater erosion than that of a leader who is out of office and, therefore, is also unable to implement actual policies that may alienate certain members of the public.

Another particularly relevant characteristic of the data obtained in this analysis is the disconnection between the themes treated in the tweets uploaded by the politician and their assistants on the one hand and the themes present in the *comments* uploaded by their followers from the general public as shown in Figures 4.2 and 4.3 below.

As assessed elsewhere in this chapter the most frequent theme in the *comments* for @marianorajoy is the figure of Rajoy himself – categorised as *political leader* – but this theme is never present in his own tweets which are mostly concerned with his activities – categorised under *political activity*. The Prime Minister's political engagements, in turn, are hardly ever mentioned in the *comments*. *National politics* occupy twice as many *comments* as original tweets although there are similar numbers of tweets and *comments* that deal with the *economy*. *Social problems* – essentially political corruption – appear in 10 per cent of all *comments*, but are not mentioned in the original tweets. *education, environment, employment* and *regional politics* are also issues never mentioned in the original tweet but present, even if exceptionally so, in the *comments*.

In @rubalcaba's case the most frequently addressed theme – with a considerably higher percentage of tweets than justified by the interest of users expressed in the *comments* – is *justice*, particularly with the legal proceedings dealing with corruption cases and the new legal framework addressing abortion.

Other themes also covered by @rubalcaba are: the *electoral campaign*, *political leader* and *political activity* in the field of political dramatization. *Population* and *employment*, from the field of meaningful politics, are also present in @rubalcaba's tweets. Through their comments, users of @

74 Elena Cebrián Guinovart et al.

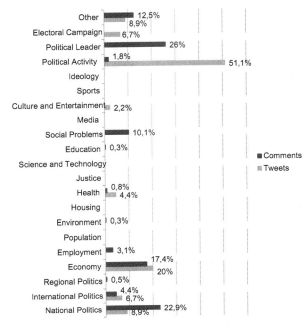

Figure 4.2 @marianorajoy's tweets and comments by theme.

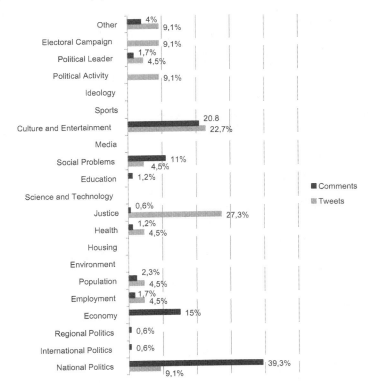

Figure 4.3 @rubalcaba's tweets and comments by theme.

rubalcaba express an interest in *national politics, the economy* and *social problems,* which are not accorded the same degree of attention by the politican's tweets.

There is, therefore, no correlation between the public's interests as expressed by the *comments* uploaded by users in @marianorajoy and @rubalcaba and the interests expressed by the political leaders in their accounts. This divergence is present both in terms of the themes covered and of the quantity of messages devoted to each theme. The range of interests displayed by users from the general public is broader than the politicians and includes issues of significant political value rather than matters of political theatralisation This disparity bodes ill for political participation because if tweets uploaded by political leaders and the responses that these elicit do not match each other, dialogue is impossible.

As Table 4.7 shows, almost three out of four *comments* uploaded by the general public criticise the politicians on both accounts.

Table 4.7 Comments by intention

	@*marianorajoy*		@*rubalcaba*	
	Frequency	%	*Frequency*	%
Favourable	30	7,8	17	9,8
Unfavourable	285	74,0	121	69,9
Neutral	21	5,5	2	1,2
Question	10	2,6	5	2,9
Not Evaluable	24	6,2	27	15,6
Others	15	3,9	1	0,6
Total	385	100	173	100

Although the range of critical *comments* is considerably broad, insults, plain abuse and denunciations of the politician's deficiencies are dominant. Citizens doubtlessly used Twitter as a tool to exert criticism. This seems to contradict the received wisdom generated by 'big data' analyses, and which assumes an ideological correlation between the political accounts on Twitter and the citizens that interact with them (Barberá, 2015; D'heer and Verdegem, 2014; Larsson, 2014). In the case of the prime minister's account, the intent to criticise becomes ever more apparent through the fact that Rajoy himself is the main theme of *comments* is also taken into account.

This analysis of *comments* concludes with an evaluation of their quality. In the first place, the analysis of *comments* according to consistency shows significant differences between the two accounts. *Comments* uploaded to @rubalcaba are mostly – 76 per cent – coherent whereas this is exceptional in Rajoy's case – where only 37 per cent of *comments* are coherent. The prime minister's account seems to elicit *comments* that are unrelated to the content of the original tweets.

76   *Elena Cebrián Guinovart et al.*

In the second place, the *comments* uploaded in @rubalcaba also show greater relevance: almost all (91 per cent) the *comments* received by this accountdeal with a politically relevant issue, while only slightly over half (53 per cent) of the *comments* uploaded in @marianorajoy can be defined as relevant.

These rather significant differences in coherency and relevancy can be interpreted as indicating two distinct forms of political interaction within the limited range of possibilities offered by the way in which these politicians employ Twitter. *Comments* uploaded in @rubalcaba seem to indicate a form of political participation guided by the politician's political agenda. Comments uploaded in @marianorajoy seem to indicate a form of political interaction aimed at satisfying the need of members of the public to release steam, by uploading *comments* unrelated to the politician's interests and with little content of political substance.

The attitude can also be found by examining *conversations*, the form of political participation which involves users interacting with each other in relation to a politician's account. If eight out of ten tweets posted on both of the politicians' accounts do generate comments from the public, in the case of @marianorajoy about 25 per cent of the authors of these comments also engage in conversations and interact between themselves. Yet the politicians' accounts themselves are distinctly unresponsive to a type of participation that they cannot control – as demonstrated by the fact, as seen earlier, that most meaningful *comments* are actually highly critical. From within the thirteen conversations between followers present in the sample – all located in @marianorajoy – five are devoted to *employment*. Rajoy himself is the second most frequent object of discussion, appearing in three conversations in which he, again, happens to be negatively valued. The political class generally (also negatively valued) is present in one conversation, while the three remaining conversations focus on sport, the death of a Spanish soldier posted in Lebanon and the cost of the funeral honours accorded to Adolfo Suarez, the then recently deceased first democratically elected Spanish prime minister.

4.4 Conclusions

The results of the analysis developed throughout this chapter allow us to conclude that:

1 Neither Mariano Rajoy nor Alfredo Pérez Rubalcaba understand their Twitter accounts as opportunities to foster political dialogue with the public.

   1.1 The differences between the usages of Twitter in each account, their "twitterstyles", are merely quantitative. Although @marianorajoy posts twice as many tweets as @rubalcaba does and these elicit double the number of responses, these differences are entirely irrelevant from the viewpoint of fostering political participation.

Is Twitter Invigorating Spanish Democracy? 77

1.2 There is an equilibrium between tweets and retweets in @marianorajoy, whereas in @rubalcaba's case the number of retweets almost doubles the number of original tweets. Still, both accounts employ re-tweeting so as to reinforce their own political messages rather than to foster citizen participation.

1.3 The *intentions* of the messages published in both accounts do not contribute to invigorate political participation, either: the most frequent tweets merely provide information about public engagements or reproduce statements delivered in said public engagements. Issues that may elicit political debate are entirely absent from @marianorajoy and only rarely found in @rubalcaba.

1.4 Along similar lines, the themes with which both accounts concern themselves seem aimed at increasing public exposure of the politicians' activities and of the pre-established political stands of the politicians and their parties. Ideological issues that may foster greater political participation are consistently neglected.

1.5 Hashtags, mentions and links are present in both accounts although with varying frequency. Both accounts employ hashtags in a similar proportion but *mentions* are more heavily used in @rubalcaba and links in @marianorajoy. These resources, however, are not employed to increase political participation in either account. Whenever other people or places are mentioned or linked, it is invariably done to reinforce the position and image of either the politician or his party. Far from seeking to invigorate political life these resources are only used at the service of the politicians' self-promotion.

1.6 Neither profile seems to acknowledge Twitter as a medium to foster dialogue between the electorate and the candidates for at no point there is the slightest indication to followers that they may engage in meaningful dialogue with the politicians. In the Prime Minister's account, this is so despite the fact that followers do understand Twitter's potential to foster dialogue as demonstrated when they engage in *conversations* with each other in no less than three out of every ten occasions.

2 Some aspects of the behaviour of followers of @marianorajoy and @rubalcaba seem to indicate a genuine interest in interacting with the politicians but either the context does not allow them to do so or users themselves fail to take full advantage of the possibilities of bi-directionality afforded by Twitter.

2.1 Participation by followers takes shape predominantly in the form of retweets in both accounts. In the case of @marianorajoy, the second most oft-used tool is favourites while @rubalcaba followers prefer comments. The lower level of activity present in the latter means, however, that automated and less demanding forms of participation predominate overall.

2.2 Comments are almost invariably written by private citizens which indeed confirms Twitter's potential as a venue where the voters and candidates may meet.

2.3 There is considerable disparity between the issues posted by politicians and those raised by the citizens through their comments. Politicians prefer issues related to their own activities or of interest to their party – that is, they prefer to engage in political theatralisation while citizens write about affairs related to political issues and pertaining either to the economic situation or to cases of corruption.

2.4 Since near three quarters of the messages posted by the public include negative impressions about politicians it seems that Twitter is used as a platform for criticism.

2.5 Together with the negative slant of the public's messages, it is also worthwhile to note the significant presence of *irrelevant* and *inconsistent* messages in the Prime Minister's account. The quality of messages from the general public is higher in @rubalcaba, where there is a higher proportion of messages deemed consistent and relevant.

Globally, it is possible to conclude that the diverging aims of politicians on the one hand and of common citizens on the other make meaningful dialogue difficult. The politicians employ Twitter as a tool for self-promotion and to support their own, pre-established political agendas. Politicians, moreover, never provide adequate answers to the concerns of common citizens as expressed in their responses. On the other hand Twitter does serve as a channel to display dissatisfaction with the politicians which may be considered a form, albeit limited, of political participation.

Works cited

Barberá, Pablo, and Rivero, Gonzalo. 2014. "Understanding the Political Representativeness of Twitter Users". *Social Science Computer Review,* December 1: 1–18.

Barberá, Pablo. 2015. "Birds of the Same Feather Tweet Together. Bayesian Ideal Point Estimation Using Twitter Data". *Political Analysis,* 23 (1): 76–91.

Cebrián Guinovart, Elena, Vázquez Barrio, Tamara, and Olabarrieta Vallejo, Ane. 2013. "¿Participación y democracia en los medios sociales?: El caso de Twitter en las elecciones vascas de 2012". *adComunica,* 6: 39–63.

Cebrián, Elena, and Vázquez, Tamara. 2013. "@marianorajoy VS @conRubalcaba: La campaña electoral de 2011 en las cuentas oficiales de Twitter de los candidatos del PP y del PSOE". In *Miradas a las pantallas en el bolsillo,* edited by Max Römer. Madrid: Universidad Camilo José Cela.

Dahlgren, Peter, and Alvares, Claudia. 2013. "Political Participation in an Age of Mediatisation. Towards a New Research Agenda". *Javnost - The Public: Journal of the European Institute for Communication and Culture,* 20 (2): 47–66.

Deltell, Luís, Florencia Claes, and José Miguel Osteso. 2013. "Predicción de tendencia política por Twitter: Elecciones Andaluzas 2012." *Ámbitos. Revista Internacional de Comunicación,* 22: 91–100. Accessed March 29, 2015. http://www.ambitos

comunicacion.com/2013/prediccion-de-tendencia-politica-por-twitter-elecciones-andaluzas-2012/.

Deltell, Luís. 2012. "Estudio del uso de Twitter, Facebook y YouTube en la campaña electoral de 2011 en España. El insólito caso de eQuo". Accessed March 29, 2015. http://eprints.ucm.es/15544/.

D'heer, Evelien, and Verdegem, Pier. 2014. "An Intermedia Understanding of the Networked Twitter Ecology. The 2012 Local elections in Belgium". In *Social Media in Politics. Case Studies on the Political Power of Social Media*, edited by Bogdan Patrut and Mónica Patrut. New York: Springer.

Ferreras, Eva María. 2011. "Redes sociales y cambio social. El movimiento 15-M y su evolución en Twitter". *Telos. Cuadernos de comunicación e innovación*, 89: 61–73.

García Ortega, Carmela, and Zugasti Azagra, Ricardo. 2012. "Twitter en campaña: el caso de Mariano Rajoy en las elecciones generales de 2011". Accessed March 29, 2015. http://www.alice-comunicacionpolitica.com/abrir-ponencia.php?f=250F50000aba2501342180026-ponencia-1.pdf.

Larsson, Anders Olof. 2015. "Everyday elites, citizens, or extremists? Assessing the use and users of non-election political hashtags". *MedieKultur. Journal of media and communication research*. Accessed March 29, 2015. http://ojs.statsbiblioteket.dk/index.php/mediekultur/article/view/8951.

Larsson, Anders Olof, and Moe, Hallvard. 2011. "Studying political microblogging: Twitter users in the 2010 Swedish election campaign". Accessed March 29, 2015. http://nms.sagepub.com/content/early/2011/11/21/1461444811422894.full.pdf+html.

Macnamara, Jim. 2011. "Pre- and post-election 2010 online: What happened to the conversation?" *Communication, Politics, and Culture*, 44(2): 18–36. Accessed March 29, 2015. https://opus.lib.uts.edu.au/research/bitstream/handle/10453/17356/2011000743.pdf?sequence=1.

Mancera, Ana, and Ana Pano. 2013. *El discurso político en Twitter. Análisis de mensajes que "trinan"*. Barcelona: Antropos.

Manlow, Veronica, Weiser, Linda, and Friedman, Hersey H. 2009. "Barack Obama 2.0: The Power of New Media in Achieving and Sustaining Presidential Charisma". *John Ben Shepperd Journal of Practical Leadership*, 4 (Spring): 77–85. Accessed March 29, 2015. http://www.researchgate.net/publication/263767717_Barack_Obama_2.0_The_Power_of_New_Media_in_Achieving_and_Sustaining_Presidential_Charisma.

Menéndez, María Cristina. 2011. "Las redes sociales y su efecto político: ¿Nuevas Fuenteovejunas digitales?" *Telos. Cuadernos de comunicación e innovación*, 89: 74–83.

Observatorio político 2.0/ Ketchum Pleon. 2011. "La campaña electoral [noviembre 2011] en las redes sociales". Accessed December 15, 2011. http://www.adesis.com/lps/comunicacion-20/index.asp.

Parmelee, John .H, and Bichard, Shanon L. 2011. *Politics and the twitter revolution: How tweets influence the relationship between political leaders and the public*. Maryland: Lexington Books.

Pérez Díaz, Luís, Pedro, Berná Sicilia, Celia, and Langa, Enrique Arroyas. 2013. "La interpretación simbólica de los desahucios en España a través del frame: un análisis semántico de la conversación en Twitter". Accessed March 29, 2015. http://reunir.unir.net/handle/123456789/1752.

Romero, Ana. 2011. "Las redes sociales y el 15-M en España". *Telos. Cuadernos de comunicación e innovación*, 89: 111–116.

Talbot, David. 2008. "How Obama Really Did It. The social networking strategy that took an obscure senator to the doors of the White House". *MIT Technology Review, September/October*. Accessed March 29, 2015. http://www.technology-review.com/featuredstory/410644/how-obama-really-did-it/.

Varona, David. 2011. "Una campaña electoral en las redes sociales, spanish style". Accessed March 29, 2015. http://blog.rtve.es/redessociales/2011/11/una-campa%C3%B1a-electoral-en-las-redes-sociales-a-su-estilo.html.

Zurutuza Muñoz, Cristina. 2012. "¿De qué habla Rubalcaba cuando twitea? La campaña del candidato socialista en Twitter para las elecciones del 20N". Accessed March 29, 2015. http://www.alice-comunicacionpolitica.com/files/ponencias/249-F50000aa32491342180003-ponencia-1.pdf.

5 Candidate Orientation to ICTs in Canadian Municipal Elections

Angelia Wagner

Introduction[1]

Politicians and civic activists both use information and communication technologies (ICTs) to build public support for their campaigns, but similarities in either the logics or forms of their online activities often ends there. Most national politicians apply a one-to-many communication style to online campaigning, treating ICTs as another type of advertising medium through which to broadcast information to voters and seek material resources such as time and donations from supporters (Karlsen 2009; Hendricks and Denton 2010; Nickerson 2009; Panagopoulos and Bergan 2009; Small 2007, 2010, 2012). Politicians appear less interested in using ICTs to engage in discussion with citizens (Williams and Tedesco 2006). Many activists, on the other hand, embrace the interactive nature of digital media. They rely on a many-to-many communication style to encourage public deliberation and collective action on a particular issue, with the goal of achieving a political remedy or societal change (Karpf 2010; Obar, Zube and Lampe 2012). So while both group of actors want to energize their supporters, they often take different approaches to ICTs to achieve this goal.

But if politicians differ from activists in their rationale for and approach to online campaigning, they can also differ from one another. Many municipal politicians, for example, do not need to appeal to as large an electorate as their national counterparts. Candidates in towns, villages and rural areas have only a few hundred or few thousand voters to reach. ICTs are of greater benefit to city candidates, who must engage tens of thousands of voters. Internet services are also not as widely available in every municipality or to every voter. While more than three-quarters of Canadian households had Internet access in 2010 (Statistics Canada 2013), broadband service is much more developed in the cities, which continue to have the advantage in terms of quality and scope of critical Internet infrastructure over their rural counterparts. This digital disparity is arguably not as crucial to the online strategies of national political parties. We must therefore consider electoral context when investigating the logic behind politicians' online campaigning. This chapter explores the specific stance of Canadian municipal candidates toward the use of ICTs.

5.1 Advantages of Internet Campaigning

Municipal candidates have several incentives to campaign online. First, ICTs allow them to send campaign messages directly to voters. Candidates have traditionally relied on the news media to act as a major conduit through which to reach voters. But journalists are not simple stenographers. Candidates face a challenge in getting journalists to cover the issues they want in the manner they want (Ansolabehere and Iyengar 1995). More importantly, many candidates struggle to get news coverage in the first place. Dwindling political reporting is a growing issue (Waddell 2012) and is a particular concern for those in lower levels of government (Dunn 1995). Media inattention can have serious consequences for candidates. Jay Bryant (1995, 90) argues that name recognition is key in politics because "most people will vote for a candidate they know and do not like if they have never heard of the opponent, and if they do not recognize either name, many voters will simply not vote at all for that office".

ICTs enable candidates to make themselves and their ideas more visible to voters. Unlike brick-and-mortar offices, a candidate's electronic headquarters are always open to the public (Small 2004). Their ease of access is complemented by their immediacy. Candidates can swiftly send messages to supporters through their ICT platforms (Pole 2010). But direct entreaties to voters are not the only appeal of ICTs: candidates can use them to court journalists as well, who scour social media sites looking for stories (Cunningham 2008; Gueorguieva 2008; Lilleker, Pack and Jackson 2010). Examining the 2004 Canadian federal election, Tamara A. Small (2007) found political parties presented information on their websites in a ready-made news format that would appeal to journalists. ICTs, therefore, facilitate a multi-pronged strategy: candidates can use them to build name recognition as well as to elicit and influence the content of news coverage.

Research has also found that ICTs can be powerful organizational tools, especially for mobilizing volunteers, supporters and donations (Gibson and Ward 2009; Smith 2010). Barack Obama's successful bid for the American presidency in 2008 is held up as *the* benchmark for online politicking in elections. Not only was he able to use ICTs to generate significant resources for his campaign but also to hurt the image of his Republican competitor; Obama used John McCain's inability to send an email because of a physical injury to portray him as old and out of touch (Waite 2010). The desire to appear modern has driven many politicians to adopt ICTs, even if they are not entirely familiar with them (Bentivegna 2008; Bowers-Brown 2003; Kluver 2008). Politicians have also used online platforms "to support, ridicule and/or refute the statements and claims made by" others (Elmer 2013, 21) or to launch their own attacks (Pole 2010; Small 2012).

Politicians' motivations for participating in online campaigning, however, are largely derived from observations of ICT use by political parties and elite politicians in national elections. We should not presume that the rationales and online practices of national politicians are also those of municipal politicians in the absence of empirical evidence. Municipal politicians likely adopt an ICT logic based on their electoral circumstances. In the case of Canada, local candidates need to appeal to smaller electorates in a non-partisan environment. Finally, it is often assumed that politicians' tendency not to use the interactivity capabilities of ICTs means they do not want to engage in online deliberation. This is not necessarily the case. We know little about how politicians themselves understand and/or justify the role of ICTs in politics in general and in their campaigns in particular.

5.2 Disadvantages of Online Campaigning

Even though ICTs have many electoral advantages, they also have a number of shortcomings. Primary among them is the time-consuming nature of regularly producing content. Managing online sites must compete with the myriad of other tasks a candidate must do during an election (Pole 2010). Candidates must also possess a certain amount of technical know-how to be able to operate them. The perfunctory nature of many political portals suggests some candidates are not familiar with ICTs but have gone online anyway to signal to voters that they are part of the modern world (Southern and Ward 2011). Younger candidates socialized to digital media (Carlson and Strandberg 2007), and well-funded candidates who can hire consultants (Ward and Gibson 2003) have typically been in the best position to develop a network of professional-looking ICTs.

A second shortcoming of ICTs is their small audience size in comparison to traditional media (Boas 2008; Howard 2005). Just because a candidate has established an online headquarters does not mean voters will walk through the virtual doors. As Kate A. Mirandilla notes (2007, 110; italics in the original), "citizens must possess a certain degree of *motivation* to avail themselves of the services offered by the Internet". The small number of voters exacerbates this problem at the local level—municipal election sites are likely to attract far fewer visitors than national ones. And even if some voters are interested in accessing political information online, candidates might find ICTs unnecessary in smaller communities where "everyone knows everyone in person" (Lev-On 2013, 163). Traditional techniques such as direct contact might be more effective in soliciting votes. Municipal candidates therefore need to be more judicious about whether or not to use ICTs (Smith 2010).

5.3 Method

The data for this chapter are drawn from a survey of candidates who sought municipal office in Canada between 2010 and 2012. Because this study stems from a larger project examining the role of gender in municipal

84 *Angelia Wagner*

political communication, the sampling frame consisted of an approximately even number of women and men candidates in the four main regions of Canada. A total of 1,007 individuals were invited to participate in the project after their respective local elections had concluded, with 385 candidates filling out a questionnaire for a response rate of 33.5 per cent. Since this chapter examines how candidates used ICTs in their campaigns, respondents who were acclaimed to office have been excluded from this analysis. The data has been weighted to compensate for the deliberate oversampling of gender by region.

The key independent variables are type of municipality, electoral outcome, age, gender, office sought, incumbency and financial resources. Overall, women comprised 54.7 per cent of the non-acclaimed respondents while 38.5 per cent of the participants were from the central region of the country, 29.2 per cent from the west, 28.5 per cent from the east, and 3.8 per cent from the north. The average age was about 54 (SD = 10.7). Mayoral candidates comprised 13.4 per cent of the sample, with the other respondents striving to become a councillor, regional councillor, or deputy mayor. Incumbents made up 32.5 per cent of the sample while winning candidates were 61.6 per cent. In terms of municipality type, 40.8 per cent of respondents sought office in a town, followed by 25.9 per cent in a rural municipality, 22.7 per cent in a city, 9.1 per cent in a village or hamlet, and 1.6 per cent in some other type of municipality. Overall, candidates raised an average of $2,546.28 for their campaigns but spent more than $3,700, of which almost $2,400 was for communications.

As for dependent variables, the questionnaire incorporated a number of items designed to assess the extent to which candidates used ICTs in their campaigns. An open-ended question also enabled respondents to provide a qualitative assessment of the campaign value of ICTs, while six respondents were later interviewed for their thoughts on the advantages and disadvantages of social media in municipal elections.

5.4 ICT Use in Canadian Municipal Elections

Survey data indicate that many Canadian municipal candidates are reluctant to use ICTs to reach out to voters. About half (49.8 per cent) of respondents who needed votes to get elected reported using Internet-based applications in their campaigns. Bivariate comparisons found gender, age, incumbency status and type of office had no influence on a candidate's decision to go online. Only electoral outcome and financial resources were important. The more money candidates had, the more likely they were to incorporate ICTs into their campaigns. Likewise, candidates who ended up losing the election were almost twice as likely as winning candidates to report using ICTs. The latter result, though, was driven by differences between winners and losers in smaller municipalities. City council hopefuls politicked online in equal numbers regardless of eventual electoral outcome: more than three-quarters of city respondents employed ICTs while just over one-third of those in towns, villages, and rural areas did the same.

Table 5.1 Logistic regression results for Canadian municipal candidate use of ICTs in their recent campaigns

Variable	Used Information and Communication Technologies in Campaign		
	B	S.E.	Exp(B)
Gender Female = 1	−.232	.377	.793
Municipality type City = 1	−.715	.392	.489
Incumbency Incumbent = 1	−.630	.353	.533
Type of office Mayoral candidate = 1	.109	.399	1.115
Electoral outcome Winner = 1	1.218	.337	3.379***
Age (in years)	−.059	.017	.943***
Communications spending (in dollars)	.000	.000	1.000***
N		240	
Nagelkerke R^2		.389	

Note: *** $p < 0.001$. Weighted data.

Municipality type ceased to play an important role in a candidate's orientation to ICTs, however, when the analysis controlled for other factors. Table 5.1 demonstrates that electoral outcome, age, and communications spending were far more important in determining whether or not a candidate used ICTs, though not always in the expected direction. Eventual winners were actually three times more likely than eventual losers to campaign online when all factors were considered, indicating the Internet might be a component of a successful communications strategy after all. As before, the younger in age and the better financed a candidate was, the more likely she or he was to set up an online platform. The multivariate results suggest the unique characteristics of city candidates, rather than the need to reach a larger electorate, is behind greater ICT use in city campaigns. City candidates in Canada are significantly younger than their non-city counterparts. And since younger people as a group tend to be more comfortable with digital media, they have been at the forefront of online campaigning in municipal elections. Online campaigning, therefore, should become more prevalent in non-city campaigns when the number of younger candidates in towns, villages and rural areas increases.

86 Angelia Wagner

Table 5.2 Summary of reasons why Canadian municipal candidates did use ICTs in their recent campaigns

	Very important		Important		Neutral/ Undecided		Not important		Not very important	
	%	(N)	%	(N)	%	(N)	%	(N)	%	(N)
Reaching voters	66.1%	(93)	24.7%	(35)	8.0%	(11)	0.0%	(0)	1.3%	(2)
Making themselves more visible	62.4%	(86)	31.1%	(43)	6.5%	(9)	0.0%	(0)	0.0%	(0)
Reaching voters	66.1%	(93)	24.7%	(35)	8.0%	(11)	0.0%	(0)	1.3%	(2)
Making themselves more visible	62.4%	(86)	31.1%	(43)	6.5%	(9)	0.0%	(0)	0.0%	(0)
Making their views more visible	53.8%	(73)	39.3%	(54)	6.7%	(9)	0.0%	(0)	0.2%	(0*)
Organizing their campaign	30.8%	(42)	18.4%	(25)	30.0%	(41)	18.1%	(25)	2.8%	(4)
Gaining visibility in traditional media	40.6%	(55)	22.9%	(31)	24.7%	(34)	10.8%	(15)	0.9%	(1)
Appearing modern	31.7%	(44)	39.8%	(56)	17.4%	(24)	10.5%	(15)	0.6%	(1)
Counteracting rumours/ falsehoods	16.4%	(22)	18.7%	(26)	19.9%	(27)	28.4%	(39)	16.7%	(23)
Critiquing other candidates	3.6%	(5)	10.2%	(14)	22.3%	(31)	26.3%	(36)	37.5%	(51)

Note: The N = 142. * Weighted data.

5.5 Reasons for Using ICTs

While only half of Canadian municipal candidates currently campaign online, survey and interview responses indicate they approach ICTs as just another advertising medium through which they can promote their candidacies to voters and journalists alike. Table 5.2 outlines how local politicians rated the importance of seven reasons for using ICTs in their campaigns. A clear majority identified reaching voters, promoting themselves and sharing their views as key goals while two-thirds also used ICTs to attract media attention. A female town candidate said in an interview that ICTs could encourage public participation in local politics: "For people interested in an issue, it can be, if it's used properly, a very efficient way of getting information out. It allows people a chance to feel that they are participating". A male city council candidate asserted that candidates could use ICTs to build name recognition months in advance of the formal campaigning period:

> It's reaching such a large population so easily, so quickly ... So at a minimum, even if they don't like what you're saying, they know you are out there. There's no possibility of walking into the polls and then finding [my name] on the ballot and going, "Gee, I wonder who that person is".

Not only can ICTs draw voter attention, several respondents felt it can play a crucial role in gaining media support. One male candidate commented on the survey that "social media connected me to more residents and mainstream media. Social media was one of the key reasons [why] the local daily paper endorsed my campaign". Three-quarters of respondents who used ICTs also wanted to project an image of modern leadership. A male candidate noted he "established local street cred ... for using these tools successfully". About half of respondents felt it was important to use ICTs as an organizational aid.

In contrast, many municipal candidates did not see ICTs as a conduit through which to counteract rumours or falsehoods, with only one-third of respondents saying this function was important or very important to them. They were even more emphatic about *not* using their online platforms to critique their competitors. Two conclusions can be drawn from this data. First, municipal candidates appear keen to avoid online behaviour or comments that could direct media or public attention to their opponents. They prefer to keep their communications focused on themselves and not on their competitors. Second, many municipal candidates are reluctant to engage in negative campaigning, preferring to run a 'clean' campaign and focus on policy and qualifications rather than on personal character.

But do all types of candidates take this promotional and informational approach? A series of *t*-tests and bivariate correlations (results not shown) reveal that candidates generally shared the same motivations for using ICTs with only a few significant differences based on personal traits, electoral situation and financial resources. For example, younger candidates were significantly more likely than their older counterparts to use ICTs to reach voters, make themselves more visible and organize their campaigns but they were much more strongly against using ICTs to critique other candidates. Challengers, for their part, were more apt than incumbents to report using their online platforms to try to catch the eye of journalists. Media visibility was also a strong incentive for some city candidates, such as younger competitors, challengers and mayoral hopefuls. In fact, mayoral contenders treated their ICTs as part of an overall strategy to build public visibility in their cities: they not only wanted to generate more news coverage of their campaigns but also to directly transmit information about themselves and their policy ideas to as many voters as possible.

88 Angelia Wagner

Table 5.3 Summary of reasons why Canadian municipal candidates did not use specific ICTs in their recent campaigns

	Too costly		Time consuming		Ineffective		Unnecessary		Not familiar with it	
	%	(N)	%	(N)	%	(N)	%	(N)	%	(N)
Websites	4.1%	(6)	8.4%	(12)	13.5%	(19)	48.1%	(67)	26.0%	(36)
Blogs	1.3%	(2)	2.4%	(3)	13.0%	(18)	44.4%	(62)	39.0%	(55)
Facebook	0.0%	(0)	6.6%	(9)	12.3%	(17)	47.7%	(67)	33.4%	(47)
Twitter	1.3%	(2)	3.9%	(6)	10.3%	(15)	45.1%	(63)	39.4%	(55)
YouTube	1.3%	(2)	2.3%	(3)	10.6%	(15)	48.6%	(67)	37.2%	(51)
Flickr	1.3%	(2)	0.3%	(0)*	8.6%	(12)	39.3%	(55)	50.6%	(71)

Note: N = 143. * Weighted data.

5.6 Reasons for Rejecting ICTs

Even though many respondents see public and media visibility as an important motivation to use ICTs in their campaigns, a large number of Canadian municipal candidates have opted not to go online at all. The survey asked these respondents to select the main reason why they did not use websites, blogs, Facebook, Twitter, YouTube or Flickr. Their responses, presented in Table 5.3, indicate municipal candidates have been slow to incorporate ICTs because they do not yet view them as necessary components of a successful communication strategy. This could simply be justification, though, as many other candidates admitted to not being sufficiently versed in digital technologies for their online campaigning to be effective. Very few respondents rejected an ICT because they thought it was too expensive. Breaking down results by candidate characteristics, winners, non-city candidates and those with fewer financial resources were significantly more likely than their respective counterparts to claim that a specific ICT was not necessary for their campaigns, while losers and city candidates believed an ICT would be ineffective in helping them to win. Retrospective rationalization is probably at work in some of these assessments. Winners might have viewed their electoral success as validation of their campaign choices, while losers might not have believed ICTs would have made a difference in their campaigns. Meanwhile, less well-funded candidates might have tried to justify the low-tech nature of their campaigns by asserting that it was the ICT that did not matter, not the lack of funds.

Other candidates' preferences probably resulted from a pragmatic approach to their electoral circumstances. With fewer voters to reach, candidates in towns, villages and rural areas might have opted for a simple campaign. Well-financed candidates, who are in the best position to adopt Internet-based applications, were most likely to find them too costly and, to a lesser degree, time consuming. Their answers might have been because of the cost of hiring consultants to produce professional-looking websites and

Candidate Orientation to ICTs in Canadian Municipal Elections   89

the need to constantly refresh content to keep voters returning to the site. As presumably viable contenders, well-funded candidates could afford to use a greater variety of campaign techniques, including lobbying for votes in person, through advertising appeals, or in news media interviews. Non-mayoral candidates, for their part, found ICTs to be too time consuming. As for other types of candidates, older candidates reported not using certain ICTs because of a lack of familiarity with them. No major trends were found for gender or incumbency.

The qualitative evidence reveals that many municipal candidates, including those who went online, are leery of the interactive capabilities of ICTs not because they wish to avoid public deliberation of local issues but because of the strong potential to lose control of their campaign message. The comment function on social media allows members of the public to respond to policy ideas that candidates put forward on their own sites. A female mayoral candidate noted that the resulting online discussion could quickly spin out of control and away from a focus on the candidate:

> Once you post something, such as, "We must build a library down-town", which is a local issue, people will come in and start posting and say, 'No, that's a stupid place to put the library.' And then the argument starts between all the people who are posting, and you lose control of the argument. And as you post back, you simply become one of many who are posting.

In those instances when candidates want to initiate a public debate about local issues, she warned that the borderless nature of the Internet enables people who do not live in a municipality to join the discussion and influence its direction, and they can do so without identifying themselves as non-residents. Candidates are also concerned about the potential for misinformation to circulate on the web. A female town candidate chose not to create any campaign ICTs and did not provide public access to her personal Facebook page during the election for this reason:

> I don't want to be on Facebook having to defend myself against things that may or may not be accurate. It just becomes a tit for tat kind of thing, and I'm not interested in that. If someone has an issue to raise with me, call me and let's talk about it.

She also disapproved of the way online debates can devolve into little more than bickering between political factions and of how some posters express their disapproval of political officials using violent language.

On the surface, these critiques of social media express a concern about the nature of online political debate in Canadian municipalities. While local candidates are generally not afraid of political debate, some believe

90 *Angelia Wagner*

debates should be based on civility and accurate information. Yet what these critiques also reveal is a deeper anxiety triggered by the global nature of the Internet: How can municipal candidates be sure they are reaching *their* voters? The audience is key to understanding municipal candidates' logic of ICT use. Some candidates are still struggling to figure out how to work with digital technology to develop and maintain their support base. A female candidate who lost her bid for re-election said she wished she had kept an electronic record of all the constituents she helped while on city council so she had a list of potential supporters when the next election rolled around:

> I should have started a Facebook account when I was first elected and built my structure. And I should have been databasing my emails from when I was first elected, but I just never got on top of that. I was pretty busy. That was definitely something I did afterwards ... I was doing it after I lost. It was some sort of therapy.

Even candidates who have experimented more with digital media have discovered that not all ICTs are ideal for communicating with voters. "I find [Twitter] rather useless, frankly," said a male city candidate, who used the microblogging site in his re-election campaign. "Yeah, it gets you out there, it gives you visibility, but you can't say much. You've got 140 characters for whatever it is that you are trying to comment on. Frankly, I find it a total waste of time". His comments indicate a growing awareness among politicians of the type of campaigning possible on each Internet-based application. The unique structure and function of each ICT determines the nature of the political engagement it can facilitate. This has, in turn, shaped the audience that each one reaches: Twitter is popular with journalists and other politically interested individuals while Facebook has a more general audience (Small 2011; Ross and Burger 2014).

The task before municipal candidates is to find the best mix of digital tools. They need to select online utilities that have the greatest likelihood of reaching their supporters and other electors who can be swayed to vote for them. But candidates also realize they need to be careful about the extent to which they go high-tech. Not all voters want to be reached by social media. Some citizens still prefer old-fashioned personal contact. One female respondent argued that "one must be careful about over-using Facebook to promote anything. There are a lot of seniors in this area who were annoyed by talk of websites and social media, so it was a balancing act". Likewise, not all voters *can* be reached by social media. A number of respondents noted that social media was just starting to emerge as an election tool in 2010 and many voters were not yet familiar with it. Considering the speed at which digital media is evolving and the inevitable variation in popularity of different social networking sites, municipal politicians will always encounter large pockets of voters who are not familiar with the latest ICT.

Lag time between the introduction of new forms of Internet-based applications and their effectiveness as campaign tools means municipal politicians need to give serious consideration not only to whether or not they should use the Internet in their campaigns but also *which* ICTs to use if they do.

Yet even though many candidates are reluctant to use ICTs, an evolution in the municipal form of online campaigning is afoot. Some respondents believe generational change in municipal leaders will soon make ICTs an essential component of local electioneering. A female mayoral candidate predicted "social media will be, at least in the next decade, the arena where people do have discussions" about local political issues, especially as tech-savvy young people get older and become more politically active. A male candidate believes a contagion effect will help this process along:

> As more people use it, that's the thing, they get drawn into it. If you've got a certain amount of people running for a particular position, and three-quarters are using social media and the other quarter aren't, they might get left behind. What used to be is no longer the way of doing business.

But the evidence presented in this chapter suggests scholars need to be cautious about over-estimating the extent to which ICTs will become part of local campaigning. They are only one set of tools among many that candidates have at their disposal to promote their policies and qualifications to voters.

5.7 Discussion and Conclusions

The rationales and forms of digital campaigning are under-studied in the municipal context even though most candidates who seek elected office in Western countries do so at the local level. While only half of Canadian municipal candidates use ICTs in their campaigns, their numbers still far outstrip the number of national candidates who create election sites. Municipal politicians (and civic activists, for that matter) help shape the political dimensions of digital media. Thus, any theory that attempts to provide a comprehensive explanation of the role of ICTs in public deliberation and political participation must take into account the orientations of municipal politicians toward ICT use.

This chapter demonstrates that Canadian municipal candidates currently take a cautious and functionalist stance toward ICTs in election campaigns. Personal characteristics and electoral circumstances strongly influence the manner in which municipal candidates use ICTs and their motivations for doing so. Many local candidates adopt a one-to-many communication approach to ICTs not out of a desire to limit political debate so much as to get elected. Yet once their goal has been achieved, some municipal politicians turn to ICTs to facilitate public participation in local political issues. Just a few months after his election, one mayor launched a social media campaign to encourage citizens to join the city's efforts to lobby the federal and provincial governments for additional transit funding (City of Edmonton 2014). The campaign, which was ultimately successful, included a website, Twitter hashtag, and YouTube videos.

This mayor's willingness to use a many-to-many communication style once in office suggests municipal politicians might follow different logics of ICT use depending upon the context: they might treat ICTs as little more than a campaign tool during an election but as a democratic tool once in office (Karlsen, 2009). In other words, politicians might change their orientation to ICTs depending upon whether they are seeking public support to get elected or to achieve a policy aim. Future research needs to explore the factors that make the interactive features of ICTs more amenable to use in local governance than in local elections. In the meantime, this chapter demonstrates that Canadian municipal candidates' approach to ICTs is strongly informed by an assessment of their utility. Candidates' primary goal during an election is to secure public office, and they will only campaign online if they believe ICTs can help them to achieve that goal.

Note

1. This project was funded through scholarships from the Social Sciences and Humanities Research Council of Canada, Government of Alberta, and the Department of Political Science at the University of Alberta.

Works Cited

Ansolabehere, Steven, and Iyengar, Shanto. 1995. "Winning Through Advertising: It's All in the Context". In Campaigns and Elections American Style, edited by James A. Thurber and Candice J. Nelson. Boulder: Westview Press.

Bentivegna, Sara. 2008. "Italy: The Evolution of E-campaigning 1996–2006". In Making a Difference: A Comparative View of the Role of the Internet in Election Politics, edited by Stephen Ward, Diana Owen, Richard Davis, and David Taras. Lanham: Lexington Books.

Boas, Taylor C. 2008. "Chile: Promoting the Personal Connection—The Internet and Presidential Election Campaigns". In Making a Difference: A Comparative View of the Role of the Internet in Election Politics, edited by Stephen Ward, Diana Owen, Richard Davis and David Taras. Lanham: Lexington Books.

Bowers-Brown, Julian. 2003. "A Marriage Made in Cyberspace? Political Marketing and UK Party Websites". In Political Parties and the Internet: Net Gain?, edited by Rachel Gibson, Paul Nixon, and Stephen Ward. New York: Routledge.

Bryant, Jay. 1995. "Paid Media Advertising". In Campaigns and Elections American Style, edited by James A. Thurber and Candice J. Nelson. Boulder: Westview Press.

Carlson, Tom, and Strandberg, Kim. 2007. "Finland: The European Parliament Election in a Candidate-centered Electoral System". In The Internet and National Elections: A Comparative Study of Web Campaigning, edited by Randolph Kluver, Nicholas W. Jankowski, Kirsten A. Foot and Steven M. Schneider. New York and London: Routledge.

Candidate Orientation to ICTs in Canadian Municipal Elections 93

City of Edmonton. 2014. "City Launches Social Media Campaign to Build Support for LRT Funding". Accessed March 27, 2015. http://www.edmonton.ca/city_government/news/2014/city-launches-social-media-campaign-to-build-support-for-lrt-funding.aspx.

Cunningham, Stuart. 2008. "Political and Media Leadership in the Age of YouTube". In Public Leadership: Perspectives and Practices, edited by Paul 't Hart and John Uhr. Canberra: The Australian National University E Press.

Dunn, Anita. 1995. "The Best Campaign Wins: Local Press Coverage of Nonpresidential Races". In Campaigns and Elections American Style, edited by James A. Thurber and Candice J. Nelson. Boulder: Westview Press.

Elmer, Greg. 2013. "Live Research: Twittering an Election Debate". New Media & Society 15 (1): 18–30.

Gibson, Rachel, and Ward, Stephen. 2009. "Parties in the Digital Age—A Review Article". Representation 45 (1): 87–100.

Gueorguieva, Vassia. 2008. "Voters, MySpace, and YouTube: The Impact of Alternative Communication Channels on the 2006 Election Cycle and Beyond". Social Science Computer Review 26 (3): 288–300.

Hendricks, John Allen, and Denton, Robert E., Jr. 2010. "Political Campaigns and Communicating with the Electorate in the Twenty-First Century". In Communicator-in-Chief: How Barack Obama Used New Media Technology to Win the White House, edited by John Allen Hendricks and Robert E. Denton, Jr. Lanham: Lexington Books.

Howard, Philip N. 2005. "Deep Democracy, Thin Citizenship: The Impact of Digital Media in Political Campaign Strategy". Annals of the American Academy of Political and Social Science 597: 153–170.

Karlsen, Rune. 2009. "Campaign Communication and the Internet: Strategy in the 2005 Norwegian Election Campaign". Journal of Elections, Public Opinion and Parties 19 (2): 183–202.

Karpf, David. 2010. "Online Political Mobilization from the Advocacy Group's Perspective: Looking Beyond Clicktivism". Policy and Internet 2 (4): 7–41.

Kluver, Randolph. 2008. "Singapore: Elections and the Internet—Online Activism and Offline Quiescence". In Making a Difference: A Comparative View of the Role of the Internet in Election Politics, edited by Stephen Ward, Diana Owen, Richard Davis and David Taras. Lanham: Lexington Books.

Lev-On, Azi. 2013. "Another Flew over the Digital Divide: Internet Usage in the Arab-Palestinian Sector in Israel During Municipal Election Campaigns, 2008". Israel Affairs 19 (1): 154–169.

Lilleker, Darren G., Pack, Mark, and Jackson, Nigel. 2010. "Political Parties and Web 2.0: The Liberal Democrat Perspective". Politics 30 (2): 105–112.

Mirandilla, Kate A. 2007. "Philippines: Poli-clicking as Politicking: Online Campaigning and Civic Action in the 2004 National Election". In The Internet and National Elections: A Comparative Study of Web Campaigning, edited by Randolph Kluver, Nicholas W. Jankowski, Kirsten A. Foot, and Steven M. Schneider. New York and London: Routledge.

Nickerson, David W. 2009. "The Impact of E-mail Campaigns on Voter Mobilization: Evidence From a Field Experiment". In Politicking Online: The Transformation of Election Campaign Communications, edited by Costas Panagopoulos. New Brunswick, N.J.: Rutgers University Press.

Obar, Jonathan A., Zube, Paul, and Lampe, Clifford. 2012. "Advocacy 2.0: An Analysis of How Advocacy Groups in the United States Perceive and Use Social Media as Tools for Facilitating Civic Engagement and Collective Action". Journal of Information Policy 2: 1–25.

Panagopoulos, Costas, and Bergan, Daniel. 2009. "Clicking for Cash: Campaigns, Donors, and the Emergence of Online Fund-raising". In Politicking Online: The Transformation of Election Campaign Communications, edited by Costas Panagopoulos. New Brunswick, N.J.: Rutgers University Press.

Pole, Antoinette. 2010. Blogging the Political: Politics and Participation in a Networked Society. New York: Routledge.

Ross, Karen, and Burger, Tobias. 2014. "Face to Face(book): Social Media, Political Campaigning and the Unbearable Lightness of Being There". Political Science 66 (1): 46–62.

Small, Tamara A. 2004. "parties@canada: The Internet and the 2004 Cyber-campaign". In The Canadian General Election of 2004, edited by Jon H. Pammett and Christopher Dornan. Toronto: Dundurn Press.

Small, Tamara A. 2007. "Canadian Cyberparties: Reflections on Internet-based Campaigning and Party Systems". Canadian Journal of Political Science 40 (3): 639–657.

Small, Tamara A. 2010. "Still Waiting for an Internet Prime Minister: Online Campaigning by Canadian Political Parties". In Election, edited by Heather MacIvor. Toronto: Emond Montgomery Publications.

Small, Tamara A. 2011. "What the Hashtag? A Content Analysis of Canadian Politics on Twitter". Information, Communication and Society 14 (6): 872–895.

Small, Tamara A. 2012. "Are We Friends Yet? Online Relationship Marketing by Political Parties". In Political Marketing in Canada, edited by Alex Marland, Thierry Giasson, and Jennier Lees-Marshment. Vancouver: UBC Press.

Smith, Melissa S. 2010. "Political Campaigns in the Twenty-first Century: Implications of New Media Technology". In Communicator-in-Chief: How Barack Obama Used New Media Technology to Win the White House, edited by John Allen Hendricks and Robert E. Denton, Jr. Lanham: Lexington Books.

Southern, Rosalynd, and Ward, Stephen. 2011. "Below the Radar? Online Campaigning at the Local Level in the 2010 Election". In Political Communication in Britain: The Leader Debates, the Campaign and the Media in the 2010 General Election, edited by Dominic Wring, Roger Mortimore and Simon Atkinson. Basingstoke: Palgrave Macmillan.

Statistics Canada. 2013. Canadian Internet Use Survey, 2012. Ottawa: Minister of Industry.

Waddell, Christopher. 2012. "Berry'd Alive: The Media, Technology, and the Death of Political Coverage". In How Canadians Communicate IV: Media and Politics, edited by David Taras and Christopher Waddell. Edmonton: Athabasca University Press.

Waite, Brandon C. 2010. "E-mail and Electoral Fortunes: Obama's Campaign Internet Insurgency". In Communicator-in-Chief: How Barack Obama Used New Media Technology to Win the White House, edited by John Allen Hendricks and Robert E. Denton, Jr. Lanham: Lexington Books.

Ward, Stephen, and Gibson, Rachel. 2003. "On-line and on Message? Candidate Websites in the 2001 General Election". British Journal of Politics and International Relations 5 (2): 188–205.

Williams, Andrew Paul, and Tedesco, John C., eds. 2006. The Internet Election: Perspectives on the Web in Campaign 2004. Lanham: Rowman & Littlefield Publishers.

6 "I show off, therefore I am"
The Politics of the Selfie

Christelle Serée-Chaussinand

Introduction

In a special issue published in May 2013 and entitled "The Me Me Me Generation," *Time Magazine* focused on millennials ("Generation Y") who came of age amid the rise of new media and interact all day through screens: these "digital natives" record their daily steps on FitBit, list their whereabouts every hour of every day on PlaceMe, post selfies on Twitter, Instagram, Snapchat or Facebook while being constantly anxious about missing out on something better or being missed out themselves (Palfrey-Gasser, 2008). Although they belong to the older generations of Baby Boomers and Generation X, today's political leaders, heads of state and government, seem to have fully taken on the younger generation's habits, making extensive use of social media for networking and communication purposes. In 2014, 68 percent of all world leaders had personal accounts on Twitter, vying for attention, connections and followers on the social network.[1]

This new trend has long been studied by scholars. In a milestone book about political communication, Dan Schill shows for instance how "stagecraft" has replaced "statecraft" in modern times when the general public and the electorate "understand politics through the mass media [and] political knowledge is mediated and socially constructed" (Schill, 2009: 1). He demonstrates that mediagenic events are purposely created by advance staff in politicians' entourage to influence the news media, generate coverage and excitement, construct favorable political images and persuade voters. In the same vein, French scholars like Marc Abélès have commented upon the "political show" – "*le spectacle du pouvoir*" – and the mutations of the liberal democratic nation-state as locus of political power and legitimacy under the combined influence of globalization and digital media.[2] Christian Salmon similarly investigates the shift of political action and debates from traditional spaces for the exercise of power to the stage offered by news media, the Internet and social networks where performance is the rule. This shift results, Salmon argues following in the steps of American scholars and political commentators, in the advent of storytelling in politics to the point that "in hypermedia societies, the ability to build a political identity, not with rational arguments but by telling stories, has become the key to the conquest of power." (Salmon, 2012: 33)

96 Christelle Serée-Chaussinand

In such a context, it is not at all surprising that, over the last two years or so, political leaders should have massively jumped on the bandwagon of selfies, using them as a new digital-age tool to self-promote and interact with prospective voters and society at large.[3] Selfies are indeed a worldwide trans-generational phenomenon; their use skyrocketed by 17,000% in 2012 leading the neologism to be declared word of the year for 2013 by *Oxford University Dictionaries* as best reflecting the mood of our times. Bursting from the confines of Instagram and Twitter, "selfie" has become a mainstream shorthand for any self-taken photograph, although the majority of such portraits are smartphone self-portraits.

This chapter focuses on selfies from a digital humanities point of view: how can this digital practice be defined and analysed in relation with more traditional humanities-based objects of inquiry? More specifically, how are selfies used in political communication? How do these non-official self-portraits compare with more traditional forms of political portraiture? This paper thus draws on existing literature in political science (in particular studies probing the digital revolution in politics) but also literature on royal and political portraiture, to examine how distinctive features and usage of traditional political portraits can be seen to translate into the digital world in the form of selfies.[4]

6.1 Celebrity Politics

The use of selfies by world leaders, heads of state and government is first a signal of the evolution of political action and campaigning towards performance as emphasized by Schill, Abélès or Salmon (*supra*). Political events acquire full meaning and importance only when presented on TV or computer or smartphone screen. Media exposure has become crucial: political leaders exist on the media stage, and their actions acquire a theatrical dimension. As Andrew White remarks, digital media practices have reformed identity, including political identity: "identity has become more performative (pertaining to the art of performance) or dramaturgical as a result of the need to be noticed online. [...] Dramaturgical identities have in turn exacerbated the trend towards celebrity or informational politics" – that is, politics fundamentally and essentially framed by the logic of mass and hypermedia (White, 2014: 63–4). Many world leaders thus use the power of pictures (selfies or other types of pictures and videos) in their feeds to increase effect and therewith engagement, the gain being of 63 percent according to a recent study of Twitter accounts by the social network itself.[5]

Likewise, the advent of storytelling is accompanied by a growing interest in the person and the "stories" surrounding that person or their entourage. With the dividing line between public and private realms becoming increasingly porous and leaky, the private lives of political leaders have come to be considered as an acceptable subject for journalistic revelation and

"I show off, therefore I am" 97

self-disclosure. Political leaders are not just familiar figures for the citizen, they become "intimate strangers" (Stanyer, 2007: 72) and people seek more and more access into their private sphere, relishing confidential or stolen pictures, anecdotes, gibes and one-liners, confessions or scandals, far more than doctrine or articles of political faith. Selfies respond in part to this new demand, especially this appetite for images, this specular drive or voyeurism. The famous election embrace posted by Barack Obama in November 2012 together with the tweet "Four more years" partakes fully in this new trend: political victory is here construed as conjugal bliss, the picture bearing only a metaphorical link to the actual event it illustrates but offering access to the president's intimate family album.[6]

6.2 Political Communication Revisited

While they help assess the evolution of politics, selfies also reshape the modalities of the relationship between political leaders and citizens. In fact, selfies recreate the way one looks at politics and political events. With selfies, the emphasis shifts from the collective to the individual, from the official and traditional to the anecdotal, from the ceremonial to the informal. The relaxation and joviality of selfies sharply contrasts, for instance, with the rigidity and smirk on glossy campaign posters. Similarly, the emphasis shifts from events to the margins or periphery of events as selfies are neither totally outside, totally disconnected from events nor totally inside them either. Richard Quest's selfie challenge in Davos in January 2014 is a good example of such a transfer of interest and focus.[7] The CNN business journalist took the opportunity of the annual gathering of international political and business leaders for the World Economic Forum to make offbeat coverage of the event. This did not interfere with the normal round of interviews he made as CNN special correspondent in Switzerland but his uncustomary pictures and short videos got thousands of views, a sign of their popularity. Quest's selfies implied a change of perspective and attitude: the decorum of official ceremonies and conventional interviews characterized by static poses, diplomatic or deferential distance and represented in official pictures was replaced with relaxed postures, friendly accolades and a jokey tone in his selfies. Additionally, his selfies introduced a form of anachronism as though they were taken in a parallel time zone, disconnected with the pressure of breaking news.

Selfies also allow more direct communication for political leaders introducing some sort of trivialization and erasing signs of mediation. Selfies seem indeed to eliminate any barrier to entry for the viewer. Although very few political leaders are conversational on social networks; although relatively few of them may do their own tweeting, and posts on "mundane" Internet tools such as Facebook, Twitter or political blogs are more often the responsibility of communication experts in their entourage, an emotional bond and a form of exchange is specially generated by selfies. There seems

98   *Christelle Serée-Chaussinand*

to be no middle-man and no distance between the public and politicians; a mutual specular relationship seems to be created, if only virtually. Not only do politicians "look *like* us" but it seems that they "look *at us*" as much as *we* look at them, what is more in a cheerful, friendly and casual way. The fact that selfie-portraits are necessarily taken close up actually reinforces the impression of proximity and maximizes fascination.[8] Besides, selfies plant memorable and powerful images in the voters' heads, such as Joe Biden's selfie with Julia Louis-Dreyfus who plays the part of vice president, and subsequent president, of the United States, in the American TV series "Veep."[9] So political leaders may use selfies not only to try to look "hip" but above all for political leadership – in a bid to increase their popularity, to come closer to their electorate and presumably to engage people in the political process – in particular young people, an always sought-after voting bloc. In this respect, one may wonder whether "selfie-ing" corresponds to deft electoral strategy; whether increased political participation is not the underlying aim. Journalists have sometimes been tempted to make the link, as suggested by the headlines of the *Wall Street Journal* on the eve of the General Election in Australia in August 2013: "Australia Leader Tries 'Selfie' Snapshots to Connect with Youth Vote." In fact, it proves especially hazardous to affirm that selfies have an actual impact either on conventional participation (voting, party affiliation, joining political meetings, etc.) or on alternative, more informal participation (interest in *res politica*, social or civic engagement, etc.). Intentionality on the part of political leaders is also hard to establish, though it appears reasonable to assume that such practices often aim, at least in part, to generate popularity and visibility.

6.3 Seeking Visibility

In social media, being popular does not only mean "being regarded with approval or affection" by a vast majority, it is above all synonymous with "being visible" and being "active." Selfies are part of a strategy to reach maximum visibility and presence. Some selfies become viral and proliferate or spread widely on social media, catapulting individuals to sudden media stardom. Heads of state and government do not necessarily seek extra fame, rather extra presence. Using selfies and tweets allows them to be in the public eye, to stand centre stage all the time. Their fantasy of omnipresence, of being "there" all the time – that betrays a fantasy of omnipotence – does not differ from rulers of all times. It is even, as Pascal Lardellier argues, consubstantial with power. In an essay entitled "*L'Image incarnée : Une généalogie du portrait politique*," Lardellier explains that "power and rulers cannot endure being absent, yet they cannot be omnipresent. So representation – not just diplomatic, but also symbolical and aesthetical – has become a powerful and efficient tool for them to overcome this aporia." (Lardellier, 1997: 26 – my translation) Among others, Lardellier cites Michel Foucault: "to an extremely important extent, power is exerted through the production

"I show off, therefore I am" 99

and exchange of signs." (Foucault, 1990: 53)[10] Selfies fall into this category of signs that are produced and exchanged for the integrity, continuity and magnification of power and in that sense, they do not differ much from the more traditional political portraits that Lardellier examines. In particular, he points to the Copernican-like revolution that followed the invention of copperplate engraving which allowed the mass production of reproductions of royal portraits. The greatly increased circulation of royal portraits contributed to reinforce the power of monarchs by increasing their visibility. Lardellier insists on the "performative dimension" of those portraits as they generate a mutual qualification of the ruler by the public and vice versa, the former being confirmed as the incarnation of power, the latter being constituted as a social group. (Lardellier, 1997: 32)[11] Today's political leaders are undoubtedly aware of the performative value of public images: using the exponential faculty of multiplication of images on social networks, they seek maximum visibility and thereby maximum endorsement with the selfies that they have circulate together with official pictures. How influential they are is measured by the number of views, likes or retweets they get. This is presumably what Joe Biden had in mind when he sent his first ever Instagram selfie.[12] The latter includes Biden and President Obama in the back of the presidential limo showing off their best smiles to the camera phone. This first selfie got more than 65,000 likes and was widely retweeted including by President Obama, a savvy selfie-maker himself, with the brief but unequivocal tag: "Pals".[13] Even "unselfies" – in which people take pictures of themselves hiding their faces behind a board branding their favourite charitable campaign – may paradoxically serve this aim of omnipresence, omnipotence and endorsement. Once their popularity is well established and they are recognizable enough, leaders may play with the code and post so-to-speak 'selfless' selfies, like John Kerry who took part in an "unselfie campaign" to support relief aid for the Philippines after super typhoon disaster.[14]

Altogether, selfies help political leaders to be recognized not only in the literal sense of "knowing or identifying from past experience or knowledge" but also in a more practical sense, namely "giving formal acknowledgment of the status, reality, validity or legality of something." As such, selfies contribute to reinforce a political identity, not only through identification but also through promotion and empowerment.

6.4 Of Identity, Authenticity and Control

The question of identity is in fact essential when one deals with selfies. The use of selfies by "digital natives" is motivated by such factors as peer interrelation, the pursuit of fame, notoriety and self-expression. This use is, to a great extent, a symptom of the Narcissism epidemic studied by JM Twenge and Keith Campbell: "Celebrity culture and the media tempt people with the idea of fame – often fame awarded for the amount of attention drawn to themselves rather than actual accomplishment. The Internet allows people to present an inflated and self-focused view of themselves to the world, and encourages them to spend hours each day contemplating their images" (Twenge-Campbell, 2013: x). In the case of political selfies, narcissism does not seem so prominent. What is at stake is not so much the image that heads of state and government have of themselves as the image they want to impose in people's eyes. Political marketing prevails over self-reflexivity and self-expression in the shrewdest way. Because of their relaxed casualness and their surface simplicity, selfies are good ways for political leaders to convey such messages as "I am this", "this is me, my true and simple self". They pick up on the natural tendency to conflate the selfie with the real self or to assume that smartphone self-portraits are revealing of personalities and possibly of hidden traits. But selfies pertain to careful image-making and the tweeted and retweeted image is but a mask, an imago – that is, the reflection of an online identity or online persona that does not coincide with the offline or core identity. In fact, as Christian Salmon argues in *La Cérémonie cannibale*, under the influence of neoliberalism and hypermedia, the *"homo politicus"* was "self-devoured" and political leaders today appear less like symbols of authority than brands or consumer goods denied of actual power and likely to evolve according to the demands of the electorate: "political figures are less and less considered as symbols of authority, as people to obey, more and more as consumer goods; less and less as norm-makers, more and more as by-products of mass-culture, as artefacts or fictions comparable to fictional characters in TV series and quiz shows" (Salmon, 2013: 8). So their digital self-portraits amount to brand advertising rather than self-revelation. Or to say things differently, postures in selfies often if not always turn out to be commercial impostures; selfies lack dearly in authenticity.

Here, we reach an essential question about political selfies: the question of their authenticity. They prove delusively close, delusively spontaneous. Whereas they look like impromptu snapshots taken on casual occasions, selfies are in fact all about control. The people featuring next to the political figure, the tags and other kinds of metadata posted with the selfies, the choice of a particular shot rather than another one, the timing for the tweet, all those editorial choices make selfies all but candid and artless. Biden's inaugural selfie with President Obama well illustrates this: the choice of his very first selfie partner is totally calculated; the text tweeted with the photograph is shrewdly written and not at all off-hand: "Found a friend to join my first selfie on Instagram." The Presidential Seal that is half visible behind their backs also plays a key part: the selfie becomes an all the more valuable snapshot as it is taken in one of the most intimate and secret loci of power, the presidential limo.

Of course, "selfie-ing" does not come without risks. There are times when selfies get out of control and even backfire on the political selfie-maker. The most famous example of such selfie goofs is of course the selfie that Barack Obama took with David Cameron and Danish Prime Minister Helle Thorning-Schmidt at Mandela's memorial service.[15] Paparazzi caught

"*I show off, therefore I am*" 101

the party unawares as they were taking selfies under Michelle's reproachful eyes. The world media exploited this "selfigate" to the full, either pointing to a poor sense of etiquette and proprieties or playing more ribald sexually connoted keys. Other examples of such digital *faux pas* include an embarrassing selfie that President Obama accepted to take with Red Sox player David Ortiz who had a secret contract with Samsung to promote their new cellphone.[16] The next day, a White House spokesman had to publicly deny any form of complicity on the part of the president. One may also refer to a picture taken by BBC *Look East* presenter Alex Dolan with David Cameron where the latter appears under an unflattering angle. The next day *The Mirror* made fun of the prime minister's "double chin and neck fat overhang," suggesting he should go on a diet to lose a few post-Christmas pounds.[17] Yet another and final example is Thomas Wieder's selfie in the Oval Office while covering François Hollande's American tour for *Le Monde*.[18] The reversal of perspective is as stunning as the reversal in *Las Meniñas* by Velàsquez but, contrary to the classical masterpiece, this picture is deliberately though jestingly irreverent: the journalist's face occupies the foreground whereas the two heads of state are saucily relegated in the background.[19]

6.5 Endorsing Proximity

Despite these few mishaps and their surface casualness, selfies more often pertain to careful image-making. This is especially obvious in the choice of partners of selfies. Political selfies are never or rarely solipsistic; other people constantly appear next to the selfie-maker. Depending on the identity and status of selfie-companions, the selfie strategy proves radically different.

If the other person on the selfie is a peer or a recognizable figure, the tweeted self-portrait is endowed with a particular meaning. The created proximity has indeed a clear endorsing value: there is a positive cumulative effect in the photographic encounter between two celebrities whatever their respective spheres of influence, their individual fames reinforcing one another. Such selfies are very common among politicians like Bill Clinton's selfie of himself with Bill Gates posted on Twitter at the occasion of the Clinton Global Initiative 2013 Conference.[20] The combination of the picture and following tag: "Two Bills, one selfie. Already having fun at CGI 2013 Meeting" allowed the former president to attract onto himself some of the qualities incarnated by Bill Gates such as inventiveness, success, vision and philanthropy, but also to point to the exceptionality of his connections and thereby to his maintained status as a man of influence. Similarly, the ostentatious complicity between Meryl Streep and Hillary Clinton at the occasion of the Kennedy Centre Honours Gala in 2012 was meant for reciprocal endorsement: the fact that the two ladies look like perfect chums suggests common values and culture.[21] As for Jimmy Kimmel's selfie with the Clintons at The Ellen Show in March 2014, it is a sample of clever media recycling.[22] The tweet posted alongside with the picture by Jimmy Kimmel

102 *Christelle Serée-Chaussinand*

read: "No Brad Cooper but 3 Clintons & a Kimmel", highlighting the fact that it was remake of Ellen DeGeneres's Oscars selfie, a selfie that smashed the retweet record previously held by Barack Obama with his post-election embrace. Despite a veneer of candidness, this picture is astute image-making too: playing the parts of Julia Roberts, Brad Pitt, Angelina Jolie and Bradley Cooper in the original photograph, the new Clinton-cum-Kimmel party covers itself partially in the prestige and glamour of the originals. Besides they look cool and capable of mild self-mockery, two highly valued qualities in politics.

On the contrary, if the person next to the political leader or the crowd surrounding him are not recognizable, the significance of the selfie is diametrically different. As in the previous case, the created proximity is well-calculated and meaningful. But the form of exchange or reciprocity that could be traced before virtually disappears here. Only an illusion of horizontal integration or assimilation is staged in such political selfies; the viewer is presented with a parody of proximity. As such, selfies are not subversive or "carnivalesque", to use Mikhaïl Bakhtin's terminology: they reinforce established hierarchies rather than they turn them upside down.[23] In fact, a vertical relationship is fundamentally maintained together with a possible form of instrumentalization, the anonymous crowd serving as foils or *faire-valoir* to the political leader. Differences and distance are maintained if not reinforced and the powerful is doubly magnified: not only is the crowd forever unrecognizable and clearly distinguished from the recognizable leader but it seems people are thankful for having the chance to appear on a picture near such a celebrity and to benefit from his/her aura.[24] This double enhancement shows for instance in a young girl's selfie request to President Obama on a visit in Seoul (which he actually snubbed) and is confirmed by such selfies as Pope Francis's selfie with young pilgrims in Rome or John Kerry's with students in Jakarta in February 2014.[25]

6.6 Converging Lines and Focal Points

As we come close to the end of this exploration of modern self-portraits in the political sphere, it appears that selfies are not fully comparable with grand portraits of monarchs and rulers, at least with regard to form. The solemnity and style of the latter radically contrast with the relaxation and absence of protocol characteristic of selfies where the pose is hardly calculated and caught on the spur of the moment. The absence of background and codified attributes in selfies is also a difference with traditional portraiture where accoutrements such as columns and swags, bookshelves and palaces hint at grandeur beyond; where globes, maps, medals or elegant clothes point to a profession or eminent deeds. However, a couple of shared characteristics can be identified between the two pictorial genres. Both "Grand Manner" portraits (full-size portraits of kings or official presidential photographs) and selfies serve for personal propaganda and visually

"*I show off, therefore I am*"   103

emphasize the superior nature and status of the sitter. Likewise, the composition of both classical portraits and selfies hinges on a similar principle. In traditional courtly or presidential portraiture, all the structuring lines in the painting or photograph are organized so as to converge towards one focal point which coincides exactly with the place where the monarch or leader stands or sits. This is for instance the case in Anthony Van Dyck's portrait of Charles I hunting or Philippe de Champaigne's full-length portrait of Richelieu: the bent head of the horse and the gaze of the second stable boy in the former, the diagonal of the curtain in the latter focus the viewer's gaze on the central figure.[26] In the case of selfies, a similar phenomenon is to be observed: the main structuring line of the smartphone self-portrait runs on from the extended arm of the person who holds the camera to take the picture and the direction of this line is determined by the selfie-maker's effort to "capture" or "frame" the political leader with him/herself in the picture. As a result, even if the leader is not exactly at the centre of the composition as is generally the case in classical portraiture, s/he is in fact central – that is, essential – to the composition of the selfie.

Conclusion

In mediatized society, success in politics depends, it seems, on the online activities of the political institutions and leaders: media-exposure – combined with a degree of self-disclosure – is essential. In this context, heads of state and government, politicians in general, are perfectly aware that the act of "selfie-ing" has become a cultural marker and many use it extensively. No scientific study, for obvious reasons, will be able to establish a direct causal link between the use of selfies by politicians and an increase in citizen participation, be it conventional (voting, party affiliation, attending political meetings, etc.) or alternative (interest in *res politica*, social or civic engagement, etc.). One may argue that selfies have an influence on the electorate as they engage people (if only for non-political reasons) by attracting them imperceptibly toward the political stage, by having them take part in the political show and by exposing them fully to political propaganda. But I would as strongly argue that, despite their own specificities, selfies derive directly from the tradition of courtly and presidential portraiture and that their use by politicians is analogous. Today's political leaders are *not* primarily interested in participation when they use social media; like their predecessors, they rather seek maximum visibility and empowerment for themselves and obey their own logics of self-promotion. Selfies are part of these logics.

Notes

1. *Twiplomacy Study 2014* (http://twiplomacy.com/blog/twiplomacy-study-2014/). Page accessed on 20th April 2015. World leaders and political figures have been on Twitter almost since it was launched in 2006. Obama sent his first tweet in

104   *Christelle Serée-Chaussinand*

2007, Mitt Romney and John McCain in 2009; on this side of the Atlantic, Nick Clegg first tweeted in 2008, Ed Miliband in 2009, David Cameron in 2012.

2. Marc Abélès, *Le Spectacle du Pouvoir*, Paris, Cahier de l'Herne, 2007.

3. Many politicians present on Twitter (more than two-thirds of all world leaders – see above) have recently taken on the habit of posting selfies or accepting to pose in other people's selfies. Although no exact figures are available, it is certain that the number of political selfies has soared in the past few years.

4. The chapter draws on a selection of online articles about political selfies, published on British and American newspaper and TV channel websites between November 2012 and February 2015 (*The Telegraph*, *The Guardian*, *The Mirror*, *The Huffington Post*, *USAToday*, CNN, NBCNews).

5. Results of a study by Twitter to determine how adding a hashtag, photo or video to tweets affects user engagement. 2 million tweets sent in the US by thousands of verified users across different fields (government, music, news, sports and TV) were analyzed over the course of one month. It clearly appeared that retweets were impressively boosted by additional photos (+35%) or videos (+28%). https://blog.twitter.com/2014/what-fuels-a-tweets-engagement. Accessed on 20th April 2015.

6. Picture available at http://www.telegraph.co.uk/news/worldnews/us-election/9660533/Barack-Obamas-four-more-years-tweet-most-popular-ever.html. Accessed on 20th April 2015.

7. Video available at http://edition.cnn.com/videos/business/2014/01/24/qmb-davos-2014-richard-quest-selfie-challenge-natpkg.cnn. Accessed on 20th April 2015.

8. In a memorable and thought-provoking formula, Jean-Luc Nancy notes that every portrait comprises three dimensions: "it resembles somebody (and me); it reminds me of somebody (and me); it gazes (at me)". (Jean-Luc Nancy, *Le Regard du portrait*, Paris, Galilée, 2000, p. 35 – my translation).

9. Picture available at http://www.straitstimes.com/breaking-news/world/story/politicians-who-whip-their-phones-selfie-20131115. Accessed on 20th April 2015.

10. Quoted by Pascal Lardellier, « L'Image incarnée : Une généalogie du portrait politique », *op. cit.*, p. 31.

11. In a political context, representation takes on the meaning and value of delegation of power, as Jean-Luc Nancy argues. The royal or political portrait as representation of the monarch or leader or master is the mandated agent of a mandater. Not only does the portrait reproduce and evoke the ruler but it becomes his/her proxyholder, reproducing, evoking and exerting his/her authority itself (or something of his/her authority). (Jean-Luc Nancy, *L'autre portrait*, Paris, Galilée, 2014, p. 17). In *Le Portrait du roi*, Louis Marin also emphasizes that representation and power are "of the same nature", arguing that representation is the means and foundation of power, that power is "produced" by representation: "the king is king – that is, monarch – only in images. They are his real presence: people must believe in the efficiency and operativeness of such iconic representations, otherwise the monarch loses his substance completely due to a lack of transubstantiation and all that remains is a simulacrum" (Louis Marin, *Le Portrait du roi*, Paris, Minuit, 1981, pp. 11–13 – my translation).

12. Picture available at http://www.nbcnews.com/news/us-news/biden-takes-selfie-obama-n82626. Accessed on 20th April 2015.

13. Barack Obama seems to keep on the frontline of social media usage: he is the first political leader to have set up a Twitter account in 2007. He also tops the world

"*I show off, therefore I am*" 105

leaders' list with the greatest number of followers: 43.7 million in 2014. *Twiplomacy Study 2014* (http://twiplomacy.com/blog/twiplomacy-study-2014/). Most recently, he innovated again with an unusual video produced to drive subscriptions in healthcare plans. In this Buzzfeed video he jestfully plays with his own image, presidential etiquette and common selfie practice, walking around the White House with a selfie stick. The video had almost 1.6m views after about an hour. Video available at http://www.theguardian.com/us-news/2015/feb/12/obama-selfie-stick-buzzfeed-video-healthcare. Accessed on 20th April 2015.

14. Picture available at http://www.cidi.org/unselfie-for-haiyan/#.VTYw7iHtmko. Accessed on 20th April 2015.

15. Picture and analysis of the consequences of this gaffe (in particular on Helle Thorning-Schmidt's image and reputation) available at http://www.theguardian.com/world/2013/dec/14/helle-thorning-schmidt-selfie-mandela-denmark. Accessed on 20th April 2015.

16. Picture available at http://ftw.usatoday.com/2014/04/david-ortiz-barack-obama-selfies. Accessed on 20th April 2015.

17. Article and picture available at http://www.mirror.co.uk/news/uk-news/david-cameron-selfie-reveals-trying-3037988. Accessed on 20th April 2015.

18. Picture available at http://www.france24.com/en/20140212-pictures-white-house-not-amused-french-journalists-selfies/. Accessed on 20th April 2015.

19. *Las Meñinas*, by Diego Velásquez, 1656, Oil on canvas, Madrid, Museo Nacional del Prado.

20. Picture available at http://www.huffingtonpost.com/2013/09/24/bill-clinton-bill-gates-selfie_n_3981192.html. Accessed on 20th April 2015.

21. Picture available at http://www.huffingtonpost.com/2012/12/02/hillary-clinton-meryl-streep_n_2228274.html. Accessed on 20th April 2015.

22. Pictures available at http://www.nydailynews.com/news/politics/jimmy-kimmel-tweets-hilarious-selfie-clinton-family-article-1.1731113. Accessed on 20th April 2015.

23. Mikhaïl Bakhtin, *Rabelais and his world*, Bloomington, Indiana University Press, 1941.

24. In this respect, it must be noticed that the craze for autographs has been replaced with selfies. Autograph hunting, which amounted to obtaining a manuscript relic of the powerful and being somehow elevated by it, has turned into selfie hunting.

25. Pictures available at http://www.dailymail.co.uk/news/article-2614185/Obama-DENIES-13-year-old-girls-touching-request-selfie-South-Korea.html; at http://www.telegraph.co.uk/news/worldnews/the-pope/10277934/Pope-Francis-and-the-first-Papal-selfie.html; at http://www.abc.net.au/news/2014-02-17/john-kerry-with-group-students-in-jakarta/5263348. Pages accessed on 20th April 2015.

26. *Charles I At the Hunt*, by Anthony Van Dyck, c. 1635, Oil on canvas, Paris, Musée du Louvre. *Richelieu*, by Philippe de Champaigne, c. 1639, Oil on canvas, Paris, Musée du Louvre.

Works Cited

Abèles, Marc. 2007. *Le Spectacle du Pouvoir*. Paris Cahier de l'Herne.
Bakhtin, Mikhaïl. 1941. *Rabelais and his world*. Bloomington: Indiana University Press.
Foucault, Michel. 1990. *Les représentations symboliques du pouvoir*. L. Turgeon, ed. Québec: Septentrion.

Lardellier, Pascal. 1997. *L'Image incarnée: Une généalogie du portrait politique*. *Médiation et Informations*, 7: 26–42.

Marin, Louis. 1981. *Le Portrait du roi*. Paris: Minuit.

Nancy, Jean-Luc. 2014. *L'autre portrait*. Paris: Galilée.

Nancy, Jean-Luc. 2000. *Le Regard du portrait*. Paris: Galilée.

Palfrey, John, and Gasser, Urs. 2008. *Born Digital: Understanding the First Generation of Digital Natives*. New York: Basic Books.

Salmon, Christian. 2012. *De Sarkosy à Obama: Ces histoires qui nous gouvernent*. Paris: JC Gawsewitch.

Salmon, Christian. 2013. *La Cérémonie Cannibale*. Paris: Fayard.

Schill, Dan. 2009. *Stagecraft and Statecraft: Advance and Media Events in Political Communication*. Lanham: Lexington Books.

Stanyer, James. 2007. *Modern Political Communication: Mediated Politics in Uncertain Terms*. Cambridge: Polity Press.

Twenge, Jean, and Campbell, W. Keith. 2013. *The Narcissism Epidemic: Living in the Age of Entitlement*. 2nd ed. New York: Atria Paperback.

Twiplomacy Study 2014 (http://twiplomacy.com/blog/twiplomacy-study-2014/). Accessed on 20th April 2015.

White, Andrew. 2014. *Digital Media and Society: Transforming Economics, Politics and Social Practices*. Basingstoke: Palgrave Macmillan.

Part II

Emerging Forms of Digital Media-based Political Participation by Citizens and Civic Activists

7 Re-Imagining the Meaning of Participation for a Digital Age

Darren G. Lilleker

Introduction: Political Participation and the Digital Age

Participation is central to the notion of democracy. Without participation in civic life there is no democracy. The central importance of participation for democracy has led to clear definitions of what is and, therefore, what is not, political participation. For example, we find the common definition expressed as: "By political participation we mean activity by private citizens designed to influence government decision-making" (Huntington & Nelson, 1976: 3). Verba et al. (1995: 38) expanded this somewhat arguing that: "By *political* participation we refer simply to activity that has the intent or effect of influencing government action either directly by affecting the making or implementation of public policy or indirectly by influencing the selection of people who make those policies". Therefore, for any action to be political it is usually deemed to fall into one of four categories; participation is voting, campaigning, contacting elected representatives, or protesting. So to qualify as participating in civic life any citizens should get involved in a public arena to advertise and communicate demands to anyone willing to listen; for example: joining a demonstration. Alternatively, citizens must contact policy-makers in legislatures or the executive branch in order to influence policy-making, for example: signing a petition. Or, citizens should get involved in the selection process of those who aspire to legislative or executive office; for example, voting for a party or personally running for office. All of these take place in all democratic nations to varying extents. In fact, the extent to which citizens take part in one or more of these forms of activity is often taken as a measure of the health of a democracy (Benhabib, 1996). The decline in numbers of those participating in these forms of behaviour is seen by some as a worrying sign, others are more sanguine (for debate see Stolle & Hooghe, 2005). Largely though academics, journalists and politicians alike appear to agree that as less citizens demonstrate, contact elected representatives, petition legislators, join parties, campaign and go out to vote, these indicators show evidence of a deficit in democracy. Simply put, is the decline in political participation taking the demos out of democracy?

Digital technologies have long been heralded as the panacea to a variety of problems with democracy. Forms of participation will expand, new

110 *Darren G. Lilleker*

public spheres will emerge, loci of power will be replaced and old hierarchies flattened; these are just some of the proclamations of early cyber optimists and remain a standard of thinking (see Rheingold, 1993 and for a review Zittel, 2004). However, greater empirical evidence weighs in favour of the 'politics as usual' thesis, within the online environment it is usually found that offline elites also flourish and despite the democratic mechanisms allowing total pluralism of voice, having the ability to create content online does not equate to being read or heard. In other words, online, the rich get richer and there has been no substantial shift in the balance of power (Margolis & Resnick, 2000; Hindman, 2009). However, despite the failure of digital technology to re-energise democracy, it may well have re-energised political participation. Online there are various platforms that provide an arena to advertise and communicate demands, so facilitating public protests. Yet the question is often raised as to whether communicating dissatisfaction with public policy using platforms like Facebook and Twitter has the same meaning as taking to the streets. Similarly, via a variety of means, technologies easily allow citizens to directly target and lobby policy-makers, the more citizens group together the greater the similarity to the petition. But, yet again, there are doubts that tweeting at a politician, telling her/him what you think, has the same importance as signing a petition. Through campaigns and lobbying, citizens can also become involved in the selection or even deselection of candidates and elected representatives. But would we consider promoting a party or candidate via Facebook as having the same meaning as putting a cross next to their name in a voting booth? Given the types of behaviours facilitated by digital technologies it would seem appropriate to question the definitions of political participation and what normatively are considered to be the forms of participation that benefit democracy. This chapter argues that it may be appropriate to rethink the definitions of the behaviours that constitute political participation and provides a theoretical framework of considering why this might be the case. The discussion raises a number of questions in order to point towards a research agenda that will allow a greater understanding of the positive and negative roles that digital technology does and might play in democratic life.

7.1 Participation: A Question of Motivations?

When we step away from normative judgments concerning what citizens should and ought to do in the context of a democracy, we find participation becomes a much looser term. The Oxford English Dictionary argues that participation is any "act or instance of taking part; or sharing something, as in benefits". Common uses of the term refer to people participating as audiences, sportspeople, debaters, hecklers, even late night revellers suggesting that we should consider any action involving others, even the most simple interaction, as being in some way participatory. Many forms of participation have no apparent purpose whatsoever; others simply satisfy the gratifications of the individual. Why then should participation only be classified as political if it has the purpose of influencing government action or the selection of people who make policy? The reason is that it is these are forms of participation that are deemed to be meaningful socially and/or politically. Campaigning influences other citizens, voting influences the composition of a legislature, protests and lobbying are attempts at changing legislation; yet while participating as an audience member for leaders debates is political, it has no meaning beyond the individual. Therefore we see a difference in the context of politics where political participation must have social meaning as opposed to only individual meaning.

However, this argument suggests an implied intent behind all participation and a specific set of intentions if one is to be considered to be participating in civic life. Political participation, it is suggested, must be carried out with the intention of having social meaning, any political participatory action must be intended to influence other citizens and/or legislators or the making of policy in some way. While this is a logical perspective to take, it does raise questions about whether much participation that would be classified as political falls into this category. Little research fully explains why citizens involve themselves in forms of political participation; rather their motivations are usually attributed based on the context. Protesting activities are deemed to be expressions of dissatisfaction with government policy. Campaigning during an election is deemed to indicate partisan support; issue campaigning is related to dedication to the cause. Similarly, little research explores the meaning individuals attribute to their participation. The vote is deemed an act of partisan attachment but also a citizenly duty, we also talk of protest votes; votes can be instrumental or expressive it is argued (Fiorina, 1976) but it is impossible to know the motivations behind any single vote or even the majority of votes cast. Concerns are raised over ill-informed voters, possibly swayed by image and style; equally some votes are the result of familial influence, with voters following their parents' or partner's lead. So is every vote a conscious attempt to have impact, are votes instrumental? Or is every vote an expression of support and, hence, expressive? Equally, we may enquire, does every vote have meaning? It is an uncomfortable thought if we cannot unequivocally state that every citizen attributes meaning to their vote. What is perhaps more interesting to consider, when thinking of meaning, is whether a 'like' on Facebook is just a meaningless click, something that involves no consideration, or an attempt to influence others based on the belief that the like is an endorsement. The argument is not that either is more important than the other, or even that a greater proportion of one has greater meaning than the other, it is to raise the question of meanings and motivations and the extent to which what may be seen as alternative or ephemeral forms of political expression may have meaning and intent that is consistent with our understanding of political participation.

112   Darren G. Lilleker

Currently, the trend is to dismiss what may be described as 'alternative' or 'non-traditional' forms of political expression or engagement, to deliberately not classify them as participation. Rather the common perception is that political 'likes', the sharing of content, even the signing of online petitions should not be defined as activism but clicktivism or slacktivism (Morozov, 2011). The argument is that the majority of the actions that can be performed via digital technologies to support political or social causes require little effort or time, suggesting political participation should, on the contrary, necessitate time, effort and cognitive involvement: little consideration is given to the act of the click on Facebook. The argument is very persuasive. Is there any effort or cognitive engagement when liking a funny picture of a cat, a high street brand, or a new feature film; moreover are the cognitive processes different when liking Barack Obama, the *Front National* or Christian Democrats; or Kim Kadashian, Paddington Bear or any other character or film, for that matter? All that happens is that your Facebook profile shows an endorsement of the picture, brand, film, politician or party. There is every reason to see a click as an ill-considered, momentary action resulting from finding some element of the communication attractive for a few seconds. However, there is also every reason to argue that sharing a picture of a funny cat or liking a film and telling your Facebook friends is strategic. If social media encourages or emphasises egocentric traits (Golbeck et al., 2011) then all actions on social media must carry some intention to contribute to a constructed persona and promote the self. Within a circle of friends it may be considered 'cool' to promote the latest Star Wars film, the latest Call of Duty game, One Direction's latest hit or AC/DC's album and tour. Similarly it may be cool, or deeply uncool, to show allegiance for a political party. Whether it is a neo-fascist right wing group, the charismatically-led centrist party of government or the far-left Marxists, is it cool to talk politics? The first question is therefore: is there consideration of the impact on self-image when deciding what or what not to click? The second question is: why click at all? Sharing funny cat pictures may be designed to amuse friends; liking brands may involve saying how trendy someone is or getting special offers; liking a political party may be saying to friends: "look at this party, they are saying things you might find interesting and relevant". This is surely worthy of investigation.

The question of intent and motivations is, therefore, one of interest. However, we currently have limited understanding of the meanings attributed to the various forms of participation among those who carry them out. Furthermore we have equally limited understanding of the link between non-traditional (digital platform-based) and traditional (offline) forms of participation and whether meanings differ. In closing this conceptual discussion of motivation and meaning I offer two examples. A television news reporter was asking participants in a protest organised by the Anonymous collective why they had taken to the streets on a cold night in support of a council estate in the East End of London in the UK. One response on camera

Re-Imagining the Meaning of Participation for a Digital Age   113

was "it was just for a laugh and my mate said it might be fun". The action of this participant contributes a positive tick for the health of democracy: he was a political participant in an action designed to influence legislators and change public policy; yet he attributed no meaning to his participation beyond personal gratification. In contrast, a young lady who contributed to a petition to better regulate staff working in care homes and who did this simply using one click and linking her digital signature to her Facebook account, chose to add the following text to the post on her wall: "This is really important, there's no other way to get them (assuming legislators) to do something so sign this". Such 'clicktivism' shows high engagement, high importance attached to the action and the intention to make friends and legislators listen. If these represent true representations of the motivations for forms of participation and the meaning attributed to them, then we might wish to reconsider the assumption that much of the political action taking place on digital platforms should not be classified as political participation and rather that a more nuanced perspective is required.

7.2 Digital Platforms as Places for Participation

While the preceding sections have asked interesting and important questions, the empirical evidence to support the case that scholars should reclassify actions such as the like on Facebook as political participation is lacking. Given the wealth of literature about online political engagement, expression and participation, can we construct an argument to suggest why the digital environment deserves a more positive image when considering its potential for democracy? Evidence gathered to date points to some positive indications. Certainly the Internet is an anarchically organised repository for any form of material from the very mundane to the most profound. But this means that a combination of openness to accessing diverse forms of material on the part of the individual and the ability to accidentally be exposed to material that is political can lead to an increased propensity to engage with and participate in politics.

Experiments and surveys have long indicated the power of searching and the fact that even the most basic use of the Internet for information gathering can stimulate cognitive engagement (Jennings & Zeitner, 2003). Concerns are justifiably raised as to the quality and credibility of information; however, perhaps this is less important if accessing one piece of information from one source leads to further searching and investigation in order to corroborate that information. What is clear is that once engagement is stimulated, and if there is a shift from fairly passive cognitive processing to active interrogation, then there are resultant feelings of empowerment. Empowerment is the result of feeling well informed, but that feeling is insufficient in itself. Evidence suggests that the more informed individuals are, the more empowered they feel and, *ceteris paribus*, the more likely they are to engage in some form of expressive behaviour (Shah et al., 2005; De Zuniga et al.,

114   *Darren G. Lilleker*

2009). The fact that digital technologies offer a plethora of simple ways to express oneself means that giving voice to thoughts is not only facilitated but encouraged. The motivations of expression are not just the by-product of the platforms that are created as a result of what are referred to as Web 2.0 technologies, but by social behaviours which occur online; expressive behaviour is also not the preserve of only the most politically active in society (Gibson & Cantijoch, 2013). Interactive communication encourages further interaction; therefore, those feeling informed and who express their opinions are encouraged by the expectation of receiving feedback through interactions with other users of the platforms (Puig-i-Abri & Rojas, 2007). Interactions between users can lead to the formation of communities of interest, spaces containing engaged individuals that can in part resemble an inclusive, participatory public sphere (Avril, 2014). The communities that are formed around the public sphere can be self-mobilising or they can be activated by organisations. Importantly, though, this can lead members of these online communities to become involved in offline forms of traditional participation (Rojas et al., 2007). Cumulatively, therefore, we find indications that the various opportunities to locate information and engage with materials easily can lead to a desire to express opinions online. Expressions may lead to interactions and the formation of communities of interest which then may mobilise members and direct them towards further and more outcome-oriented pathways of political participation (Rojas & Puig-i-Abril, 2009). There is also the potential that an expressive act on Facebook, for example, may gain more traction, reach and so impact than an expressive act at the ballot box.

Sceptics will argue correctly this presents something of an ideal. Any linear model that begins at the point of being encouraged to seek information and results in adopting the full rights of a citizen within an active civic society is flawed, as it does not work for every individual and there are multiple points of exit through the process. Material accessed can cognitively turn off, make a receiver avoid material on the topic, or even in the subject area, as easily as it can lead to hot cognition where the individual is engaged and the neurons in their brain are firing. Some argue that much political communication, in particular as it follows a more negative trajectory, can act as a demotivation to engagement (Dermody & Scullion, 2005). Similarly the behaviour of online users who interact with an individual encouraged to express their thoughts and opinions can lead to negative experiences, even hearing about the so-called trolls threatening to rape a campaigner arguing that at least one UK bank note should have a women on it can lead some to reject posting any sort of controversial view online. Linearity is problematic, it is an ideal situation, but, even though there are reasons why it may not work, that is not to say that it never works at all. Perhaps initial expressions represent metaphorically dipping a toe into bath water: no responses and the atmosphere is frigid and unwelcoming; hostile responses indicate dangerously hot territory; a friend liking, saying they agree, or even

Re-Imagining the Meaning of Participation for a Digital Age   115

being supportively critical and the individual testing the water may jump in and find the experience rewarding. The fact that dipping a toe into political participation could be through liking, or sharing, adding a simple endorsement or comment, means that such actions may be important and worthy of encouragement as well as measurement.

7.3 Understanding Participation: A Behavioural Psychology Approach

Currently there is insufficient measurement of the raft of divergent actions any individual may or may not choose to make that have some relevance for politics and which are facilitated by digital technologies. Some surveys have begun to take account of the number of citizens who become followers or fans of politicians or parties (Williams & Gulati, 2012; Vesnic-Alujevic, 2012), a smaller number ask about authoring posts or tweets about politics (Koc-Michalska & Lilleker, 2014), likes and shares are counted on profiles but not in surveys of users and, most importantly, no studies to date have explored the meanings individuals attribute to different actions. In order to test the extent that individuals do follow some form of linear path towards engagement we need more sophisticated understandings of those individuals and the psychology of social media usage incorporating motivations and intent. Focusing purely on Facebook use, Joinson (2008) identified seven uses and gratifications, three of which seem pertinent to mention as they offer hints at the psychology of engagement. First, Facebook is used by people for social investigation, learning about the world around them, their contacts, what is 'in' and what is 'passé' or 'out'. Second, he notes that Facebook users seek social connections, establishing and maintaining relationships with their network. Third, users build shared identities within those networks, becoming part of a community which sets norms of behaviour and rules for engagement. These three motivations all suggest that strategic considerations influence the usage of social media.

Research into the social investigation motivation is extensive. Accessing news is an activity that social media are widely used for, a Pew Research Report found 62%per cent of Reddit users, 52 per cent of Facebook users and 47 per cent of Twitter users access the platforms for news; 65 per cent of all those who go online in the United States use the Internet for news (Holcomb et al., 2013). However, the content of the news most sought, written about or commented on is usually of a non-political nature. For the week of May 14–18, 2014, the X Factor was the No. 1 subject on Twitter and the No. 5 story on blogs (Guskin & Tan, 2012). This chimes well with the findings that one in ten Americans are political bystanders, who are not registered to vote, rarely or never follow current affairs and have never contributed to a campaign. Furthermore, Pew data suggests few Americans beyond that 10 percent are serial participants in consuming or contributing

116 *Darren G. Lilleker*

to discourse around politics (Pew Research Center, 2014). Political participation of any variety is an occasional or rare activity for the vast majority.

In terms of political engagement, which can be argued to be a precursor for participation, what we do not know is what factors initially lead to a first interest, which is required for engagement. Whether engagement naturally leads to forms of expression, be they likes, shares, comments and beyond, may depend on the value attributed to such actions. In the environment of a social media platform the value may be personal, where it is perceived that contributing in these ways confers status within a network. Equally, however, it may be an attempt to be more connected into a network. Connectedness, or a desire for connectedness, measured by the amount of interactions received in return for expression, can give the impression of being at the heart of a network. Networks can be perceived as communities, awarding belonging. Belonging within a community, being connected to other members through common interests, issue positions or ideologies mean that any expression comes with the promise of connectedness. The promise of connectedness in turn acts as an encouragement, a form of mobilisation that comes from being part of a community and acting in conduit with the norms of that community.

Belonging, however, may not be sufficient in order to sustain engagement. Having influence, or the potential for influence, is argued to act as a powerful motivational force (Irvin & Stansbury, 2004). We must, therefore, consider to what extent having the ability to express views is in itself empowering? Or rather, is it the ability to be heard that is empowering? In either case we can consider that feelings of empowerment are important for sustaining engagement and acting as a participant in any form of activity.

These are inter-related and interdependent; they each are likely to cause and sustain one another. The inter-relations can be explained using theories normally used in the field of consumer psychology. Ajzen (1991) proposed three calculations that determine a behavioural decision, put simply these are: firstly a personal weighting on the behaviour itself and its outcomes; secondly, a calculation of others' weightings regarding the behaviour and its outcomes; thirdly, whether there are insurmountable barriers to behaving in the way desired. The theory has been applied to simple consumer decision-making situations as well as health and well-being choices but only recently to the realm of political participation (Lilleker, 2014: 167–170).

We can propose a number of simple precursors that we would expect should determine any form of political participation, using any platform, which involves some form of cognitive consideration. First and perhaps of ultimate importance, there needs to be an underlying interest in politics. Perhaps not electoral politics but either in public affairs generally, a specific cause with political implications or in a specific area of policy or its impact. Second and focusing on the actual action, any behaviour needs to be perceived as having a positive outcome, either for the individual (drawing on egocentric motivations) of for broader society (the potential for social or

Re-Imagining the Meaning of Participation for a Digital Age   117

political influence, communitarian motivations). The public nature of much non-traditional political participation means mixed motivations are likely, blending the egocentric and the communitarian. Signing a petition was a private act, but with many online petitions the signatory is encouraged to publicly share a link with their endorsement to the petition. This neatly leads to the third precursor for behaviour, perceptions of how the action will be received by others. The power of social norms within any community should determine how any member will behave to some extent. In particular the desire for rewards (perhaps likes or messages of support) and fear of censure (if only through statements like: "we don't do politics") will determine the likelihood of an action taking place. Finally, we consider the barriers to an action. Traditionally Ajzen ties barriers exclusively to perceived ability: smokers will only quit if they feel they are able, a consumer will only purchase an item if it is available and within their economic means, notwithstanding the availability of credit. However, when considering political participation, barriers may be linked more to the ability to achieve a goal than to commit any action. An online petition takes minimal effort, but if the chances of the mechanism having an impact are perceived to be low it is unlikely for many who consider their behaviour to sign up. Similarly, if there is little chance of a niche party gaining election, for example in first past the post systems like the United States and United Kingdom, but that is the only party to which one has an allegiance, there may seem no point in voting. Therefore, we can use this theory as a simple heuristic to provide some insights into a range of behaviours. The key is to understand the motivations and whether these are egocentric, communitarian, a combination or indeed related to other aspects of an individual's personality or world view. Ajzen's theory of planned behaviour offers a loose framework for understanding the motivations for taking part in non-traditional forms of political participation if they are considered actions and so to what extent they might mirror motivations that are implied when defining actions which constitute political participation.

It is true that individual clicks may have no meaning; they certainly require little effort. However, this may equally be considered more carefully. Within most cultures, political expression is outside social norms, showing party allegiance is not a common public act for the majority, so for any individual who is not a seasoned and habitual campaigner to express their political views should involve some cognitive decision-making process. For those driven by either egocentric or communitarian motives, a click may represent the first stage in seeking whether to become more involved, it is dipping a toe into the murky waters of political participation in order to see what happens. Is there a reward (from the network or through joining forces with others and gaining influence) or censure (criticism, ridicule and disempowerment)?

The fact that much research suggests that any action can lead to subsequent interactions and that, in turn, the subsequent interactions lead to

118 *Darren G. Lilleker*

greater engagement and involvement in participatory actions suggests that within a digital media environment a reaction is sought. If further participation is indeed dependent upon being rewarded, then there needs to be a recognised norm for this form of behaviour. The reinforcement of that norm leads to a desire to participate further and online participation may lead to offline participation if an individual is motivated to do so by rewards within their network and provided the barriers to participation (in terms of commitment) are not perceived as being too high. *Ceteris paribus*, punishments are demotivating and lead to non-participation in any actions that are censured.

Therefore, with stimuli from a network, any act of participation can lead to further participatory acts and political participation can become a norm of behaviour. What the digital age offers are myriad means to gain interest, to become engaged, to perform small actions to test the reaction, to interact with others, to gain instantaneous feedback and, in theory, for any individual to feel motivated to move along the participation continuum from the click to something more profound and, to recognise the longstanding perspectives in the area, a form of traditional political participation. While there may be some vestige of communitarian interest it must also be recognised that the intended outcome from non-traditional political participation may not purely aim at influencing policy, rather egocentric motivations relating to connecting into a network, forming communities and achieving status may be of equal or greater importance and be as or more empowering than the pursuit of communitarian goals.

7.3 Political Participation Online: The Murky Reality

Whereas online political participation can be lauded, this rests on a theoretical perspective rather than any in-depth study of what form non-traditional political participation actually takes. While there are some activities identified as traditional which can simply take place within an online environment (such as petitions becoming e-petitions, or letters to representatives being more likely to be sent via email) much non-traditional participation shares more with political talk in a bar. I use a short case study to provide some indication of the nature and form of the type of non-traditional political participation many engage with. The best description for this activity would be some form of broad, general discussion, an activity which involves some degree of interest, cognition and may exist within communities governed by social norms. The observations raise both positives and negatives of conceptualising online political participation as meaningful.

The referendum to determine Scotland remaining in the United Kingdom or becoming independent encouraged extraordinary high levels of engagement and participation: the turnout of 84.59 per cent is unheard of in recent years beyond nations with compulsory voting. The online environment was equally vibrant and active. Data on that vibrancy was taken a week after the referendum took place, 25 September 2014. The YES Campaign, in favour of independence, which lost but gained support among 44.7 per cent of voters, had a 73,298 strong community on Facebook. In terms of engagement there was an average of 809 likes, 240 shares and 89 comments per post. The victorious NO Campaign gained 55.3 per cent of the vote and has a 69,182 strong community on Facebook averaging 562 likes, 77 shares and 169 comments per post. One can instantly see a disparity and note that neither vibrancy nor reach matched the result. One can also note that the easier action of liking was most popular; sharing to a network of followers or another group less popular than liking, whereas commenting shows a more complex pattern in terms of volume. The nature of the comments was assessed through simply reading the nature of comments and making an evaluation regarding the extent to which conversations were taking place and whether commenters appeared informed or not and whether they sought responses and so making qualitative judgments regarding the forms of communication engaged in. Given the scale of data there is no attempt at quantification and, regardless, numbers are not the point. The purpose of the case study is to consider what this form of online participation takes.

The Facebook users who engaged with either side constituted no more than a maximum of 12 per cent of the total electorate and this is assuming that all members were from Scotland and joined one side only. However, this is equally only one snapshot of a bigger conversation which encompassed Twitter, YouTube and various other social spaces such as weblogs and forums. The question is what meanings were attributed when joining one or both campaigns, what outcomes were desired and realised, to what extent norms of behaviour encouraged greater interaction, and so on. Without using a targeted large-scale survey, we cannot know exactly; what does become apparent, from the trail of text left by users, is that as we can describe some actions as participation. Users were having input into a conversation that could shape the opinions, attitudes and ultimately voting behaviour of others and so shape the future of their nation. Furthermore, reading Facebook as a space for open contributions by anyone interested, we can describe the form(s) that expressive non-traditional participation took.

A myriad of forms of communication can be found, though this is not an attempt to quantify scientifically the types of expression, rather to identify the range. Some contributors posted highly informed commentary, quoted facts and statistics, as well as linking these facts to the experiences of ordinary people; this was particularly the case with concerns relating to what could happen if an independent Scotland was left with a floundering currency that was linked to neither the British pound nor the Euro. While the facts, often supported by hyperlinks, tended to replicate the campaigns of one of the sides, it shows a high degree of engagement. Much of this sort of expression was persuasive to an extent, though arguably a large proportion of the content of the profiles of both campaigns could be described as

120   *Darren G. Lilleker*

persuasive. The persuasive expression took various forms. One did not have to look far to find a large amount of uninformed commentary, statements that may have been phrased as fact but did not even contain cues to suggest there was any factual basis. Equally, many of the contributions were nothing more than individual observations about the campaign or rather random expressions of opinion regarding individuals, organisations or particular arguments. Some took to simply insulting figures from the campaign, Scottish Nationalist and YES campaign figurehead Alex Salmond and NO campaigner and Labour party leader in Scotland Jim Murphy received numerous and often highly personal insults across both campaign profiles. All these forms of expression could sit alongside the informed expressions and a record was included on what the 'audience' appreciated. Likes for comments and posts were distributed fairly across all forms of expression, there was no sense that more informed posts or comments got a greater or lesser number of likes than any other forms of expression. As would be expected in what was a rather heated politically charged environment, there were more simple expressions of support for the campaign or a specific argument as well as heckling from opponents than informed commentary. Equally, many of the expressions could be described as 'graffiti', single contributions like writing on a physical wall, expressing opinions such as "Salmond is a dick" or suggesting ill-considered actions like "Kick traitors like Murphy out of Scotland". In these cases there is no indication that a response was desired or sought.

But can we normatively ascribe greater meaning and intent to any one type of participation and argue it to be in some way better or more important? More importantly, should any of the forms of expression that can be located be classified as beyond the description of political participation? The question lies in the motivations for participation, were they self-oriented, communitarian, or should we also argue that expressing a view of any form, which may influence others, should be classified as participation in the digital age? Could the act of insulting a politician in public be a form of demonstration, for example?

The forms the comments took in relation to referendum can be classified in a number of ways that elide to some extent with definitions for campaigning, contacting elected representatives, or protesting which are at the heart of traditional political participation. Whether in the form of informed and measured argument or insulting an opponent there were examples of activism, all of which suggest many were taking part in campaigning activities. Some comments were clear attempts to applying pressure on others through persuasion, especially those that used emotive calls to 'duty'. Some comments sought to influence the campaign itself, showing support for the campaign yet opposing a specific argument. The 1,993 users who liked and shared the vow from the party leaders backing the NO campaign to give more powers to the Scottish people were engaged in a concerted, crowd-sourced, campaign to ensure promises were kept. Others could be argued

Re-Imagining the Meaning of Participation for a Digital Age   121

to be forms of protest. About the procedures, the campaign styles, the arguments, the individual campaign leaders and their motives. We could argue that the 364 citizens who opposed Jim Murphy's 'scaremongering' video on potential NHS cuts were acting as part of a demonstration, coherent and crowdsourced to exact influence. So much non-traditional political participation may actually be a form of traditional participation using other means.

However, arguably many contributions represent little more than simple actions which appear to have involved little consideration. Demonstrations of support or opposition are unorchestrated and spread across different posts indicating a lack of cohesion and organisation. The communication is anarchic with few genuine interactions to other users or even about the original post. Similarly there appears no sense of there being an intended outcome from much of the activity. Applying Ajzen's theory of planned behaviour it is difficult to see what positive outcomes were perceived to be possible from the contributions, whether the social norms went beyond the simple act of contributing or whether there was any sense of perceived empowerment. If we return to the bar analogy it would appear one in thirty contributions were informed; the rest were incoherent interjections by those who maybe had had one too many drinks. While this may be true for those who take to the streets to demonstrate, one can still see that the whole event has some level of organisation that is missing from the dialogic milieu that can be read on either of the Facebook profiles of the respective sides in the referendum.

7.3 A New Research Agenda

A cyber-optimist can view this as wholly positive evidence that digital technologies are facilitating political engagement and participation in a big conversation. Cyber-pessimists, in contrast, can view this as largely uninformed, anarchic and ultimately pointless. The middle ground is that it is both, though possibly to varying extents, and this may depend more upon the individual and their motivations than actual outcomes. A street demonstration or petition can be fruitless but empowering; can the same empowerment be gained by commenting on a post about politics on Facebook?

Researchers need data in order for us to understand the users who contribute to political discussions. What are their levels of political interest, are they seasoned campaigners or new to any form of participation, what did they hope to achieve, if anything and how did they feel as a result of taking part? These are all valid and important questions at the heart of understanding this relatively new but seemingly well-embedded phenomenon. A second raft of questions concerns each specific action. Was the act of liking, sharing or commenting pre-meditated or spontaneous and what are the different perceptions for each action? Do users search Facebook for spaces to make comments, or are they inspired into momentary 'hot cognition' by something that they read? When liking or sharing, to what extent are

122 *Darren G. Lilleker*

possible reactions from their network considered, equally what reactions are most desired? When deciding to contribute a comment, is this thought through, agonised over, edited and revised, or is it spur of the moment and ill-considered and what form do comments take that result from these different preparatory processes? Furthermore to what extent does the form of contribution mirror other user contributions, or to what extent is behaviour shaped by that of others within a specific network (members of a profile) or the personal network of a user? In order to mature, the study of digital political communication must draw on more scientific methods of examination in order to understand exactly what processes occur to lead to participation in what Chadwick (2011) describes as 'the political information cycle' where each contribution becomes part of a diegesis, a multi-authored narrative (Lilleker, 2014), around a debate or event of political significance.

7.4 Conclusion

The digital age allows anyone with access to broadband or 3G to take part in a variety of forms of political participation. The debate is not whether this happens, but whether this is political participation in any meaningful sense. We need to reconsider the importance of non-traditional forms of participation, in terms of their impact on individual participants, their networks and to the health of democracy generally. Any reconsideration must investigate the motivations for taking part and the meanings attributed by the individual participant. The dominant perspective of traditional political participation as outcome oriented, with the focus being on communitarian outcomes, may be outdated. Much online participation about politics may have no intended outcome that we would recognise as 'political' but it may have highly significant personal impacts and these may shape attitudes to other forms of participation that are ascribed as being meaningful. Research shows that engagement occurs and some is related to political events of significance, but too often such engagement is discounted, it is dismissed as effortless slacktivism rather than being considered as a form of activism. When we consider the diversity of forms of participation, the diversity of those who participate and so the diversity of motivations and meanings, can we judge the discounting to be fair? We need more understanding, which means more research and in particular specialist research, on the meanings of clicks and likes and random interjections in order to know what political participation means in a digital age.

Works Cited

Ajzen, Icek. 1991. "The theory of planned behaviour." *Organizational behavior and human decision processes*, 50 (2): 179–211.

Avril, Emmanuel. 2014. Democracy, Participation and Contestation Civil society, governance and the future of liberal democracy, London: Routledge.

Re-Imagining the Meaning of Participation for a Digital Age 123

Benhabib, Seyla. 1996. Democracy and difference: Contesting the boundaries of the political. Princeton, NJ: Princeton University Press.

Chadwick, Andrew. 2011. "The political information cycle in a hybrid news system: The British prime minister and the "bullygate" affair." *The International Journal of Press/Politics*, 16 (1): 3–29.

Dermody, Janine, and Scullion, Richard. 2005. "Young people's attitudes towards British political advertising: nurturing or impeding voter engagement?". *Journal of Nonprofit & Public Sector Marketing*, 14 (1–2): 129–149.

De Zúñiga, Homero, Gil, Eulalia Puig-I-Abril, and Rojas, Hernando. 2009. "Weblogs, traditional sources online and political participation: an assessment of how the internet is changing the political environment". *New Media & Society*, 11 (4): 553–574.

Fiorina, Morris. P. 1976. "The voting decision: instrumental and expressive aspects". *The Journal of Politics*, 38 (2): 390–413.

Gibson, Rachel, and Cantijoch, Marta. 2013. "Conceptualizing and measuring participation in the age of the internet: Is online political engagement really different to offline?" *The Journal of Politics*, 75 (3): 701–716.

Golbeck, Jennifer, Robles, Cristina, and Turner, Karen. 2011. "Predicting personality with social media". *CHI'11 Extended Abstracts on Human Factors in Computing Systems* (pp. 253–262). ACM.

Guskin, Emily, and Tan, Suvini. 2012. "Pop Culture is King in Social Media". Accessed 16 August 2014. http://www.journalism.org/2012/05/24/pop-culture-king-social-media/.

Hindman, Matthew. 2008. *The myth of digital democracy*. Princeton: Princeton University Press.

Holcomb, Jesse, Gottfried, Jeffrey, and Mitchell, Amy. 2013. "News Use Across Social Media Platforms". Accessed 16 August 2014. http://www.journalism.org/2013/11/14/news-use-across-social-media-platforms/.

Huntington, Samuel P., and Nelson, Joan M. 1976. *No Easy Choice: Political Participation in Developing Countries*. Cambridge, Mass: Harvard University Press.

Irvin, Renee. A, and Stansbury, John. 2004. "Citizen participation in decision making: is it worth the effort?" *Public administration review*, 64 (1): 55–65.

Jennings, M. Kent, and Zeitner, Vicki. 2003. "Internet use and civic engagement: A longitudinal analysis". *Public Opinion Quarterly*, 67 (3): 311–334.

Joinson, Adam. N. 2008. "Looking at, looking up or keeping up with people?: motives and use of facebook." In *Proceedings of the SIGCHI conference on Human Factors in Computing Systems* (pp. 1027–1036). ACM.

Koc-Michalska, Karolina, and Lilleker, Darren G. 2014. "Evolving In Step or Poles Apart?: Online Audiences and Networking During Poland and France 2011–12 Election Campaign". *International Journal of E-Politics (IJEP)*, 5 (1): 41–60.

Lilleker, Darren. G. 2014. "Autobiography and Political Marketing: Narrative and the Obama Brand". In *Real Lives, Celebrity Stories: Narratives of Ordinary and Extraordinary People Across Media*, edited by Julia Round and Bronwen Thomas. London, Bloomsbury.

Margolis, Michael, and Resnick, David. 2000. *Politics as Usual: The Cyberspace Revolution*. New York: Sage.

Pew Research Center. 2014. "Beyond Red vs. Blue: The Political Typology" Accessed 16 August 2014. http://www.people-press.org/2014/06/26/the-political-typology-beyond-red-vs-blue/.

124   Darren G. Lilleker

Puig-i-Abril, Eulalia, and Rojas, Hernando. 2007. "Being early on the curve: Online practices and expressive political participation". *International Journal of Internet Science*, 2 (1): 28–44.

Rheingold, Harold. 1993. The virtual community: Finding commection in a computerized world. Boston, MA: Addison-Wesley Longman.

Rojas, Hernando, Puig-i-Abril, Eulalia, and Perez, Irma. 2007. "The Internet and civic engagement: How online news, political messaging and blog use matter for participation". Paper presented at the annual meeting of the *Association for Internet Researchers-AOIR annual meeting*, Oct, 18–20: Vancouver.

Rojas, Hernando, and Puig-i-Abril, Eulalia. 2009. "Mobilizers mobilized: Information, expression, mobilization and participation in the digital age". *Journal of Computer-Mediated Communication*, 14 (4): 902–927.

Shah, Dhavan, Cho, V. Jaeho, Eveland, William P., and Kwak, Nojin. 2005. "Information and expression in a digital age modeling Internet effects on civic participation". *Communication research*, 32 (5): 531–565.

Stolle, Dietlind, and Hooghe, Mark. 2005. "Inaccurate, exceptional, one-sided or irrelevant? The debate about the alleged decline of social capital and civic engagement in Western societies". *British journal of political science*, 35 (1): 149–167.

Verba, Stanley, Schlozman, Kay L., and Brady, Henry E. 1995. *Voice and equality: Civic voluntarism in American politics*. Cambridge, Mass: Harvard University Press.

Vesnic-Alujevic, Lucia. 2012. "Political participation and Web 2.0 in Europe: A case study of Facebook". *Public Relations Review*, 38 (3): 466–470.

Williams, Christine, and Gulati, Girish J. (2012). "Social networks in political campaigns: Facebook and the congressional elections of 2006 and 2008". *New Media & Society*, 15 (1): 52–71.

Zittel, Thomas. 2004. "Political Communication and Electronic Democracy". In *Comparing political communication: Theories, cases and challenges*, edited by Frank Esser and Barbara Pfetsch. London: Cambridge University Press.

8 Who's Afraid of Clicktivism? Exploring Citizens' Use of Social Media and Political Participation in the Czech Republic

Jaromír Mazák and Václav Štětka

Introduction[1]

The recent explosion of social network sites and other Web 2.0 applications has been accompanied by a rapidly growing body of research exploring their role in civic engagement and political participation. Optimistic perspectives have stressed the potential of these new communication technologies to rejuvenate democracy, mainly by enabling for greater interactivity and user participation in the creation of online political content, as well as by facilitating new forms of civic and political activism (Jenkins 2006; Bruns 2008; Shirky 2008; Castells 2012; Bennett and Segerberg 2013). However, claims about the importance of online media in enhancing citizens' involvement in political affairs and bringing previously disaffected members of the public into the arena of democratic politics soon started to be challenged by more skeptical arguments, according to which online engagement has no connection to (or impact on) the "real life". Denouncing social media activism as "clicktivism" or "slacktivism" (Morozov 2009; White 2010a), these critics have alleged that there is a profound gap between peoples' actions in the online and in the offline world and that engaging in this form of participation might even lead to increasing passivity in relation to offline politics.

Given the increasing adoption of social media by political candidates and parties across the Western world for electoral campaigning (see e.g., Lilleker and Jackson 2010; Larsson and Moe 2012; Strandberg 2013; Gibson 2013), the incentive to study the relationship between online and offline forms of political engagement is obviously even more relevant. However, so far the evidence about whether online and traditional campaign tools mobilize the same kind of people and whether and how the online participatory activities translate into political engagement offline has been fragmented and is still rather inconclusive (Boulianne 2009; Gibson and Cantijoch 2013).

Drawing on these debates, this chapter aims to empirically investigate the connection between offline political/civic engagement and a specific form of political engagement carried out in the online environment, namely online political expression (Gil de Zuniga et al. 2014), in the context of the 2013 Czech Parliamentary Elections. Driven by the main research question "*How*

126 *Jaromír Mazák and Václav Štětka*

does social media use relate to election turnout and offline forms of political participation?", this study uses data collected by means of a representative survey of the Czech adult population (N = 1603), distributed directly following the 2013 elections. The analysis further explores the relationship between traditional forms of political participation and the use of social media for online political expression, taking into account other factors such as political interest, political efficacy and social-demographic variables, with the ambition to provide a more detailed understanding of online political engagement and its correlates.

8.1 Clicktivism or Expressive Political Action? Participation in the Age of Social Buttons

The intertwined concepts of "clicktivism" / "slacktivism" have been recently popularized as a critical answer to the initial optimistic narratives about the ability of the Internet and social media to uplift and intensify democratic participation and to arm citizens with effective instruments to mobilize for collective action (Gladwell 2010; Popova 2010; White 2010b; Christensen 2011; Zuckerman 2014). For the critics, activities such as signing online petitions, sharing content on social network sites or demonstrating support or solidarity via the "social buttons" (such as Facebook's "Like" button) represent a low-key or "thin form of engagement" (Halupka 2014: 117), which does not express a full-fledged political commitment. Instead, its main role is seen in making the Internet users feel good about themselves, while avoiding a "real" involvement that might be more demanding in terms of time and effort. In the words of one of the leading proponents of the slacktivism thesis, Evgeny Morozov, this is an "ideal type of activism for a lazy generation", giving "to those who participate in 'slacktivist' campaigns an illusion of having a meaningful impact on the world without demanding anything more than joining a Facebook group" (Morozov 2009). Aside from allegedly having "zero political or social impact", Morozov denounces slacktivism for potentially turning people "away from conventional (and proven) forms of activism (demonstrations, sit-ins, confrontation with police, strategic litigation, etc.)" (Morozov 2009). Micah White, one of the Occupy Wall Street initiators, goes even further down this line of thought, expressing an opinion that clicktivism actually damages genuine political movements, alienating potential supporters by an overt reliance on online marketing strategies. As he puts it,

> Digital activism is a danger to the left. Its ineffectual marketing campaigns spread political cynicism and draw attention away from genuinely radical movements. Political passivity is the end result of replacing salient political critique with the logic of advertising.
>
> (White 2010a)

Notwithstanding such criticism dismissing the impact of clicktivism on offline political behaviour as either negligible or negative, empirical scholarship has been seeking to provide evidence for a spillover effect from online engagement over to offline participation. Using individual web survey data from Norway, Enjolras et al. (2013) found that social media mobilize specific socio-demographic segments and that "participation in Facebook groups has a strong and independent effect on mobilization" (Enjolras et al. 2013: 904). Based on a student survey before the 2008 U.S. presidential elections, Vitak et al. (2011) found that political activity on Facebook is a significant predictor of other forms of political participation. In response to the need for a more nuanced approach towards examining political participation in the social media environment, the concept of online political expression (or e-expression) has recently been introduced by several authors attempting to describe online activities such as posting or sharing politically relevant comments, befriending or following politicians and candidates – in other words, activities regularly labelled as "clicktivism" – without the negative connotations associated with that term (Rojas and Puig-i-Abril 2009; Gil de Zúñiga, Jung and Valenzuela 2012; Gil de Zúñiga, Molyneux and Zheng 2014). Focusing on "the public expression of political orientations" (Rojas and Puig-i-Abril 2009: 906), this e-expressive mode of participation (Gibson and Cantijoch 2013) has been found by the above-quoted studies to be significantly related to political participation both online (through donating money, volunteering, writing emails, etc.) and – even more importantly – offline. In light of such findings, Gil de Zúñiga et al. have argued that:

> Political discussion in person and offline expression, while not being less important, may now be complemented by supplemental paths to political involvement via social media. This supplementary connection to political expression in social media use is promising for the development of a politically active future, especially for younger people (2014: 627).

However, despite these outcomes indicating a possible rehabilitation of clicktivism as a "legitimate political action" (Halupka 2014), existing research is far from providing a clear-cut answer concerning the link between political expression on social media platforms and other forms of political engagement. This study attempts to contribute to this still emerging research territory by examining the above mentioned relationship using empirical data from the Czech Republic, a country where social media have only very recently started playing a more significant role in political communication. Inspired by the pioneering campaign of the presidential candidate Karel Schwarzenberg in January 2013, which was particularly successful in mobilizing young voters via Facebook (Štětka, Macková and Fialová 2014), most politicians and political parties lifted their pace of adoption of social media for electoral communication. In consequence, the 2013 parliamentary

128 Jaromír Mazák and Václav Štětka

elections campaign, which took place less than a year after the presidential election, was marked by the intensive use of Facebook by the majority of relevant parties (see Štětka and Vochocová 2014). This situation has given us an opportunity to empirically analyze the responsiveness of the Czech citizens to the electoral mobilization via social network sites by parties and candidates, as well as to examine the intensity of political use of social media by the Czech online population.

8.2 Research Aims and Methods

Drawing on the above presented theoretical framework, the main aim of our study was to investigate if there is a link between online political expression during the election campaign and traditional forms of political participation among Czech Facebook users. Following the above-quoted studies (Rojas and Puig-i-Abril 2009; Vitak et al. 2011; Gil de Zúñiga, Jung and Valenzuela 2012; Gil de Zúñiga, Molyneux and Zheng 2014) we expected (H1) that online political expression during the campaign will be positively correlated with traditional, mostly offline forms of political participation. Online political expression was measured using a composite index of altogether nine selected activities during the 2013 parliamentary elections on Facebook (liking politician's or party post; commenting on a friend's contribution about the campaign; sharing contributions by politicians or political parties; becoming a fan of a politician or a political party, commenting on posts by politicians or political parties; adding comments or information concerning elections on one's own profile; becoming a fan of another political initiative related to elections) and on Internet discussion forums (reading online forums about the elections; contributing to these forums). For traditional forms of political participation we included following variables: discussing politics offline; signing petitions; attending a demonstration; attending a local community-related gathering; working for a club or local organization; and finally voting in the 2013 parliamentary elections.

Furthermore, we decided to include political interest as a control variable in our analysis. Political interest has been traditionally considered an important resource for political participation (Brady, Verba and Schlozman 1995; Norris 2000) and recent empirical studies have confirmed that this relationship extends into the domain of online participation as well (Vitak et al. 2011; Boulianne 2011; Holt et al. 2013). In tackling the slacktivism thesis, we therefore wanted to see if the expected correlations between online political expression and traditional forms of political participation will still hold when controlling for declared political interest.

The second goal of this study was to propose an exploratory typology based on combining people's electoral participation and their online political expression and then to test whether different clusters of respondents (particularly those who go to the elections *and* display at least some level of online political expression versus the rest) differ in selected other characteristics, namely political efficacy (measured by the question whether people can change anything by participating in elections, as well as by the question whether there is a political party in the country sufficiently representing the respondent's opinions) and using preferential voting in the 2013 parliamentary elections. Following previous studies on online participation, which have included measures of political efficacy (Gil de Zúñiga, Jung and Valenzuela 2012; Lariscy, Tinkham and Sweetser 2011; Jung, Kim and Gil de Zúñiga 2011), we expected (H2) that high political efficacy will be positively correlated to voting participation and online political expression.

The data set we drew on in this study was obtained by means of a quota sample (N = 1653) representative of the adult Czech population with regards to region (NUTS 3), size of residence, gender, age and education. However, since our indicator of online political expression was primarily based on activities displayed by Facebook users during the election campaign period, we only used the subset of Facebook users (N = 743) for our analysis.[2] The survey was administered using face-to-face interviews between 28 October and 11 November 2013, immediately following the early parliamentary elections that took place on 25 – 26 October 2013. Table 8.1 shows the socio-demographic distribution of the sample as well as shares of the Internet and Facebook users within individual socio-demographic categories. For example, among the 298 people in the sample aged 65 and more, 24 per cent use the Internet and 9 per cent use the Facebook. This means that about one in three Internet users in this age category also uses Facebook.

Table 8.1 Sample distribution and shares of Internet/Facebook users within individual socio-demographic categories

		% of Internet users within the sample	% of Facebook users within Internet users (the sample)
Gender	Male (816)	70	66 (46)
	Female (835)	67	66 (44)
Age	18 - 24 (181)	91	94 (86)
	25 - 34 (296)	88	84 (74)
	35 - 44 (308)	85	68 (58)
	45 - 54 (264)	75	46 (35)
	55 - 64 (273)	56	43 (24)
	65+ (298)	24	36 (9)
Education	primary (269)	46	81 (37)
	lower secondary (560)	59	66 (39)
	higher secondary (538)	82	64 (52)
	tertiary (261)	89	62 (55)

Note: Numbers in parenthesis in the second column indicate the number of respondents falling into the category within the whole sample (N = 1,653) with missing values omitted.

8.3 Testing the Relationship between Online Political Expression and Traditional Forms of Political Participation

In order to study online political expression, we asked the respondents (Facebook users only) whether they engaged during the election campaign period in the following specific activities on Facebook and online discussion forums. The prevalence of these activities is displayed in Figure 8.1.

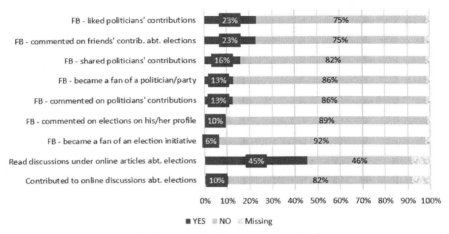

Figure 8.1 Prevalence of online political expression in the election campaign period (Facebook users only, N = 743).

As the graph shows, the most predominant activities on Facebook in response to the election campaign were "liking" politician's (or a political candidate's) status – the sort of activity most often mentioned when illustrating the phenomenon of slacktivism (Fuchs 2013) – and commenting on an election-related status by friends. However, reading discussions under Internet news articles about the elections has been by far the most frequent activity of all, with almost half of the sub-sample (45 per cent) of Facebook users engaging in it.

The dependent variable in our model was derived from a composite index constructed from the nine items in Figure 8.1 (Cronbach alpha 0.83) representing online political expression.[3] For the purpose of our statistical model, the index of online political expression has been transformed into three levels:

- No online political expression (45 per cent of Facebook users)[4]
- Lower online political expression (one or two of the nine items in the Figure 8.1 during the campaign; 31 per cent of Facebook users)
- Higher online political expression (at least three of the nine items, 24 per cent of Facebook users)

Before inspecting the dependency model, we take a closer look at the independent variables. Table 8.2 shows percentage of Facebook users who claim to have pursued the selected forms of traditional political participation (first column) and the predictive capacity of these items in relation to online political expression (second column).

Table 8.2 Traditional participatory activities and their predictive capacity in relation to online political expression

	Percentage of FB users (sample)[5]	Provided the FB user pursued the given form of political participation (list to the left), how likely was he/she to also engage in online political expression (either lower or higher)?
Signed petition	22 (18) %	74%
Attended demonstration	16 (15) %	87%
Local public gathering	25 (24) %	72%
Work for club, local organization	17 (16) %	73%
Discussing politics offline	29 (27) %	84%
Voted in the 2013 elections	67 (68) %	68%

Note: The first column in the table gives the share of Facebook users (N = 743) and of the whole sample (in brackets, N = 1,653) who participated in the respective form of traditional political participation in the previous 12 months.

Whereas only 55 per cent of Facebook users in the sample engaged in some sort of online political expression before the elections, this number rises to 74 per cent for those who signed a petition in the twelve months prior to the survey and is even higher for those who attended a demonstration or discussed politics offline. All the individual forms of traditional political participation in the Table 8.2 show positive association with online political expression.

Do these positive relationships hold when we control for the influence of declared interest in politics? The interest in politics was measured using four categories in the survey, but we had to transform them into three due to the low number of respondents very much interested in politics. The resulting three-level variable had the following distribution for the subset of Facebook users: higher interest (combining the original categories "very much interested" and "quite a bit interested") = 19 per cent, lower interest = 54 percent, no interest = 28 per cent.

Due to the fact that the dependent variable (online political expression) was coded as an ordered categorical variable with three categories, we have used ordinal logistic regression to statistically test our model.[5]

The final model is displayed in Table 8.3. Even when controlling for the strong influence of declared interest in politics, traditional forms of political participation – discussing politics offline at least once a week, signing a

132   *Jaromír Mazák and Václav Štětka*

petition in the previous twelve months and attending a demonstration in the previous twelve months – were all by themselves significant predictors of online political expression during the election campaign. Voting in the elections is also significantly positively associated with online political expression. This suggests that one of the main assumptions of the hypothesis about clicktivism which argues that pressing the "like button" is rarely accompanied by showing up for elections, does not find much support in our data, according to which voting is associated with online political expression even when we control for the remaining variables in the model.

On the other hand, neither attending public gatherings on local community issues, nor working for a local club or organization in the previous twelve months turned out to be significant predictors of online political expression during elections in the model.

Table 8.3 Ordinal logistic regression analysis with online political expression as dependent variable (population: Facebook users, N = 686)

Parameter	Estimate (S.E.)	Odds Ratio
Threshold (online - none)	2 (0,32) ***	7,40
Threshold (online - lower)	3,89 (0,35) ***	48,91
Age (centred)	**-0,02 (0,01) ***	0,99
Female	-0,02 (0,16)	0,98
Edu. - tertiary	0,13 (0,30)	1,14
Edu. - higher secondary	0,36 (0,27)	1,43
Edu. - lower secondary	0,32 (0,28)	1,37
Discuss politics offline	**1,12 (0,19) ***	3,06
Petition	**0,54 (0,20) ***	1,71
Demonstration	**0,90 (0,24) ***	2,46
Local gathering	0,07 (0,21)	1,07
Work for club	-0,02 (0,23)	0,99
Voting	**0,77 (0,19) ***	2,16
Political interest - higher	**2,08 (0,30) ***	7,96
Political interest - lower	**0,93 (0,21) ***	2,53

Note: pseudo R^2 = .34 (Cox & Snell), .38 (Nagelkerke). Model chi-square (13) = 280, p < .0005, N = 686.
* p < .05, ** p < .01, *** p < .0005. Multicolinearity diagnosis: No variance inflation factor exceeded 3.
Education categories are compared to primary education, political interest categories are compared to the base category of no political interest. Other variables in the model are binaries or continuous (age).

While declared political interest is clearly indicative of higher online engagement, the standard control variables of gender, age and education do not seem to be very important for explaining online political expression. Of all these three variables, only age has some statistically significant effect: older Facebook users are somewhat less likely to be politically active online.

To estimate the size effects of the individual variables when controlling for all the other variables in the model, see the odds ration column in Table 8.3. It explains that, for example, the likelihood of higher online political expression is 8 times (2.5 times) greater for people with higher (lower) political interest than people with no political interest. Due to the nature of the ordinal logistic regression model, the same can be said for the joint likelihood of higher and lower online political expression.

8.4 Toward a Typology of Online Political Expression and Voting Behaviour

In the previous section, we have demonstrated that our cross-sectional data indicate a positive association between online political expression and at least some forms of traditional, mostly offline political participation (voting, demonstration, petition, discussing politics offline) as well as declared interest in politics. Our further goal was to conduct an exploratory analysis of a typology based on a combination of online political expression and voting as the arguably most import form of traditional political participation. Not only did we want to see how often online political expression and voting actually concur among the Facebook users during the campaign, but we were especially interested in examining how the people who participate by casting the ballot as well as by making politically related expressions on Facebook differ from those who either only go to the elections, or only express themselves online, or do none of these activities.

Our typology is based on a simple quadrant scheme (Table 8.4). For online political expression, we only differentiate between those who positively replied to any one of the nine items in Figure 8.1 and the others.

Table 8.4 Online political expression vs. voting behaviour: typology and frequencies

		Voting	
		YES	NO
Online political expression	YES	Expressive voters 330 (46 %)	Expressive non-voters 75 (10 %)
	NO	Non-expressive voters 154 (21 %)	Non-expressive non-voters 165 (23 %)

Note: The figures in each of the four quadrants indicate the number of Facebook users and their percentage from the total N=724 who entered the analysis.

Looking at the outcomes, it is clear that voting and online political expression concur fairly often during the campaign. More than two thirds of the Facebook users who cast the ballot also engaged in at least some form of online political expression. Among the non-voters, the ratio is the opposite: only less than a third of them engaged in online political expression.

With regards to the results from the regression model presented in the previous part of this chapter, it does not come as much of a surprise that expressive voters show much higher levels of declared political interest than all the remaining groups (35 per cent of them claim to be very or quite a lot interested in politics as opposed to 7 per cent among non-expressive voters and 3 per cent among both the other two categories of our typology). However, it turns out that they are also quite different when it comes to the issue of political efficacy, measured by asking the respondents whether they thought voting for a certain party "can change anything". The expressive voters in the sample perceived voting as more effective than the other groups, as shown in the following Figure 8.2.

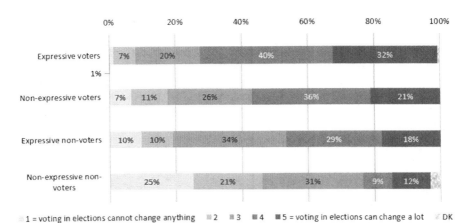

Figure 8.2 Political efficacy – can voting in the elections change anything?

Similarly, expressive voters are much more likely than the others to think that some party expresses their own opinions and attitudes well enough. Specifically, 64 per cent of expressive voters answered "yes" in this binary question as opposed to 39 per cent of non-expressive voters, 24 per cent of expressive non-voters and only 8 per cent of non-expressive non-voters.

Furthermore, when we compare only expressive and non-expressive voters in their usage of preference votes, enabling voters to select individual candidates on the party's ballot as opposed to accepting the order of candidates as suggested by the party, there is again a notable difference. Whereas 44 per cent of the expressive voters claim to have used the preference votes, this only holds for 25 per cent of non-expressive voters in the sample. As long as preference votes can be considered an indicator of a better informed or at least more engaged voting, online political expression is positively associated with it.

8.5 Discussion and Conclusions

The results of this study, as displayed above, suggest that the use of social media for political expression is positively correlated with some forms of traditional, mainly offline political participation, thereby lending support to our first hypothesis (H1). Furthermore, our study has offered some more in-depth insights into the relationship between these two forms of political participation by demonstrating that the cluster of "expressive voters" – that is those voters actively engaging in online political expression during the campaign – are also more likely to display higher levels of political efficacy (believing that voting in elections will make a difference) and also to use the instrument of preferential voting more often than their fellow citizens who are not active online during the campaign. It is also worth stressing that our analysis found a positive relationship between online political expression and respondents' declared political interest, which remains strong even when controlling for the selected types of traditional political participation.

How can these findings inform the contemporary discussion about the validity of the concept of clicktivism? Even though we obviously cannot address all aspects featured in the rather complex debate, as outlined in the first part of our chapter, we have demonstrated that the same people who engage in relatively effortless politically expressive activities such as mere liking, sharing or commenting online political content, can be also considered as more engaged citizens when it comes to the more traditional forms of participation, particularly attending demonstrations, signing petitions or debating politics outside of the Internet. While this might seem to be a rather minor empirical challenge to an arguably broader theoretical thesis, it directly questions one of its cores assumptions, namely that there is a deep gap between being politically active in the SNS environment and in the "real world". In our opinion, the evidence is compelling enough to allow us to argue that the clicktivism thesis in its crudest version – portraying Facebook political enthusiasts as disconnected from offline participatory mechanisms and practices – has little ground when tested against our data.

By rejecting this assumption, based on our data from the 2013 Czech parliamentary elections, we of course do not want to go as far as to claim that online political expression itself paves way for other types of participatory activities, including voting. The cross-sectional design of our study did not enable us to test the possible causal effect of online participation on offline engagement, as has been explored elsewhere, for example by Holt et al. (2013) in their panel study, so our findings must remain on the level of establishing correlation between these activities. Another limitation of our study which we duly acknowledge concerns the fact that it was set within the rather specific period of the election campaign. While we found out that expressing political stances via Facebook's social buttons during the campaign is positively correlated with subsequent voting as well as other offline participatory activities, we are also aware of the fact that the time of the campaign usually increases citizens' interest in politics and the levels of their engagement. Future research should therefore target more routine periods of the election cycle and examine whether the Internet users – and particularly those from among the group of voters – will continue to be politically active online and use social network sites for political expression even without the additional stimulation provided by electoral mobilization.

Despite these limitations, we believe the outcomes of our study add to the growing amount of empirical support for the argument that online political expression on social media platforms should be viewed as an activity which is complementing, rather than substituting, offline forms of civic and political engagement (e.g., Gil de Zúñiga et al. 2014). The fact that the number of Facebook users we called "expressive voters" in our sample turned out to be more than four times higher than the number of "expressive non-voters" (that is, those "clicktivists" who do not transfer their online engagement with the campaign into casting a ballot) suggests that the alleged divide between online and offline modes of political participation is probably much smaller than sometimes predicted (or even feared), at least when it comes to electoral behaviour. Therefore, instead of disdaining social buttons as instruments of participation, we think further research should rather seek inspiration by those who propose to treat clicktivism as a legitimate political act (see Halupka 2014), and focus on more detailed explorations of the particular ways and mechanisms through which online activism, and especially activism exercised via social network sites, translates into offline political and civic engagement.

Notes

1. This research was supported by the Czech Science Foundation (GACR), Standard Grant Nr 14–05575S "The Role of Social Media in the Transformation of Political Communication and Citizen Participation in the Czech Republic".
2. The alternative solution to include all respondents regardless of their internet use might result in mislabelling a significant number of people as politically inactive online, while the primary reason for their lack of online political participation would be in fact the decision not to use Facebook or the Internet in the first place.
3. The reason why the online political expression is dependent whereas traditional, mostly offline forms of political participation are independent variables is purely technical we do not propose any causality by the model, rather we examine the mutual association between these variables.
4. The total here is 731, not 743 as some Facebook users did not answer at least seven of the nine items, which was our arbitrary condition for inclusion.
5. Model PLUM in SPSS, test of parallel lines chi-square = 17; df = 13, p = 0.20.

Works Cited

Bennett, Lance W., and Segerberg, Alexandra. 2013. The logic of connective action: Digital media and the personalization of contentious politics. Cambridge: Cambridge University Press.

Who's Afraid of Clicktivism? 137

Boulianne, Shelley. 2009. "Does Internet use affect engagement? A meta-analysis of research". Political communication 26 (2): 193–211.

Boulianne, Shelley. 2011. "Stimulating or Reinforcing Political Interest: Using Panel Data to Examine Reciprocal Effects Between News Media and Political Interest". Political Communication 28 (2): 147–162.

Brady, Henry E., Verba, Sidney, and Schlozman, Kay Lehman. 1995. "Beyond SES: A resource model of political participation". American Political Science Review 89 (02): 271–294.

Bruns, Axel. 2008. Blogs, Wikipedia, Second Life, and beyond: From production to produsage. Vol. 45. Peter Lang.

Castells, Manuel. 2012. Networks of outrage and hope: Social movements in the internet age. Cambridge, UK; Malden, MA: Polity.

Christensen, Henrik Serup. 2011. "Political activities on the Internet: 'Slacktivism' or political participation by other means"? First Monday 16 (2).

Dahlgren, Peter. 2013. The political web: media, participation and alternative democracy. Basingstoke, New York: Palgrave Macmillan.

Enjolras, B., Steen-Johnsen, K., and Wollebæk, D. 2013. "Social media and mobilization to offline demonstrations: Transcending participatory divides"? New Media & Society, 15 (6): 890–908.

Fuchs, Christian. 2013. Social media: A critical introduction. London: Sage.

Gibson, Rachel K. 2013. "Party Change, Social Media and the Rise of 'Citizen-Initiated' Campaigning". Party Politics, January, 1354068812472575. doi:10.1177/1354068812472575.

Gibson, Rachel, and Cantijoch, Marta. 2013. "Conceptualizing and measuring participation in the age of the internet: Is online political engagement really different to offline"? The Journal of Politics, 75 (03): 701–716.

Gil de Zúñiga, Homero, Jung, Nakwon, and Valenzuela, Sebastián. 2012. "Social Media Use for News and Individuals' Social Capital, Civic Engagement and Political Participation". Journal of Computer-Mediated Communication 17 (3): 319–36.

Gil de Zúñiga, Homero, Molyneux, Logan, and Zheng, Pei. 2014. "Social Media, Political Expression, and Political Participation: Panel Analysis of Lagged and Concurrent Relationships". Journal of Communication 64 (4): 612–34.

Gladwell, Malcolm. 2010. "Small Change: Why the revolution will not be tweeted." The New Yorker, 4 Oct 2010. Available online at: http://www.newyorker.com/magazine/2010/10/04/small-change-3 (accessed 16/4/2015).

Halupka, Max. 2014. "Clicktivism: A Systematic Heuristic". Policy & Internet 6 (2): 115–32.

Holt, Kristoffer, Shehata, Adam, Strömbäck, Jesper, and Ljungberg, Elisabet. 2013. "Age and the Effects of News Media Attention and Social Media Use on Political Interest and Participation: Do Social Media Function as Leveller"? European Journal of Communication 28 (1): 19–34.

Jenkins, Henry. 2006. Convergence culture: Where old and new media collide. New York: NYU Press.

Jung, Nakwon, Kim, Yonghwan, and Gil de Zúñiga, Homero. 2011. "The Mediating Role of Knowledge and Efficacy in the Effects of Communication on Political Participation". Mass Communication and Society 14 (4): 407–30.

Lariscy, Ruthann Weaver, Tinkham, Spencer F., and Sweetser, Kaye D. 2011. "Kids These Days: Examining Differences in Political Uses and Gratifications, Internet

138 *Jaromír Mazák and Václav Štětka*

Political Participation, Political Information Efficacy, and Cynicism on the Basis of Age". American Behavioral Scientist 55 (6): 749–64.

Larsson, Anders Olof, and Moe, Hallvard. 2012. "Studying Political Microblogging: Twitter Users in the 2010 Swedish Election Campaign". New Media & Society 14 (5): 729–47.

Lilleker, Darren G, and Jackson, Nigel A. 2010. "Towards a More Participatory Style of Election Campaigning: The Impact of Web 2.0 on the UK 2010 General Election". Policy & Internet 2 (3): 67–96.

Morozov, Evgeny. 2009. "The brave new world of slacktivism". *Foreign Policy*, May 19. Accessed June 12, 2014. http://neteffect.foreignpolicy.com/posts/2009/05/19/the_brave_new_world_of_slacktivism.

Norris, Pippa. 2000. A virtuous circle: Political communications in postindustrial societies. Cambridge: Cambridge University Press.

Popova, Maria. 2010. "Malcolm Gladwell Is #Wrong". The Design Observer Group, 10 Jun 2010. Available online: http://designobserver.com/feature/malcolm-gladwell-is-wrong/19008/, last accessed 12 April 2015.

Rojas, Hernando, and Puig-i-Abril, Eulalia. 2009. "Mobilizers Mobilized: Information, Expression, Mobilization and Participation in the Digital Age". Journal of Computer-Mediated Communication 14 (4): 902–27.

Shirky, Clay. 2008. Here comes everybody: The power of organizing without organizations. Penguin.

Štětka, Václav, Macková, Alena, and Fialová, Marta. 2014. "A Winding Road from 'Likes' to Votes". In Social Media in Politics, edited by Bogdan Pătruţ and Monica Pătruţ, 225–44. Public Administration and Information Technology 13. Springer International Publishing.

Štětka, Václav, and Vochocová, Lenka. 2014. "A dialogue of the deaf, or communities of debate? The use of Facebook for campaign communication and citizen participation in the 2013 Czech Parliamentary elections". Teorija in praksa, 6 (2014): 1361–1380.

Strandberg, Kim. 2013. "A Social Media Revolution or Just a Case of History Repeating Itself? The Use of Social Media in the 2011 Finnish Parliamentary Elections". New Media & Society 15 (8): 1329–47.

Vitak, Jessica, Zube, Paul, Smock, Andrew, Carr, Caleb T., Ellison, Nicole, and Lampe, Cliff. 2011. "It's Complicated: Facebook Users' Political Participation in the 2008 Election". Cyberpsychology, Behavior, and Social Networking 14 (3): 107–14.

White, Micah. 2010a. "Clicktivism is ruining leftist activism". TheGuardian, August 12. Accessed April 12, 2015. http://www.theguardian.com/commentisfree/2010/aug/12/clicktivism-ruining-leftist-activism.

White, Micah. 2010b. "Why Gladwell is wrong". Adbusters, October 8. Accessed April 12, 2015.

Zuckerman, Ethan. 2014. "New Media, New Civics"? Policy & Internet 6 (2): 151–68.

9 Twitter as a Counterpublic Sphere
Polemics in the Twittersphere During French Electoral Campaigns

Arnaud Mercier

Introduction

The rise of the political use of social media in France has occurred in a climate of strong opposition to political leaders and traditional parties, marked by a certain level of civic protest. The first studies on the use of social media insist on strong personal and emotional involvement in the published messages (Boyd 2008). There is also evidence that existing political forces have integrated social media into their repertoire of collective action (Mercier 2015), especially during election campaigns. This makes Twitter accounts, Facebook, Instagram and others an extension of the technologies of web campaigning.

This paper sheds light on the ways French citizens use Twitter during campaigns to participate critically in the electoral process. As the chapter will argue, these spaces of expression are often used for the purposes of polemic;[1] that is, to formulate political criticism, on at least three levels: (1) to destabilise a political opponent for tactical and ideological reasons; (2) to criticise as a whole the politicians and the partisans in play; and (3) to associate other players in the electoral game with this criticism of politics – the media and journalists. Everything is done through games of posturing and by exchanging generally aggressive and radical messages, which often have common characteristics: irony, ridiculing personal attacks, sarcastic photomontages, and arguments undermining the legitimacy or credibility of those targeted.

Twitter and other networks have become tools that help in social mobilisation, promoting "connective actions" (Bennett and Segerberg 2013). However, they favour, above all, a protest form of political participation. A considerable number of citizens use Twitter as a tool of denunciation, either in the logic of emotional reactivity or by employing tactics thought to destabilise the political process.

First, we will examine how social media are used politically insofar as they are associated with the freedom to express one's opinions. Within a highly critical political context, we will demonstrate that we can then consider the Twitter network to be home to the expression of a counterpublic sphere. Our next step will be to introduce some of the tactics used in an electoral context (the 2012 French presidential election and 2014 local

140 *Arnaud Mercier*

elections) in order to study the way in which Twitter has become integrated into the repertoire of protest.

9.1 Social Media as a Place to Express Opinions without Restraint

Social networking sites (SNS) have recorded strong growth over the past ten years, thanks to the expressive potential they offer users. The success of blogs some fifteen years ago can be attributed to the idea of free and easily shared personal expression, and this success has continued with the popularity of social media platforms such as Facebook, Tumblr or Twitter. These websites are associated with a desire for self-assertion, that Allard and Vandenberghe (2003) term "expressive individualism".

From a Goffmanian point of view, we can consider social networking sites to be a stage on which we can observe social roles and faces being [organised and] played in new ways. On social media, expressive individualism often follows a logic of release from certain social frameworks and conventions that govern ordinary social interactions. The success and popularity of these technological communication systems with many users can be explained by their compatibility with social aspirations, and a process which the Dutch sociologist Cas Wouters terms "informalization".

This sociologist follows in the footsteps of Norbert Elias and his diachronic analysis of the "civilising process". He notes the rise, since 1945, of a strong desire to live as one wishes, showing less and less respect for formal constraints that have been socially imposed. He detects "increasing behavioural and emotional alternatives, socially accepted" (Wouters 2007: 57). This can be seen through a greater acceptability of familiar or vulgar forms of speech, including growing acceptance among all classes of the use of a more relaxed vocabulary, in various social situations (ranging up to swear-words). According to Wouters, this trend takes the form of a desire not to be constrained by rigid rules of social control and to overcome some of the rules that usually govern ordinary sociability.

Social networking sites (SNS) are perceived and experienced by many as a technological form encouraging self-assertiveness and the exposure, without censorship, of one's private life, tastes and personality, to the point of shamelessness. We may call this trend for self-exhibition through social media "self-expressivity", occurring as it does in a liberating and "informalized" frame.

"Self-expressivity" frequently finds an opening in politically-oriented communication. This is partly because social networks foster direct interactions in sharing communities and hence the logic of "political polarisation" can be observed (DiMaggio & al. 2001). Twitter offers a very convenient way of creating communities – including those temporarily created with a simple hashtag used as a coordination tool – while also providing a critical conversational feed about a specific event, often of a polemical nature.

Twitter as a Counterpublic Sphere 141

A keyword links together individuals who do not know or who do not necessarily follow each other. The strength of this social coordination tool is thus to build "bridges" between people who do not know each other; that is, between "the hashtag community and its own network of followers" (Brown and Burgess 2011). Thus, there are social situations in which the hashtag allows the construction of what these authors call an "ad hoc public". Indignation, tactical attacks or denunciations become constitutive factors of these groups, causing them to overlap with polemics, which are all the more likely to occur if a growing number of people share a dominantly negative image of politicians, as is the case in many Western democracies (Norris 1999) and particularly in France.

9.2 Twitter as a Counterpublic Sphere

Although Jürgen Habermas' historical-philosophical approach to the public sphere has received some criticism (Negt and Kluge 1988), we can accept the idea that modern democracy can be conceived as a facade of deliberative space where rational (but also ideological) arguments are exchanged. The mainstream media give an extra dimension to this deliberative game through the concept of media arenas. These arenas can serve as sounding boards, or enable an extended exchange of arguments, images, symbols and representations that may have a direct impact on the political space of government and legislative deliberation.

In striving to defend their cause, all the players involved have now fully integrated media variables in an attempt to derive benefits (for instance, to bring visibility to their cause, to influence the definition and representation of problems, and to expand support from a part of public opinion). In return, professional politicians have sought to control communications systems and media, thus professionalising their communication strategies (Negrine and Lilleker 2002), to the point of trying to make journalists a more or less involuntary relay of their persuasive intent.

In reaction to this, a powerful movement has arisen in many Western democracies. Defiance against the media has emerged, including the accusation that an inbred political-media class ("*classe politico-mediatique*") – even a "caste" – has emerged, imposing its own rules. Whereas previously viewed in a positive light for their role in giving people wider access to information, streaming media have become the target of "mediactivists" (Cardon and Granjon 2010) who accuse them of distorting reality in their news coverage and being too influenced (even in terms of close friendships) by the (politically or economically) powerful few. An annual survey published by the newspaper *La Croix* reflects, year after year, the extent of the distrust of French citizens towards the news media.

Moreover, these suspicions of the media are coupled with a strong distrust – even a rejection – of the political class. For fifteen years, Pascal Perrineau (2003) has been evoking a real "democratic disenchantment" of French citizens, combined with a ballot box strike (abstention rates are increasing in every election), the rise of a Far-Right party (National Front) and the institutionalisation of protest forms of political participation. Pierre Bréchon showed in 2003 that those kind non-conventional forms of political participation are increasingly accepted by the French. Judgments about "protest participation"[2] are less severe in all social and age classes. This political analyst detects "a trivialisation of the beginning of this culture of direct political action" (Bréchon 2003: 146).

Moreover, the social situation has become highly degraded in French society. Financial insecurity, chronic unemployment, poverty and the existence of abandoned zones are realities that affect a growing number of people. The geographer Christophe Guilluy speaks of "French fractures" and denounces "the invisibility of the working classes" victims of liberal globalisation who have "disappeared from the radar screens of politics and media" (Guilluy 2010: 8). Moreover, we can add to this list, young adults with few or no qualifications and little hope of finding full-time employment. Guibert and Mergier put forward the idea of a "downward social escalator" to emphasise that the French republican promise of upward mobility is not quite honoured; instead many are falling down and out of society or are afraid of doing so. In addition, such people feel society to be more and more violent. Violence is "at the heart of all social interactions"; it is perceived and experienced as "inherent in society as it has become" (Guibert and Mergier 2006: 95).

In this context, a significant number of citizens have decided to express themselves on digital social networks in order to share opinions and information. They have taken the opportunity to criticise traditional political forces and/or the media. Moreover, they attack them vehemently, sometimes with considerable anger. Social media are experienced as places where critical and iconoclastic comment is allowed, unpolished, and indeed may be given access to a certain degree of social visibility. Here one approaches the concept of Nancy Fraser's "subaltern counter publics", emerging from her critical reflection upon Habermas' theory. These subaltern counter publics are defined as "parallel discursive arenas" where dominated social groups "invent and circulate counter discourses" to produce "their own interpretation of their identities, interests and needs" (Fraser 2005: 126, 127).

Here, we would say that, far from seeking access to the media public sphere and wanting to engage therein, a majority of these Internet users are simply expressing their feelings with their affinity-based community. Peter Dahlgren already pointed out, ten years ago, that politics has increasingly become "an expressive activity" (Dahlgren 2005).

Such Internet users base part of their identity on a posture of relative marginality. However, the easy circulation of information on social networks, both immediately and virally, guarantees that many become visible. This visibility has become a "capital" (Heinich 2012: 43), in the sense that Pierre Bourdieu used the term. Hence, they obtain a sub-media social existence.

Without media recognition, these contributors can gain still greater visibility if they remain solitary within a blog. Their words can have an echo and flatter their narcissism, even when hidden under a pseudonym.

In the 'struggle for visibility', not being admitted into the world of publicised appearances generates amongst those who feel excluded, "a sense of social non-existence, of contempt and negation of themselves" (Voirol 2005: 117). Access to a public podium from which their discourse can potentially circulate virally, leading to media exposure and/or journalistic support for their cause, can be seen as social vengeance or as a challenge to what is often perceived as social domination by the political and media classes.

The concept of "recognition" as conceived by Axel Honneth, is very useful here. The latter writes that it is common for "the dominant (to) express their social superiority by not seeing those they dominate" (Honneth 2010: 226). A lack of 'recognition' in public and media spheres may find a palliative in the socio-digital sphere. Furthermore, the violence and frustration experienced through this lack of recognition and the inability to have one's voice heard or, even worse, to act, may disappear when the balance of imposed power is reversed. Just as Goffman (1963) identifies a strategy of "reversal of the stigma" employed by members of stigmatised populations, we consider that some Internet users, who experience their imposed invisibility as undignifying and violent, use social media in an attempt to turn this process on its head. Those disappointed by the politics on offer – the socially downgraded, the ideologically marginalised and those invisible in the media – find this outlet to assert themselves, regain their dignity and fight "the system", sharing this combat with a large enough number of individuals to feel less alone and to belong to a community.

Guibert and Mergier study how the downtrodden working class reacts in France, evoking in this group the temptation to vote for the *Front National*, constituting "the need for a denial, expressed in a vote" because protest votes, even if they are a sanction against dominant actors, are "mostly self-reaffirmations of voters". "The radicalism of their opinion" serves as a "lever" allowing such actors to reaffirm their dignity (Guibert and Mergier 2006: 119). Systematically criticising the elites on social media can thus be understood as an act of resistance.

Consequently, we find in election scenarios (times of intensive political activity) many controversial messages which are the expression of a true 'socio-digital counterpublic sphere', as Dimitra Milioni (2009) defines it. The distinctive character of counterpublics and "their crucial role" is "a modification of existing norms and patterns, and the actualization and, potentially, radicalization of the normative content of the critical public sphere." In these spaces people monitor, protest, denounce, deride, ridicule and insult politicians and often journalists as representatives of the hated media. The material for electoral propaganda is targeted (posters, leaflets ...) in order to thwart its potential to influence, by diverting, by parodying, in

144 *Arnaud Mercier*

the spirit of the 'meme'. Media services are sabotaged to denounce the perceived collusion between journalists and their political guests; live social TV deprecates political speeches at the very moment they are pronounced. ... Candidates and elected representatives with accounts on social networks are directly taken to task and insulted, they are parodied, caricatured or become victims of malicious rumours.

9.3 Use of Twitter in Forms of Political Participation for Protest

The data we collected on Twitter during the local election campaign taking place across 260 of France's largest cities (*cf.* Mercier 2014 for methodological details), revealed a lot of controversies and political attacks which gained a certain degree of visibility by setting the Twittersphere alight. They generated a multitude of conflicting messages, displaying agitation, acrimony and insults, denunciation and indignation. Throughout this period of observation, we encountered politicians who, through their words, their actions, or sometimes their personality, provoked very harsh campaigns of mobilisation against themselves, including *ad hominem* attacks, some of great violence. Militant postures on these networks seem to assume immunity to the ordinary rules of civility, and therefore reflect the dual logic of the operation described above: strong, unrestrained levels of self-expressivity in the framework of a renewed political struggle, one which has become digital, and is marked with irony, aggression and bitterness.

Personal Insults

The communicational contract can be thought of as the founding pact of any language exchange between two parties, one through which they recognise each other's identity traits and the social position that defines them as the subject of this act of communication, by which they agree implicitly about the target of the act and the subject of the conversation. The illocutionary force of the insult comes from its power to break the communicational contract and to transgress conventions, in order to enter into a logic of aggression without going as far as to physically assault the target. "The insult is an interlocutory speech act; it carries an emotional, even compulsive, force and seeks to belittle and call into question the image of the person at whom it is aimed. It has a dominantly perlocutionary function" (Auger et al. 2008: 639).

Pragmatically, the insulting party aims to break the conventional relational nodes that define the possible social interactions between himself and his target. In doing so he demeans the person to or about whom he is speaking. His actions threaten the recipient's status, his social position; denying him a posture of superiority generally associated with public figures, that would otherwise be imposed when speaking to or about him (rules of politeness, protocol). Insults are "direct addresses that both 'express' the poisonous emotions of speaker and devalue the listener they 'represent'" (Chastaing and Abdi 1980: 35). The use of swear-words, familiarity and direct addresses are all markers of this equalisation of statuses required by the insulter, which often sound like a form of social revenge, a reversal of the established world order. The dominated party gives himself the power of injury as a way to degrade those whom social conventions place above him, so neutralising their social power.

However, to be fully effective, an insult must imply a discursive configuration involving an audience. Those who insult and provoke need an audience in front of which they can expose their insults. In this way, they can feel a sense of triumph over social laws and gain social recognition for behaving like a protester, in many cases helping them to feel integrated into the affinity group of those who share this same desire for or practice of revolt and transgression.

SNS can thus be experienced as a 'counterpublic sphere' for those seeking to acquire social visibility, since their words are not going unnoticed, largely due to their transgressive, iconoclastic and controversial nature. The other virtue found in this polemical use of Twitter is the ability to ensure that one's target is harangued directly, to ensure that the attacks, otherwise often constrained to a small circle, reach the target directly and publicly. This is because addressing a person or a Twitter account ensures that those involved will end up knowing that they are being mentioned on the network and will therefore receive directly the salvos fired at them. Below are some examples both from the tough municipal election battle over Marseille and from the presidential campaign of 2012:

- @Bassounov: Les candidatures des #momies #Bouteflika et #Gaudin montrent la persistance de l'influence #égyptienne sur tout le bassin méditerranéen !
- @belami_ : si j'habitais à Marseille je préfère encore voter pour Gaudin que pour ce connard parachuté du FN
- @momomducoin : @AvecMennucci c'est bon avec mennucci on sens bas les couilles de cette grosse merde !!!
- @BobSalesBob : le nouveau Zéro de la République : @fhollande !!! J'espère qu'il se casse sa bête gueule de socialiste à la con ! #avec Sarkozy #RadioLondres
- @ianhazlitt : Merkel + Sarkozy = Merkozy. Merkel + Hollande = Merde.
- @gerardfiloche : ce pourri de Sarkozy veut un referendum contre les chomeurs pas contre le chomage
- @philou15200 : Sarkozy est un con et un salaud jamais je ne voterai pour ce type ! VIVE MARINE
- @laspiralee : J'compte pas voter au présidentielle apar si la salope de Marine Le Pen passe le second tour ! #JeudiConfession[3]

Indignation

Another powerful device for provoking controversy on social media is indignation. Without necessarily resorting to insult and invective, users employ this strong expressive medium to emit cries of anger against what they see as an injustice, or against acts judged un-civic or unworthy of a political representative. In this category, we find denunciations of lies and coarse manipulations of which candidates are apparently guilty (*'mensonges'*, *'menteur'* in French). Some citizens act on the SNS as social vigilantes. They also involve themselves in fact checking, not wishing to give reporters the monopoly on this activity. The most common incarnation of this posture is denouncing the lies of the candidates by circulating 'detox' articles (*'désintox'* in French) written by journalists or self-produced video *montages* in the manner of before/after, thus juxtaposing contradictory statements in the mouth of the same personality.

- *@Faboune57: @DebordValerie: Christian Jacob et la hausse d'impôts - Désintox: youtu.be/gLlJk ...*
- *@andre001: nicolas Sarkozy n'hésite jamais à balancer un gros mensonge à la télé, il sait que seule une minorité aura vent de la désintox dailymotion.com/video ...*
- *@fanfanbacquepg: Désintox : Marine Le Pen, FN et monde ouvrier - Le blog de Danactu-résistance 0z.fr/M ...*
- *@radiomokette: Hollande prend la pose mitterrandienne: copier le + grand bandit/menteur faut croire que flamby manque d'inspiration!! video.liberation.fr ...*

In a context where distrust of the political class seems to be spreading in contemporary French society, we find fairly strong campaigns against politicians who appear to benefit from undue privileges. When an article implicating a politician in corruption is published, for instance, the link to this article is very rapidly shared, often accompanied by a severe comment. This is also the case during campaigns where the intention is to denounce the turpitudes of candidates (arguments and photos used by candidates that are rigged, hidden cameras showing the dirty backstage of the campaign, publicity given to racist or xenophobic discourse pronounced in small groups, etc.).

Conspiracy

Finally, when observing closely what is shared on these networks, we also discover postures of disclosure denouncing what is apparently hidden, disguised by institutions, the media or the political elite. SNS are experienced as an alternative public sphere, providing publicity and giving visibility to what, according to these Internet users, deserves to circulate in the media and public sphere, but which occult powers otherwise lock away and hide.

In this register, a very active Far-Right Twittersphere exists, denouncing the media and their silence in regard to insufficiently highlighted facts or events. The urban riots of the extreme Left at Rennes and Nantes, during the municipal elections of winter 2014, offer a perfect illustration. The many messages in circulation do not simply express disgust at and condemn the reported acts of vandalism. They denounce what is perceived to be a double standard in the attitude of the political and police authorities towards Leftist movements in comparison to how the *Front National* or other nationalist groups are treated.

The bitterness of being stigmatised, associated with the perceived impunity of Far-Left forces, unleashes passions and leads to verbal jousting on Twitter. A vision of a more or less paranoid conspiracy-obsessed society is spread by these kinds of contents, and Twitter is often considered as a means of public expression to rectify the situation, to draw attention to what the media do not publish, and publicise issues which the Establishment would prefer to keep quiet at all costs.

- * - @SissiPatriote: Meeting #FN in Rennes: the #antifas attack the police station. Who are the fascists? Where is the threat? ==> Leftists[4]
- * - @FrkGuiot: Well @le_Parisien does not publish the identity of #Antifa masked and armed with iron bars arrested in #Rennes? http: // www.leparisien.fr / ...

But we also see the Far-Right denouncing Right-wing mayors, from Nice and Bordeaux, for their alleged hidden and unconfessed agenda: preparations to build a mosque in their city should they be re-elected. Sharing spectacular photomontages that undermine the mayor was a popular way of denouncing this. The *UMP* mayor of Nice, regarded as embodying a moderately hard nationalist Right, is nevertheless described as "Imam" in a photomontage where he appears in front of a minaret with the caption: "Tomorrow in Nice, 20 mosques?"

Outrageous remarks will spread on Twitter varying between accusations and malicious rumours, for example on the evening of the election of the Socialist President, François Hollande:

- * - @Ignomynous: We are informed that a reprint of Mao's Little Red Book will be distributed tomorrow in all schools #radiolondres

9.4 Irony and Mockery: the Success of the Protest #Radiolondres During the 2012 Presidential Election

Political mockery spreads on the Internet, thanks to videos on specialised sites and the accelerated and massive flow of cartoons, jokes or clips, like the so-called 'sarkostic' campaign of 2006–2007 had shown (a pun on Sarkozy and the adjective 'sarcastic'). Thanks to the archiving capacities of the

148 *Arnaud Mercier*

Internet, it has become easier to provide *montages* portraying politicians' inconsistencies between statements made one day and the words and deeds of another. Activists only have to reproduce these in devastating form using gif animations, memes or pastiches and then share them on networks. By changing a few words, or through edited images, collages or other graphic manipulations broadcast on their networks, "hacktivists" seek a ricochet effect to reach tens of thousands of people whom they do not know, and so participate in the battle for electoral influence.

Of course, like many forms of political activity online, these participants are more or less invested in the cause, and deserve, for some, the label of "*slacktivists*" a portmanteau term made from 'slacker' and 'activism' (see also previous chapters in this volume).[5] This term is used to refer to forms of apparent engagement online which, it is suggested, have little political impact because people are not really involved. Yet the simple use of a hashtag in an electoral context can constitute a significant subversive force! This was the case in 2012 (and for subsequent each Election Day) during the two days of voting for the presidency of the French Republic, with the hashtag #RadioLondres (Mercier 2013).

As the name suggests, #RadioLondres wants to incarnate the spirit of "resistance" (Radio London was the name given to French-language programmes broadcast from London by the Gaullist forces during the Second World War). Through the magic of the Internet's basic democracy, three activists gave substance to a word which then spread and became one of the most popular hashtags in France throughout the election sequence. Everything was said in just four tweets. One proposes the idea of choosing a keyword, another replies and a third makes a counterproposal. Finally, the second outbids the latter by proposing a formula inspired by him.

- * - @marcvasseur: Could there be a common hashtag between Twitter users for the results on Sunday?
- * -@bembelly: Is there one? @marcvasseur
- * -@remisabau: @bembelly @marcvasseur: #RadioBruxelles?
- * -@bembelly: #RadioLondres. #resistance and so on …

None of these Twitter users hide their activism on the Left. Marc Vasseur has 3,600 followers, while the other two have fewer than 1,500; therefore they cannot be said to be opinion leaders on Twitter. However, this democratic microblogging site allowed three unidentified militants to create a keyword that other users then sought to popularise, to the point that journalists and politicians also fed into the traffic generated by this feed, in order to be visible on Twitter during election days. On 22 April 2012, the hashtag set off more than 1,800 tweets per hour, allowing Sabine White, a reporter for the activist website Owni.fr, to rejoice on her Twitter feed:

- * - @sabineblanc: Was told that digital was absent from the campaign … until #Radiolondres which exploded obsolete and absurd rules.

Other activist bloggers then entered the arena to determine what to say and, in particular, how to show a spirit of resistance in this community of affinity based on electoral interest. The goal became to defy the heavy restrictions of the electoral law imposing a blanket media ban – before 8 p.m. and the closing of all polling stations – on any available information about the election results. The other purpose was to celebrate the defeat of Nicolas Sarkozy, both hoped for and expected by many of these users. Internal control was organised around the choice of easily recognisable formulae by Twitter's initiates to announce the results, while not giving them explicitly. The objective was to thwart the law without being punished.

What motivated many Twitter users to plug into this hashtag feed was the idea of challenging a ban that was considered stupid and archaic, since neighbouring French-speaking news sites in Belgium and Switzerland announced election estimates one and a half hours before the end of the embargo in France. The use of the hashtag became a contest of jokes and poetry. Here are some significant excerpts of the types of messages circulating during the first or second round:

- * - Weather update: 27° Amsterdam 25° Budapest 15° Vichy, 13° in Moscow #RadioLondres[6]

In other tweets, a typical national dish is chosen to refer each candidate. Internet users also use the tourist metaphor:

- * - Departure to Amsterdam € 68.4 from Martinique € 71.9 from French Guyana, to € 51.5 from St Martin. #RadioLondres

Decryption: the journey from Martinique to Amsterdam cost € 68.4, thus F. Hollande obtains 68.4% of the vote in Martinique.

- * - Among our Canadian cousins, 63% of loggers go paddleboating #RadioLondres

Decryption: French expatriates in Canada suddenly become loggers (stereotype of the inhabitants of Canada) where 63% voted F. Hollande (his opponent on the extreme Left accused F. Hollande of not having broad enough shoulders for the presidency, comparing him to a "paddleboat captain". The formula had been much commented on, so the allusion was widely understood).

- * - Listen to #RadioLondres it is on 53.1 on the FH band

Decryption: listening to the FM radio stations is done on what is called the FM band; therefore, if one is on the FH band, the initials of François Hollande, it means that he has won the second round with 53.1% of the vote.

150   *Arnaud Mercier*

Others play with the codes of Facebook, by targeting, ironically, the wife of Nicolas Sarkozy, the outgoing President, to signify that he has been defeated:

- * - Carla Bruni changed her FB status from 'married' to 'it's complicated'. #radioLondres

Using the hashtag #radiolondres could be viewed as an act of citizenship. It is a way both to take a position and challenge a law which no longer holds water: the prohibition on mentioning the first election estimates before 8 p.m. It could also be applauded for replaying the quarrel of the Ancients and the Moderns around the idea that the Internet is exploding codes and regulations.

- * - @brunowalter : Internet just exploded 50 years of republican traditions. #embargo-is-dead

Journalists also had the opportunity to mock their colleagues gently:

- * - @MargauxBergey: Thoughts for TV colleagues who have yet to fill 45min of airtime while we know the results #Presidential

The subversion was so clear that the pollsters who prepared the election estimates felt compelled to protect themselves, denying on Twitter that they had produced the figures:

- * - @TweetOpinionWay: No publication of digits before 8pm. OpinionWay denies all digits attributed to it in the last few minutes

9.5 Conclusion

Twitter is already an integrated part of the political and electoral repertoire. The candidates and their teams use it and journalists cover some events with it. They unearth remarks and actions on Twitter in order to give them publicity. Nonetheless, ownership by citizens is still the highlight of the political use of social media, principally because they use it as a tool of protest and mobilisation.

Live commentary (even more if it is doubled by journalistic fact-checking) may, for instance, be a powerful tool to subvert rhetorical tactics and marketing. Political speeches can be challenged at the same time as they are pronounced. In a collective framework of sharing and critical thinking, through a process of equalising the legitimacy to speak, political speech is being subjected to a new test of de-sacralisation, undergoing a process of de-legitimisation through digital disfigurement, factual criticism, verification of past actions or statements, counter arguments, irony and derision.

Consequently, through this innovative form or online participation, we can now refer to the creation of the conditions for a major shift both in how political discourse on television is received and how campaigns are tracked, one that we would call a 'social media turn'.

Notes

1. "Polemical discourse is always based upon another discourse about which it makes value judgments." (Micheli 2011). According to Catherine Kerbrat-Orecchioni (1980), "the aim of polemical discourse is to make the receiver reject information that he accepts or could accept". [Our translations].
2. Bréchon uses the expression *"participation protestataire"* in French, to define a hybrid, grey area between traditional political participation, and (violent) protest movements: "protest participation" is more based on rejection than simple participation, but not based primarily on a show of strength or violent force.
3. Even without full translations of these colourful and often grammatically challenged examples, the reader will doubtless appreciate the general gist and register based on translations of the words underlined in the text mummy (*momie* in French), asshole (*con, connard*), balls (*couilles*), big shit (*grosse merde*), rotten (*pourri*), bastard (*salaud*), bitch (*salope*).
4. * Each time a tweet is preceded by *, the translation is the author's.
5. In French, we have proposed the term '*aclictivisme*' (Mercier 2013) for this same notion of low-cost participation in political action.
6. Decryption: F. Hollande = Amsterdam, of course!; Budapest = Sarkozy because his father was Hungarian; Vichy = Le Pen because under German occupation, that was where the government which collaborated with the Nazis was based; Moscow = Mélenchon because he was supported by the Communist Party. Everyone understands, in an encrypted form, what is referred to in these election estimates.

Works Cited

Allard, Laurence, and Vandenberghe, Frédéric. 2010. "Express Yourself ! Les Pages Perso entre Légitimation Techno-politique de l'Individualisme Expressif et Authenticité Réflexive Peer-to-peer". *Réseaux* 117: 191–219.

Auger, N. Fracchiolla, B. Moïse, C., and Schultz-Romain, C. 2008. "De la Violence Verbale". In *Congrès Mondial de Linguistique Française,* edited by Durand, J. Habert, B. and Laks, B. 631–643.

Bennett, Lance, and Segerberg, Alexandra. 2013. *The Logic of Connective Action.* New York: Cambridge University Press.

Boyd, Danah. 2008. *Taken Out of Context. American Teen Sociality in Networked Publics.* PhD for the degree of Doctor of Philosophy in information management and systems, University of California, Berkeley.

Bréchon, Pierre. 2003. *Les Valeurs des Français.* Paris: Armand Colin.

Bruns, Axel, and Burgess, Jean. 2011. "The Use of Twitter Hashtags in the Formation of Ad Hoc Publics". 6th European Consortium for Political Research, Reykjavik. Accessed March 19, 2015.

Cardon, Dominique, and Granjon, Fabien. 2010. *Médiactivistes.* Paris: Presses de SciencesPo.

152 Arnaud Mercier

Chastaing, M., and Abdi, H. 1980. "Psychologie des Injures". *Journal de Psychologie Normale et Pathologique* 1: 31–62.

Christensen, Henrik. 2011. "Political Activities on the Internet: Slacktivism or Political Participation by Other Means"? *First Monday* 16 (2). Accessed March 19, 2015.

Conover, MD. Ratkiewicz, J. Francisco, M. Goncalves, B. Flammini, A., and Menczer, F. 2011. "Political Polarization on Twitter". Proc. 5th Int. AAAI Conf. Weblogs Social Media. Menlo Park, CA: AAAI Press.

Dahlgren, Peter. 2005. "The Internet, Public Spheres, and Political Communication: Dispersion and Deliberation". *Political Communication* 22: 147–162.

DiMaggio, P. Hargittai, E. Neuman, WR., and Robinson, JP. 2001. "Social implications of the Internet". *Annual Review of Sociology* 27: 307–336.

Fraser, Nancy. 2005. Qu'est-ce que la Justice Sociale? Reconnaissance et Redistribution. Paris: La Découverte.

Goffman, Erving. 1963. *Stigma: Notes on the Management of Spoiled Identity*. Englewood Cliffs, N-J.: Prentice-Hall.

Guibert, Philippe, and Mergier, Alain. 2006. *Le Descendeur Social*. Paris: Plon / Fondation Jean Jaurès.

Guilluy, Christophe. 2010. *Fractures Françaises*. Paris: François Bourin éditeur.

Heinich, Nathalie. 2012. *De la Visibilité*. Paris: Gallimard.

Honneth, Axel. 2010. *La Société du Mépris*. Paris: La Découverte.

Mercier, Arnaud. 2015 (forthcoming). "L'Intégration de Twitter au Répertoire d'Action Electorale des Campagnes Municipales Françaises de 2014". In *La Communication Electronique : Enjeux, Stratégies et Opportunités*, Limoges: éditions Lambert-Lucas.

Mercier, Arnaud. 2014. "*Décryptage des Tweet-campagnes Municipales Françaises (janvier-mars 2014)*". Actes du colloque international: Communication Electronique, Cultures et Identités, 11–13 juin, université du Havre 485–496.

Mercier, Arnaud. 2013. "Avènement du Twiléspectateur et Hashtags Contestataires". In *Présidentielle 2012: une Communication Politique bien Singulière*, edited by Philippe Maarek. Paris: L'Harmattan 165–200.

Micheli, Raphaël. 2011. "Quand l'Afrontement Porte sur les Mots *en tant que Mots* : Polémique et Réflexivité Langagière". *Semen* 31. Accessed March 28, 2015.

Milioni, Dimitra. 2009. "Probing the Online Counterpublic Sphere: the Case of Indymedia Athens". *Media Culture Society* 31(3): 409–431.

Negrine, Ralph, and Lilleker, Darren G. 2002. "The Professionalization of Political Communication. Continuities and Change in Media Practices". *European Journal of Communication* 17(3): 305–323.

Negt, Oskar, and Kluge, Alexander. 1998. "The Public Sphere and Experience". *October* 46: 60–82.

Norris, Pippa ed. 1999. Critical Citizens: Global Support for Democratic Government. Oxford: Oxford University Press.

Perrineau, Pascal. 2003. *Le Désenchantement Démocratique*. La Tour d'Aigues: éditions de l'Aube.

Voirol, Olivier. 2005. "Les Luttes pour la Visibilité". *Réseaux* 129–130: 89–121.

Wouters, Cas. 2007. Informalization. Manners and Emotions Since 1890. London: Sage.

10 Cultural Creation and Political Activism in the Digital World

Lluís Anyó and Iasa Monique Ribeiro

Introduction: A Methodological Proposal

It is often stated that new technologies democratise access to consumption of information and personal expression. We also know from extensive prior research that the designated uses of each different technology are defined by society itself through practices of production and consumption, independently of the purposes for which the technology has been created, produced and marketed. However, the radical change in the relationship between man and information, stemming from the spread of Web 2.0 and new connected devices, does not only represent the democratisation of access – or overcrowding and accumulation (Latanzi 2013, 23). It also involves change at a much deeper level involving forms of production, promotion, expression and recognition, suggesting new forms of personal relationship and, as a result, new forms of control (Latanzi 2013, 24).

This research is a response to the question of how we may describe and analyse activist creation in the digital world. Based on a limited study of three recent but very distinct cases of cultural creativity and political activism, we put forward a methodological framework focused on the study of two criteria that seem to be central to activist expressions of cultural content in the digital world.

These criteria are, firstly, the analysis of the contents created and, secondly, the analysis of their authorship. The theoretical and methodological framework was constructed at the same time as the case studies were developed, in a rich, feedback-driven relationship. However, for reasons of clarity, we will first set out the analytical criteria and will then move on to discuss the specific case studies.

The initial focus is primarily on the distinction between art and culture. Art has been fully integrated into the mercantilist logic, particularly since the abandonment of modernity and the emergence of postmodernism in the late seventies (Granés 2010) (Heath and Potter 2005). Indeed, caught up in the hegemonic model of capitalist production, art has not only been fully integrated but is even fostered. In this context, activist art introduces critical analysis, creative forms of protest and intervention regarding consumption and alters the established codes. In this sense, it differs from the classical political art of modernity. Activist art is very close to cultural creation, in

154 Lluís Anyó and Iasa Monique Ribeiro

the context of collective rather than individual action. Classic examples of collective art include *Group Material, Guerrilla Girls* and *Gran Fury*.

Teixeira Coelho (2009, 309) affirms that culture and art, which naturally share common ground, can be differentiated based on the individual and aesthetic character of art versus the far more collective and functional character of culture. Activist art is heavily involved in culture due to the social function of the creations, where often the artist is a manager or coordinator and the creation is produced by a collective.

In light of the above, we can relate political activism to the expression of realities that would otherwise be hidden, where political activists are groups of individuals or communities who criticise a reality that is not part of the hegemonic discourse. It has also been widely noted that the new digital communication technologies have produced an environment in which political activism may develop more democratically, giving a voice to groups who otherwise would not have access to the mass media: "The challenge at hand is to begin to conceive the political reality of media such as the Internet as a complex series of places embodying reconstructed models of citizenship and new forms of political activism, even as the Internet itself reproduces logics of capital and becomes co-opted by hegemonic forces" (Kellner and Kahn 2007, 618–9). This contextualisation, added to theories of communication, studies of changes of paradigm and the analysis of recent history (Castells 1996), help us to understand the present context when discussing online political activism and earlier theories of media representation, media politics and new languages (Poster 1997) (Meikle 2002). In addition, Web 2.0 also quite recently became a stage for the intersection of different areas of activity – which is not the same as platforms or practices – mainly due to its undiscriminating acceptance, where everything is allowed and where the boundaries last only briefly before being broken down by something or someone. This not only refers to a wide range of capabilities, but to the possibility of almost anything being subjected to a process of hybridisation.

Regarding the second focus of this study, information and communication technology facilitates expression in what are referred to as virtual communities. These are defined around a subject or idea of common interest, unlike traditional communities which were based on membership in a territory or kinship. This point will not be developed here, but refers to the classic opposition in sociology between 'Gemeinscrhaft' and 'Gesellschaft', 'Vergemeinschaftung' and 'Vergesellschaftung' or mechanical solidarity and organic solidarity discussed by Ferdinand Tönnies (1957), Max Weber (1978) and Émile Durkheim (2014), and carried over into the virtual environment by Howard Rheingold (2000), Nancy K. Baym (1995) and Elizabeth M. Reid (1996), among many others. Virtual communities are strongly linked to the availability of free time of individuals who, from the private sphere and motivated by their personal interest, communicate in the public sphere. We will see throughout this chapter how the communities formed

Cultural Creation and Political Activism in the Digital World 155

through social networks can be understood in relation to free time – cognitive surplus – and the dissolution of the boundary between public and private – immobile socialisation – which have a major bearing on the weak social integration of the individual in the group and the ephemeral nature of the community itself.

Accordingly, this chapter puts forward an analysis of the cultural practices of political activism in the digital sphere based on two criteria. These are presented in the theoretical and methodological section of the text and are found in the analysis of three specific cases, *Eu não mereço ser estuprada* (Brazil, 2014), *Megaphone.net* (Barcelona, 2014) *Don't be a tourist* (Barcelona, 2014). The first criterion is the art versus culture dichotomy, which, as we have seen, can be defined in terms of art's individual authorship and aesthetic nature and culture's collective authorship and a functional nature. The function of activist discourse is to give visibility to a reality that does not appear in hegemonic discourse, as we will demonstrate. This is the function of social criticism in activist cultural creation. The second criterion is the strong community versus weak community dichotomy, in the sociological definition of community in terms of inclusion of the individual. The concepts of cognitive surplus and immobile socialisation help us to define the type of community.

10.1 Activism and Technology: A Brief History

The relationship between political activism and computer technology began at the same time as the emergence of the personal computer and Internet usage through university networks, thirty years before the advent of Web 2.0, usually dated at 2004, the date when Tim O'Reilly (2005) gave a name to the phenomenon of transformation of the social uses of the internet after the dot.com debacle.

During the first half of the 2000–2010 decade, the Internet became progressively, and with increasing success, a social network facilitated by technological tools, mainly used for communication and collaboration between people with similar interests. Web 2.0 is, therefore, a social meeting place, which transforms interactivity – the previous key concept of Web 1.0 – into what has been called prosumption, as users become both consumers and producers of communicational content (Ritzer and Jorgenson 2010).

Active users of the Web 2.0 not only publish their own information but also share it with others, who can use it and share it themselves. As a consequence, the creation of content is now subsumed in a field of collective creation. Folksonomies are good examples of this phenomenon, since they classify information not based on a rigid taxonomy but in a cloud of concepts that emerges from the information itself. Moreover, the phenomenon affects the most diverse fields, either because of the format of the data – text, photography, audiovisual – or the type of content – informative or entertaining, documentary or fiction, etc. In 2003, even before the concept

156 Lluís Anyó and Iasa Monique Ribeiro

of Web 2.0 had spread, David Casacuberta had already noted that the radical changes derivable from the technologies of information and communication would become a collective creation: "by collective creation I understand a paradigm shift in the cultural creation and usage systems that puts, systematically and for the first time in history, the creative aspects in the hands of the public, which stops being merely passive and instead becomes an active participant in art and culture" (Casacuberta 2005, 15, our translation).

Both the origins of the personal computer in the 1970s, closely linked to counterculture and political activism, as well as the birth of the Internet over the following decade – once the ARPAnet military strategic network was left behind – foster the idea of a close relationship between technology-based social networks and political activism.

The very definition of hacker, in its original meaning – i.e, someone who promotes and facilitates the use of tools and forms of communication for information-sharing – and the use of the term made by the hegemonic corporations, states and their related media – as a terrorist who invades protected computer systems for evil purposes – illustrates the activist nature of the Internet itself, but also the tensions raised by technology in the political debate. At the same time, "the Internet is a contested terrain in which alternative subcultural forces and progressive political groups are being articulated in opposition to more reactionary, conservative and dominant forces" (Keller and Kahn 2007, 621).

The demonstrations of free software which can be found in publications of that time such as Ted Nelsol's *Computer Lib/Dream Machines* (1974), the *People's Computer Company Newsletter (1972)* or the *Whole Earth Catalog (1968)*, edited by Stewart Brand are based on Creative Commons, which operate beyond the technological field. The prevailing model of intellectual property in all artistic and cultural creation is brought into crisis, on Internet sites like Wired.com and Slashdot.org, as well as the anarchist community, which frequents Infoshop.org. It is necessary to distinguish, however, in the overall Web 2.0, those projects that follow the spirit of free software and computing for the people, or are genuinely collaborative, such as Wikipedia.org, and private business projects that, despite acting as tools for social communications, are not collaborative in all aspects, such as Youtube.com, Google blog sites, social networks like Facebook.com or Twitter.com, and so on.

During the first decade of the twenty-first century, the definitive popularisation of the computer and communication and creation technologies, in all forms and devices from the classic desktop to mobile technologies, was the prerequisite for the development of associated cultural and artistic practices. Those practices, mediated by technologies already established as free and non-hierarchical, are linked with political criticism and activism where references and alternative proposals are shared in a postmodern society that is suffering from lack of referents.

Criterion 1. Activism and the Choice of Culture

As stated above, online political activism, despite being a recent phenomenon, has been thoroughly studied in the field of communication and philosophy, and related to concepts of collective intelligence and digital convergence (Lévy 1997) (Holloway 2002). When political activism is expressed in an artistic form, its political nature partly determines its own status as art, given that its function is not only formal or aesthetic but also social or critical. "Activist art is a public and collective art by nature. That is, from one side is determined to produce a 'public sphere' and, from the other, to activate in it a 'consensus building' without which the public sphere would be meaningless and lack political efficacy, because it would not have built a community into it" (Aznar y Iñigo 2007).

When linking participation and the cultural environment, it is important to return to the ideas of Walter Benjamin (1975), who highlighted the potential of art as a critical and revolutionary tool. What makes art a special tool is the ability of the proletariat to learn and teach it, and hence its greatest strength: the essence of this form of production is in overcoming the social differences between the author and ordinary people. Benjamin argued that artists would develop attractive strategies geared towards those who were indifferent to art, so that they would be motivated to become producers. Susan Buck-Morrs (1993) considers Benjamin's position to be too radical and argues that, if we politicised art in this way, it would be left permanently adulterated and would no longer be art as we know it. When we observe the emergence of participatory cultural and artistic projects in demonstrations and circles of political activism, we understand that art and culture appear here as a sign of the motivation that Benjamin described. In his text, the author also argues that artists are not revolutionaries just because they are artists, and that their potential is proportional to the development of reflexive tools and the delivery of those tools to those excluded, making it possible for them to become producers (Nuñez 2009). In short, the higher the level of involvement of the individual in the cultural world, the greater their personal impact and, consequently, even higher expectations may be raised, which is particularly relevant in a society that has lost its referents, is chronically dissatisfied and is currently living on the tightrope of alienation (Bauman 2010).

As stated by Anthony Giddens (1993), participation in cultural life diversifies social discourses, creates critical notions of life and strengthens identity systems and, by expanding the discussion to the global level, the benefits of cultural participation are not limited to the individual, but are also felt by the entire community. When it comes to art specifically, the interesting study by François Matarasso (1997), about the effects of participation in different fields and social impacts (personal development, social cohesion, community empowerment, identity and local imagination and vision, and health and well-being), showed that cultural projects often promote cheap and effective solutions to different types of social problems, that interpersonal relationships play an essential part in them and that their impacts are highly visible: "What matters so much about participation in the arts is not just that it gives people the personal and practical skills to help themselves and become involved in society – although it does this – but that it opens routes into the wider democratic process and encourages people to want to take part" (Matarasso 1997, 78).

In the cases presented below, we find the core of each activist political activity to be the visibility of realities that would remain hidden, in conflict with the majority visibility of the hegemonic media. This visibility, according to Jorge Luis Marzo (2006, 5), is facilitated by the articulation of self-management and socialisation mechanisms that respond to what the community considers to be necessary. The public expression of a silenced community is only possible after a prior negotiation of a both internal and external suitable communicative context. In short, in every cultural creation activist has at least three characteristics: the creation of internal networks, the establishment of mechanisms of expression, and the criticism of hegemonic discourses. Of course, one of the most obvious problems of activism in cultural creation is its deactivation by the prevailing discourses, which can overcome the most aesthetic activism mechanisms and eliminate their social commentary, converting it into a product for consumption, a fashion or trend.

Criterion 2. Communities of Interest, Cognitive Surplus and Immobile Socialisation

To help us understand the idea of participation in Web 2.0 and the individual decision to take part in new forms of online creative collaboration, we take up Clay Shirky's concept of cognitive surplus (2010). The term aims to define the surplus of time and talent of the population in the developed world. According to the author, we all have a certain amount of free time that is part of our daily routine, and that we choose to spend according to our own priorities. The average day of an average person consists of eight hours of work, eight hours of rest and eight hours that are divided between several activities such as eating, watching television, a personal hobby or engagement in social and family life. Obviously, these eight hours can work out to be even more, inasmuch as we believe that, in the age of technology, the boundaries between work and leisure time are no longer defined, or inflexible.

It is the leisure time that, according to Shirky, has undergone a huge transformation following the advent of personal computers connected to the Internet and to open-source content platforms. With the opportunity to develop, promote and establish connections, people began to spend their spare time in actively participating in the production of online content. Among the more interesting statistics on this topic, is the comparison between the time that the American population spends watching television in a year – 200 billion hours – and the amount of time needed to create

Wikipedia – 100 million hours. The difference highlights the very powerful and well-known transformation in which individuals leave the passive state of receiving information and move to the active state of generating content, whatever it may be. The author further states that cyberspace is today, for contemporary society, what gin and tonic were for seventeenth century English society, becoming the escape from the brutal changes in contemporary life of late capitalism.

The large amount of cognitive surplus being spent on content production has generated an environment of extremely fertile and dynamic collective activities. Out of this phenomenon, many important projects have been created and then given shape thanks to the participation of individuals who do not know each other and do not share the same physical environment, but have agreed to devote their free time to the same cause or idea. From alternative educational projects to forums or human rights advocacy platforms, users have stopped just receiving knowledge, and begun to produce it based on their own criteria, thoughts and interests. The main consequence of this process, beyond the transition between consumer and prosumer, according to Shirky, is the breakdown of the barrier of exclusion and the resulting integration, generating what Shirky calls "civic value" or "public value". As a result, society gains a direct and colossal benefit from each of these projects and its collective influences.

When talking about online activist involvement in relation to the concept of cognitive surplus, in addition to the idea of the usage of free time, we are particularly interested in what happens immediately prior to the participatory activity itself: the choice of a particular activity. With so many people involved in new projects in cyberspace, one can find countless options for applying creative energy in one's free time. Even though managing a personal Facebook timeline can be considered a form of statement and creation – whether of a posture or stance toward the world – there is a big difference between 'liking' or sharing the creations of others and producing personalised content or truly engaging with a specific subject or creation practice. Clearly, each individual will choose what to do, how to do it and how much time to devote to each of their areas of interest: "Media producers are responding to these newly empowered consumers in contradictory ways, sometimes encouraging change, sometimes resisting what they see as renegade behaviour. And consumers, in turn, are perplexed by what they see as mixed signals about how much and what kinds of participation they can enjoy" (Jenkins 2006, 19).

From the outset, online political activists have understood the use of technology, Web 2.0 and collaborative creation as tools or facilitators of a process, since politically active individuals are naturally closer to the idea of participation than alienated individuals, who are unaware of the political issues experienced by their community. Thiago Soares and Allysson V. Martins (2012) analyse the collaborative journalism and the convergence strategies in the occupation protest at the Universidade de São Paulo.

160 Lluís Anyó and Iasa Monique Ribeiro

Although online political activism may be favoured by cognitive surplus, we may question its effective range, especially when it comes to offline practices. This question arises from the consideration of the type of community that develops in the virtual world, with its undoubted advantages and also its difficulties and limitations. For although these communities bring together a powerful social and cultural wealth of cognitive surplus, they are limited in their effectiveness by what Zygmunt Bauman would call "peg communities". As explained by David Bell, "the peg here is a coat peg, a place to casually hang your coat or hat, for now. Part of the perceived problem with peg communities, of course, is their very coat-pegginess, their elective ephemerality, or what Bauman names their 'superficial and perfunctory, as well as transient bonds'" (Bell 2007, 257).

The virtual community is located in the daily existence of those who articulate their lives in a fluid relationship between online and offline. The term immobile socialisation, that Maria Bakardjieva (2007) uses to analyse her ethnographic study, relates in part to this. Bakardjieva reverses Raymond Williams's concept of mobile privatisation: "unlike broadcast technology and the automobile that, according to Williams, precipitated a withdrawal of middle-class families from public spaces of association and sociability into private suburban homes, the Internet is being mobilised in a process of collective deliberation and action which engages people from their private realm" (Bakardjieva 2007, 236). Thus, immobile socialisation is part of the daily lives of real people, using available technology in terms of specific practices. This idea is interesting because it places online sociability practices in the context of offline practices, and not a superfluous or unnecessary sphere.

In any event, as we have seen, communities in the digital environment can be characterised in relation to the strength of social ties, the commitment of their members, their permanence and the ephemeral character of the group itself. In virtual communities, the participation of members can be analysed in relation to the dedication of free time, i.e., of a surplus that is used up after the 'serious' activities have taken place – cognitive surplus. The commitment is made within the private sphere of the technologically connected home, but protected from physical public commitment that requires a physical presence – immobile socialisation.

10.2 Case Studies and Discussion

Many diverse cultural content projects with activist goals have been developed over the last few years. In this section, we aim to identify and analyse just three projects, which are examples of the integration between political participation and cultural resources. In line with our proposal above, the analysis will be based on two criteria. The first relates to the type of content created, which we analyse in the relationship between the artistic and cultural nature, defined respectively as the expression of individual creation of a high aesthetic value, and expression of collective creation as a function

Cultural Creation and Political Activism in the Digital World 161

of political criticism. The second criterion refers to the type of community developing the creative process. We define the community in relation to the strength of social ties or a universe of common interest, which maintains the community on the basis of the cognitive surplus and immobile socialisation of its members, which we have called a "peg community".

#1 *Eu não mereço ser estuprada* (Brasil, 2014)

On March 27, 2014, a survey carried out by the Institute of Applied Economic Research (IPEA) among 3,810 Brazilians reported that 65 per cent of respondents agreed fully or partially with the statement "women wearing clothes that show off their bodies deserve to be attacked". Although a few days later the same Institute published an apology acknowledging that the data had been published erroneously and that, in fact, 70 per cent of the respondents disagreed totally or partially with this statement, the first published data might indicate the general belief that the access to the female body is free when women do not impose limits or dress appropriately. The following day, the journalist Nana Queiroz created a Facebook campaign, convening all women to take part. The protest consisted in the participants posting the hashtag #eunãomereçoserestuprada – I do not deserve to be raped, in Portuguese – on their own Facebook timelines. Queiroz also posted a picture of herself naked, covering her breasts with her arms, with the text "Eu não mereço ser estuprada" inked on her skin. In three days, the Facebook event created to widen the movement had more than 250,000 'likes' and 44,000 people attending. The Brazilian Facebook pages were filled with pictures of women and men accepting, customising and adding content to Queiroz's idea, posting photos of their own naked bodies and personal messages against sexism and rapists, and encouraging victims to report and condemn offenders.

Queiroz's initiative, combined with the speed and scope provided by Facebook, mushroomed and within a couple of days the protest achieved national and international visibility. Even the president of Brazil, Dilma Rousseff, posted on her official Twitter account that she endorsed the protest and that nothing could justify sexual abuse. Groups from all over the country contributed to the protest through their own actions, and countless alternative demonstrations emerged from the connection and recognition of various groups and initiatives. Among the most interesting and enduring creations is the collaboration between a number of feminist artists who joined forces to publish and highlight their protest through artistic creations. Umbigo Sujo, in umbigosujo.tumblr.com, is a collaborative illustration page in which women from around Brazil create and submit content based on verbal attacks they have witnessed, or other representative situations and thoughts.

This case study fits well with a practice of cultural creation with strong critical content in a specific field: feminism, which has a long tradition and

162   Lluís Anyó and Iasa Monique Ribeiro

contains many of the characteristics noted throughout this study. The action was initiated by the journalist Nana Queiroz, but it soon developed further, the Facebook page becoming a receptacle for public opinion, and those who sought a change of opinion. It is also a good example of cognitive surplus, as Shirky understands it, in the sense of agents using part of their leisure time for an objective of interest in a virtual community. This peg community is built on collective creation recorded in the daily lives of the people, who use technological mechanisms of expression for their own purposes, regardless of the function for which they were created. By giving visibility to a body of hidden opinion in relation to rape, they are condemning it. Furthermore, the action has extended to other areas of artistic creation, maintaining and increasing its reach and relevance.

#2 Megafone.Net (Barcelona, 2014)

Megafone.net is a project created by the multimedia artist Antoni Abad and has been running since 2004. The project seeks to explore alternative and new social and communicative uses of mobile phone technologies, through ongoing collaborative and independent content production. The main goal of *Megafone.net* is to encourage those who have been marginalised by society to express their feelings and views, and to report what is going on in their environment through personal expression. Participants use mobile phones to record audio, video, text or photo messages, and then publish them online, turning their devices into virtual megaphones. Over ten years, *Megafone.net* has developed thirteen secondary projects, an extensive participatory timeline and an even more extensive cloud of keywords. 54,312 posts have been published by 260 participants, and the project works under a Creative Commons license.

The project debates the concept of the ´communal mobile phone´, a software designed to be used and shared by multiple participants. At weekly meetings, participants talk about the content of the webcasts and help each other to publish this content.

This community web for publishing using mobile devices has given a voice to groups at risk of social exclusion, such as taxi drivers in Mexico (2004), young gypsies in Lleida and León (2005), prostitutes in Madrid (2005), Nicaraguan immigrants in San José in Costa Rica (2006), motorcycle couriers or motoboys in São Paulo (2007) and demobilised and displaced people in Colombia and young Sahrawi refugee camps near Tindouf in Algeria (2009). It has also worked with disabled groups in Barcelona (2006) and Geneva (2008) and blind and people with limited vision in Barcelona (2010).

It is a multiple action where the artist, Antoni Abad, has the role of director but is not responsible for creating the content, which is provided by the various groups to which the initiative gives a voice. The group manages the access to the mechanisms of expression, and the community inserts critical

Cultural Creation and Political Activism in the Digital World 163

content. The result is a rich and complex audio-visual production of cultural and artistic creation. Here, the use of cognitive surplus is different from the previous case, as the groups are mostly active offline and only just extend into online. They amplify their voice through participating in an act of artistic prestige

The *Megafone.net/2004–2014* exhibition took place between February and June of 2014, at the Museum of Contemporary Art (MACBA). The exhibition demonstrated the difficult balance between institutionalised artistic practice and the exploration of social and communicational uses of mobile technology in a global initiative, and notably the tension between art and culture as laid out by Teixeira Coelho (2009) (*supra*). The value of *Megafone.net*, in our view, is in creating opportunities for collective expression to groups who would not normally have access to it, and in bringing its contents without mediation to the field of institutionalised culture, in this case the contemporary museums of the art world.

#3 Don't Be a Tourist (Barcelona, 2014)

Don't be a tourist is a Facebook page – facebook.com/dontbeatouristinbarcelona – created in June 2014 by residents of Barcelona. Of the three cases discussed here, it is the most primitive and simplest. Its users and participants create and publish memes (customisable visual creations popularised online) with assertions and opinions about attitudes on the part of tourists who visit the city which they consider to be unacceptable or negative. The author of the project, Joaquim Fonolls, manages the online web pages – Tumblr and Facebook accounts – selecting and editing images and text proposed by the public. The aim of the project is not to protest against tourism, but to activate a dynamic manifesto for quality visitors, differentiated by the authors as 'guests'. The group asks for respect from visitors to Barcelona and wishes them to understand, principally, that the local population of the city is composed of ordinary, working people who are not on holiday and have to continue their day-to-day lives among the tourists, some of whom behave antisocially. Since its creation on June 28 and at the last count on September 12, 2014, forty-four images had been published, and the Facebook page had more than 3,700 likes.

The project is one of a series of measures initiated by the citizens and residents of Barcelona critical of the type of tourism that the city is experiencing. In late August, the mayor of Barcelona, Xavier Trias, waged a war against the private apartment rental network Airbnb, alleging fiscal irregularities. The measure came at the same time as the residents of the Barceloneta neighbourhood voiced their weariness and discontent with the attitude of tourists who rent private apartments and play loud music late at night, throw loud parties, start fights, damage the properties and façades and consume excessive amounts of alcohol.

164 *Lluís Anyó and Iasa Monique Ribeiro*

Although *Don't be a tourist* is the most light-hearted case study and has an clearly comic and humorous tone, of the three cases analysed, it is the most tightly linked to the idea of cognitive surplus – or is at least the easiest to become involved in. Participation takes very little time, requires no prior arrangements or meetings, and allows participants to express their views anonymously and with no direct responsibility. To sum up, the users of *Don't be a tourist* express their opposition to certain unpleasant practices linked to mass tourism, thereby creating a slight and very light-hearted impression of an offended community among users and participants of the Facebook page.

What we may observe here, as in the first case study, is that the idea of content – the universe of interest – overrides the idea of community, which, unlike the case of *Megafone.net*, is not properly constructed. Criticism here goes beyond just making the reality visible, as in the two previous cases, offering a different perspective of reality and finishing up by condemning it with irony. The page homes in on specific tourist behaviour that tends to come into conflict with the everyday lives of residents. In this case, there is no collective seeking and demanding change. The aim of the project is, through satire, to criticise uncontrolled mass tourism.

10.3 Final Thoughts

The main aim of this chapter was to develop a reflection that would help to explain the emergence of cultural projects created by political aspirations in the collaborative environment of Web 2.0. We understand participation as an effective way to re-establish the connections that have been lost or put at risk on account of the paradigmatic changes in postmodern society. Through artistic or culturally loaded creations, political activism manages to get very close to the ordinary lives of the people. The online user who has free time receives new information in an open and interesting way, makes use of the tools offered by information technologies and feels capable and motivated to contribute effectively and representatively. We have seen that the combination of online technology and cognitive surplus opens up countless possible universes of activity and hybridisation, and one of its results is this form of cultural collaborative creation motivated by political dissatisfaction and the desire to communicate.

In conclusion, and hypothetically, we can state that activist cultural creation in the digital world can be analysed based on two criteria, firstly the contrast between art and culture and secondly the contrast between a strong or weak community. As we have noted in the case studies, these two contrasts provide us with a better understanding of the various expressions of activist creation in the digital world.

It is the cultural path that allows these creations to be developed increasingly closer to people's personal worlds. Derived partly from art activism and partly from political activism, but democratised through the concepts

Cultural Creation and Political Activism in the Digital World 165

of collaboration and participation, online activism initiates cultural projects that may have greater or lesser artistic significance, whose essence is objectively political and that are full of personal, voluntary and reflexive expression.

Works Cited

Aznar, Sagrario y María Iñigo. 2007. "Arte, Política y activismo". *Concinnitas Revista do Instituto de Artes de Universidade de Rio de Janeiro*, 10 (1). http://e-spacio.uned.es/fez/view/bibliuned:536. Accessed July 19, 2014.

Bakardjieva, Maria. 2007. "Virtual togetherness. An everyday-life perspective". In *The Cybercultures reader. Second Edition*, edited by David Bell and Barbara M. Kennedy. London; New York: Routledge.

Bauman, Zygmunt. 2005. *Liquid Life*. Cambridge: Polity Press.

Baym, Nancy K. 1995. "The emergence of community in computer-mediated communication". In *Cybersociety. Computer-mediated communication and community*, edited by S.G. Jones. London: Sage.

Bell, David. 2007. "Webs as pegs". In *The Cybercultures reader. Second Edition*. edited by David Bell and Barbara M. Kennedy. London; New York: Routledge.

Benjamin, Walter. 1975. *El autor como productor*. Madrid. Taurus.

Casacuberta, David. 2003. *Creación colectiva. En Internet, el creador es el público*. Barcelona: Gedisa.

Castells, Manuel. 1996. The Rise of the Network Society. *The Information Age: Economy, Society and Culture Vol. I*. Cambridge, MA; Oxford, UK: Blackwell.

Coelho, Teixeira. 2009. "Cultura es la regla, arte la excepción". In *Diccionario crítico de política cultural. Cultura e imaginario*. Barcelona: Gedisa.

Durkheim, Émile. 2014. *The Division of Labor in Society*. New York: Simon & Schuster.

Giddens, Anthony. 1993. *Consecuencias de la modernidad*. Madrid: Alianza.

Granés, Carlos. 2010. "Revoluciones modernas, culpas posmodernas". In *Antropología: horizontes estéticos*, edited by Carmelo Lisón-Tolosana. Barcelona: Anthropos.

Heath, Joseph, and Potter, Andrew. 2005. *The rebel sell. How counterculture became consumer culture*. West Sussex: Caption.

Holloway, John. 2002. *Change the World without Taking Power*. London: Pluto Press.

Jenkins, Henry. 2006. *Convergence Culture: Where Old and New Media Collide*. New York: NYU Press.

Kellner, Douglas, and Kahn, Richard. 2007. "Technopolitics and oppositional media". In *The Cybercultures reader. Second Edition*, edited by David Bell and Barbara M. Kennedy. London; New York: Routledge.

Latanzi, Juan Pablo. 2013. "¿El poder de las nuevas tecnologías o las nuevas tecnologías del poder"? *Cuadernos del Centro de Estudios en Diseño y Comunicación*, 45: 15–25.

Lévy, Pierre. 1997. *Collective Intelligence*. Cambridge: Perseus Books.

Marzo, Jorge Luis. 2006. "Introducción: Fotografía y activismo. (Algunos) recorridos críticos en los últimos 25 años". In *Fotografía y activismo*, edited by Jorge Luis Marzo. Barcelona: Gustavo Gili.

166 *Lluís Anyó and Iasa Monique Ribeiro*

Matarasso, François. 1997. *Use or Ornament? The Social Impact of Participation in the Arts*. London: Comedia.

Meikle, G. *Future active: Media activism and the Internet*. London: Taylor & Francis, 2002.

Núñez, Tomás P. 2009. "Participación, consumo cultural e individualización: aportes teóricos y empíricos para la gestión cultural en Chile". *Primer encuentro anual de gestores y animadores culturales*. Santiago de Chile.

Nelson, Ted. 1974. *Computer Lib: You can and must understand computers now / Dream Machines: new freedoms through computer screens*. Self-published.

O'Reilly, Tim. 2005. "What is Web 2.0. Design Patterns and Business Models for the Next Generation of Software". http://www.oreilly.com/pub/a/web2/archive/what-is-web-20.html. Accessed July 19, 2014.

People's Computer Company Newsletter. 1972. http://www.digibarn.com/collections/newsletters/peoples-computer/index.html. Accessed July 19, 2014.

Poster, Mark. 1997. "Cyberdemocracy: The Internet and the Public Sphere". In *Internet Culture*, edited by D. Porter. New York: Routledge.

Reid, Elizabeth M. 1996. "Electropolis: Communication and community on Internet Relay Chat". In *High noon on the electronic frontier: Conceptual issues in cyberspace, edited by P. Ludlow*. Cambridge: MIT Press.

Rheingold, Howard. 2000. *The virtual community: homesteading on the electronic frontier*. Boston: MIT Press.

George Ritzer & Jorgenson, Nathan. 2010. Production, consumption, prosumption: the nature of capitalism in the age of the digital 'prosumer', *Journal of Consumer Culture* 10.1: 13–36.

Shirky, Clay. 2010. *Cognitive Surplus. Creativity and Generosity in a Connected Age*. London: Peguin Books.

Soares, Thiago, and Martins, Allysson V. 2012. "Convergência, transmídia e excedente congnitivo na Ocupação da USP". *Estudios em Comunicaçaõ*, 12: 135–154.

Tönnies, Ferdinand. 1957. *Community and Society*. East Lansing: Michigan State University Press.

Weber, Max. 1978. *Economy and Society*. Berkeley: University of California Press.

Williams, Raymond. 1974. *Television: Technology and Cultural Form*. London: Fontana.

Whole Earth Catalog. (1968). http://www.wholeearth.com/index.php. Accessed July 19, 2014.

11 The Mediatization of Politics and the Digital Public Sphere
The Dynamics of Mini-Publics

Caja Thimm

Introduction

In most of today's societies, many social and communicative activities implying the construction of cultural meaning are intrinsically tied to media.

There is widespread agreement that one of the most viable forces behind this development is the Internet. Particularly social media can be regarded as a key issue for the process of mediatization. Marked by characteristics like ubiquity, user-generated content (Bruns 2008), multi-mediality and more recently, portability (Chayko 2008, Bächle and Thimm 2014), the Internet has gained increasing influence on people's lives and daily interactions. But not only are private lives increasingly shaped by mediated exchanges, the public sphere is undergoing changes as well. More and more people are using the Internet as a platform and outlet for their personal opinions, criticisms and decision-making. Most notably, citizens all over the world have been taking their protests to the Internet (see Shirky 2011 for an overview), prominently during the so-called 'Arab Spring' in 2011 (Tufekci and Wilson 2012), but also in other parts of the world, like Germany (Thimm and Bürger 2012) or France (Mercier 2014, Frame and Brachotte 2015).

Some researchers characterize these changes within the public, political, secular, institutional and private spheres and in daily life as a pivotal 'meta-processes' (Krotz 2007, Hepp and Krotz 2014). This focus on the role of media as a driving force of social change is one of the main characteristics of the concept of mediatization (Lundby 2009). Looking at the changes in political participation from the perspective of mediatization as a dynamic process offers an approach to the media as a driving force of these changes, which are currently being experienced around the globe (Couldry and Hepp 2013).

11.1 The Mediatization of Politics

When regarding the mediatization of politics it is evident that social relations online play an increasingly important role. People meet on the web, organize activities and exchange information, whether on Facebook, Twitter, Instagram or in blogs. Social interaction and group formation in particular must consequently be revisited in light of social networking sites (SNS), which provide space for such diverse functions as identity-, relationship- and information-management (Baym 2010, Boyd and Ellison 2007). Social media can be conceptualized as a space of "digital sociality" (see contributions in Anastasiadis and Thimm 2011), with individuals often relating to each other along similar interests and online activities. These socio-communicative functionalities have also spawned new forms of mediatized political communication such as "pirate" cultures online (Lindgren and Lundström 2015) or cyber-protest (Donk van de, Loader, Nixon, and Rucht 2005). Lindgren and Lundström (2015) argue, for example, that Twitter and the Internet have a particularly strong potential to create a space for what Beck terms "subpolitics": politics that are not "governmental, parliamentary, and party politics", but take place in "all the other fields of society" (Beck 1997, 52). The new vigor of participation can be regarded as one of the major developments in user empowerment, as digital networks and communications were actually developed to meet the desire for interpersonal contact (Rheingold 2000). By going online, civic discourses expand and pluralize the existing systems of political communication, meaning that everyone, not only political elites, can readily express their socio-political concerns. Such civic media activity has also started to shape the news agenda, circumventing the traditional gatekeepers, such as TV or print media. Nowadays, many newspapers take up issues from the digital agenda set in social media environments, use SNS for their own news distribution, or develop their presence on social media platforms. SNS have experienced strong growth thanks, in particular, to the potential for self-expression they offer to Internet users. Linked to the idea of free self-expression and easy sharing, accounts on networks like Facebook or Twitter are associated with a desire for self-affirmation, which Allard and Vandenberghe (2003) call "expressive individualism". For a better understanding of these new participation motives on the part of the users, it seems necessary to reflect on the changing role of group formation and group coherence as well as on the changing options by social media in relation to traditional mass media. Journalistically produced mass media still have an important role for the public sphere, but as discourse circulates between digital publics in reaction to events reported in the traditional media, and their echoes on the Internet and SNS, the media agenda is increasingly influenced by discourses and topics stemming from the web.

As illustrated, media development and societal changes are closely connected. This interrelatedness is at the core of the "mediatization theory" (Hepp and Krotz 2014, Lundby 2009, Hjarvard 2013). Convincingly, Krotz (2007) argues for mediatization as a "meta-process" of social or cultural change, comparable to globalization and commercialization:

> Today, globalization, individualization, mediatization and the growing importance of the economy, which we here call commercialization, can

The Mediatization of Politics and the Digital Public Sphere 169

be seen as the relevant meta-processes that influence democracy and society, culture, politics and other conditions of life over the longer term.

(Krotz 2007, 257)

Media have become so important because of how they are used in communicative behavior within society and how they help construct reality (Krotz 2009). Thus, mediatization focuses on the increasing importance of media for work, play and social relationships (see also Hjarvard 2013), or as Strömbäck and Esser (2014, 8) define: "The essence of mediatization is that it is a long-term process of increasing media importance and direct and indirect media influence in various spheres of society". These spheres are manifold, as Hjarvard (2008, 2013) points out:

> As a concept mediatization denotes the processes through which core elements of a cultural or social activity (e.g., politics, religion, language) assume media form. As a consequence, the activity is to a greater or lesser degree performed through interaction with a medium, and the symbolic content and the structure of the social and cultural activities are influenced by media environments which they gradually become more dependent upon.
>
> (Hjarvard 2008, 3)

The approach is not without its critics. Couldry (2008) for example criticizes mediatization's focus on "single logic of transformation", and Strömbäck (2008) points to the difficulties in operationalization and empirical investigation within the framework of mediatization.

When looking at the changes politics are currently undergoing from the perspective of mediatization, it is not only political communication itself, which needs to be analyzed, but political institutions, stakeholders and social environments as well. Particularly the process orientation, which is constitutive for the mediatization approach, helps to reflect and include different influences on these developments. Taking up the perspective of the dynamics of the mediatization process, Strömbäck (2008) and Strombäck and Esser (2014, 6) see the mediatization of politics as a "long-term process through which the importance of the media and their spill-over effects on political processes, institutions organization and actors have increased". Based on this general view, Strömbäck (2008) and Strömbäck and Esser (2014) differentiate between four phases, which point to the increasing dependency of the political sphere on media and their respective logic.

In these four phases the authors assume a gradual increase of the role media play in the political process and see the media as indispensable to the political system and its protagonists. This model is presupposing media as a powerful and controlling system, in which the media logics (Altheide and Snow 1979) determine the political logics of political actors and institutions in the end.

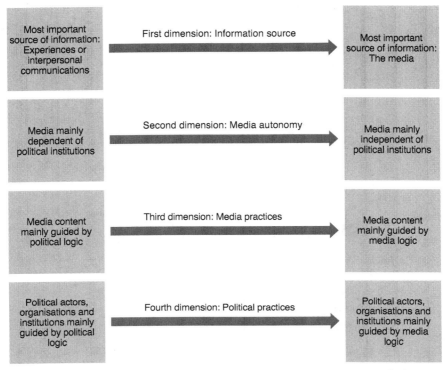

Figure 11.1 Four Phases of mediatization (Strömbäck and Esser 2014, 8)[1].

11.2 The Mediatization of the Public Sphere

Over the years, the concept of the public sphere has been applied and linked to many issues and approaches in media and communication theory (Breese 2011). The main underlying ideas, however, are based on the works of Habermas and his notion of the public sphere (Habermas 1989). At the core of Habermas' work is the description of the evolution from personal opinion to public opinion and the socio–structural transformation of the latter. With the advent of the Internet as a new driving force in society, the conceptualization of society as a "network society", which is characterized by "networks operated by information and communication technologies based in microelectronics and digital computer networks" (Castells 2005, 32), lay the ground for an understanding of the public sphere as organized on the basis of media communication networks (Castells 2008). In many works on the role of the Internet in relation to the public sphere, many authors have highlighted the potential of the Internet to advance political communication (for example, Dahlberg 2007, Dahlgren 2009, Papacharissi and De Fatima Oliveira 2012). Less optimistic perspectives point to possible downsides of political communication on the Internet such as the fragmentation or polarization of society, the digital divide (Norris 2001), the limited flow of

The Mediatization of Politics and the Digital Public Sphere 171

information due to algorithmic power in the "filter bubble" (Pariser 2011) and its intellectual "shallowness" in general (Carr 2010). More explicitly, Morozov (2011) sees the risks of surveillance by governments and calls the hopes for net-based democratic changes a "net delusion".

More recent work, particularly on social media, however, has argued that any over-generalization might not grasp the real activities of the participants and argue for a more situated and contextualized approach (see contributions in Einspänner-Pflock, Dang-Anh, and Thimm 2014). The very general perspectives might not be able to assess the ways people engage and participate in specific settings and for specific purposes, such as situated activities, which users engage in and for which the Internet is made useful from their point of view. Particularly the ease with which publicity and public attention can be generated without the gatekeeping force of the traditional mass media is an important factor for political participation online.

Overall there can be no doubt that the transition of the public sphere in the direction of a digital public sphere marks an important societal change, as digital spaces can be a venue for the renewal of public discourses on all matters. Consequently, more and more media scholars call for a 'rethinking of the public sphere' (see contributions in Lunt and Livingstone 2013).

Social Networks and the Public Sphere: "Mini-Publics"

Media use in the most diverse contexts has become normality for an entire generation of individuals who have inhabited the Internet as a true living space, which is as natural to them as a non-digital environment. Digital networks and communities were born of social and communicative needs for interpersonal contact (Rheingold 2000, Baym 2010), the motives of today's netizens, however, are no longer one-dimensional. The trend towards a dynamic-participatory medium can be described as a breakthrough in user empowerment. Although the assumption that these networks give rise to a collective intelligence and a new culture of the "wisdom of crowds" is still much debated (Surowiecki 2005), the Internet is indeed changing political participation and most likely, politics and political institutions themselves as well.

Due to new functionalities, the Internet must increasingly be included as a defining dimension of social relations: the socio-communicative functionality of the Internet is the reason for its explosive rise in use. Social interaction and identity formation in particular must be revisited in light of social networks such as Facebook, LinkedIn or Twitter, which provide space for such diverse functions as identity-, relationship- and information-management (Boyd and Ellison 2007, Thimm 2008).

Whereas in the pre-digital age, mass media played a decisive role in formatting and influencing the public sphere, digital discourse networks do not have such widespread impact. Hence it has been argued that agenda-setting processes have to be reconceptualized so as to include social media (Sayre, Bode, Wilcox and Shah 2010). SNS are perceived and experienced

172 Caja Thimm

as assertive technology, allowing users to expose their privacy, tastes, personality, and convictions, without censorship. Consequently, postures of denunciation and protest thus find a renewed space for expression. One aspect of the social utility of SNS is related to their possible use as "counter public spheres" (Downey and Fenton 2003), especially for those otherwise devoid of access to the media sphere, because of their low social visibility or their discourses considered extremist. For these Internet users, the word of the authorities (media, politicians, intellectuals and moral authorities) is questioned, challenged or even turned against them. Twitter, for example, is regularly used as a "controversial sphere" (Mercier 2014, and Chapter 9 in this volume), especially at election time. In fact, in a networked society "it can be more challenging to convince others that your way is the right way when online participants have access to online resources (information or other people) that may offer alternative points of view" (Gruzd and Wellman 2014, 1252). By providing echo chambers (Sunstein 2001) for likeminded individuals, SNS may in fact favor the emergence of counter public spheres within the global media landscape.

This goes hand in hand with a more recent observation on the emergence of "mini-publics" as an element of the public sphere. So far, mini-publics have been conceptualized as smaller circles of (better) informed groups, which engage in information exchange processes and discourses (Bohmann 2004, Goodin and Dryzek 2006). These groups engage in a convergent environment, which can be described by "transmedial" or, as Madianou and Miller (2013) called it, "polymedial". Such mini-publics become increasingly common in the online-environment: They can often be linked to specific political activities or form along certain topics and interests. However, in the digital sphere, they have to be framed differently and must be differentiated from the perspective of the user and the topic.

Mapping Mini-Publics—Perspectives and Typology

Set in the context of deliberation, the term "mini-publics" has been used to describe smaller decision-making groups. These are

> [...] designed to be groups small enough to be genuinely deliberative, and representative enough to be genuinely democratic (though rarely will they meet standards of statistical representativeness, and they are never representative in the electoral sense). Such mini-publics include Deliberative Polls, Consensus Conferences, Citizens' Juries, Planning Cells, and many others.
>
> (Goodin and Dryzek 2006, 220)

Mini-publics in this framework are closely connected to the idea of deliberation, as they are conceptualized as small groups of people who engage in (political) deliberation. These groups, however, are mostly tied to institutions,

The Mediatization of Politics and the Digital Public Sphere 173

set in the political process and have clear agendas. In the increasingly interactive world of social networks, such groups are characterized more and more by self-formation and self-selection. Mini-publics in the wider sense can thus be created for any kind of issue, whether political or personal. Some are purposely created with the aim of establishing public attention, such as celebrities using their Facebook accounts to get closer to their fans. Often these discourses emerge spontaneously, stay on the agenda for a limited time and thus can also be called "ad-hoc publics" (see also Chapter 3 in this volume).

This restricted perspective on mini-publics does not, for example, offer an approach for understanding the outbreak of intense online debates in specific circles, on blogs or Facebook pages. If we see opinion formation and debates as a central quality of political participation and political engagement, we have to regard smaller publics, such as a Facebook discussion thread, as a *constitutive subset* and element of the digital public sphere and not as a second rate public, which has fallen victim to "fragmentation" (Webster and Ksiazek 2012). Secondly, the size of the group should not be limited to a group "small enough to be genuinely deliberative", as demanded by Goodin and Dryzek (2006, 220). This condition does not reflect the online realities of many net-based groups, which are characterized by silent spectators or "lurkers", eclectically active "clicktivists", and highly engaged activists (Christensen 2011, Carpentier 2009). All of these kinds of members are to be found in political publics all over the world.

Mini-publics online are consequently understood as:

> A group of online users referring to a shared topic in a publicly visible and publicly accessible online space over a period of time, by means of individual activities such as textual or visual contributions.

The character of such mini-publics is influenced by factors such as user roles, topic evolvement and time frames. The following types of mini-publics shall be differentiated:

1 *User-initiated mini-publics*: the topic in question can be initiated or instigated by a user, who might take on the role of a moderator (such as in blogs).
2 *Event-driven mini-publics*: real world events can cause intensive participation and online activities on the event in question. Often these are natural catastrophes, political events (such as elections), big events (such as sports), or scandals of any sort. These mini-publics can be brief and may die down as the event recedes into the past, or stay "dormant" in a smaller public which gets reactivated with new information on the event. Mostly these mini-publics start as ad hoc mini-publics (see below).
3 *Commercially launched mini-publics*: more and more businesses have discovered the power of smaller and intense debates on products or company policies as tools for online marketing and consumer attention.

174   *Caja Thimm*

These commercially launched mini-publics might, however, not always result in the positive consequences the companies wish for. If not done according to net cultures, such campaigns can result in "digital firestorms" or "shitstorms" (Bieber, Härthe, and Thimm 2015).

To identify the role such mini-publics can play for the public sphere in general and for political participation in particular, it is important to include the time factor into the concept. Two aspects will be differentiated:

- *Ad-hoc mini-publics*: these publics are reactions to incidents of all kinds, e.g., from catastrophes, show business, sports events or politics. They are characterized by a short duration and high intensity. Usually, in these mini-publics, longer-lasting communities are not created, but activities can be rekindled if new information appears on the topic.
- *Over-time mini-publics*: these mini-publics exist over longer periods of time and are characterized by variable levels of activity. Often the issues targeted in these publics are unresolved political issues (such as the one presented further down), long-lasting general topics structured around political interests or very general issues, such as hobbies.

Many mini-publics relate to the traditional media by cross-referencing to mainstream media content in various ways, thereby being polymedial by nature. Others never reach a larger public and stay online exclusively. This category should hence also be included when assessing the quality and reach of online mini-publics:

- Platform-based mini-publics: these mini-publics exist on one media platform only and are based on the media logics of the digital environment (like YouTube mini-publics).
- Polymedia mini-publics: these mini-publics are defined by their inter- and transmediality. They are either started online and are picked up by the traditional media or vice versa. They are characterized by a high intensity and frequent activities on all types of media and are mostly engaging a larger public.

Overall, these mini-publics can be regarded as both initiators of topics as well as reactive publics, where discussion and exchanges form the central core of online dynamics.

During the process of establishing mini-publics, the media logics of the technology in question can have formatting influences. For example, on Twitter the introduction of a hashtag can often be regarded as the beginning of the formation of a mini-public if picked up by others. If the topic gets attention from a wider audience, the phenomenon of the formation of a "hashtag family" can be observed. For example, in the case of the Paris murders of Charlie Hebdo staff members in January 2015, a large variety of hashtags could be observed, such as #CharlieHebdo, #WeAreAllCharlie,

The Mediatization of Politics and the Digital Public Sphere   175

#NousSommesCharlie, #JeSuisCharlie. The more activities mini-publics generate, the more positions can be symbolized by creating new hashtags of the same family, such as in the case of Charlie Hebdo. Here, connected hashtags were, for example: #JeSuisAhmed (in memory of the murdered policeman), or #JeNeSuisPasCharlie (as a counter argument), #ContreLes-Terroristes or references to connected events such as #MarcheRepublicaine.

An important approach to characterize the discursive connectedness of such publics was found in a study on Twitter network structures. Smith, Rainie, Himelboim and Shneiderman (2014) tracked one hashtag related to the U.S. budget deficit crisis (#my2k) in 2014 over two days. They found "large dense groups that have little inter-connection or bridge between them", corresponding to a "liberal group" and a "conservative group." Not only do the two groups rarely talk to each other, they also use different hashtags and link to different websites within their tweets. Only a very limited amount of users has links to both groups. Consequently Smith et al. call this type of mini-public a "polarized crowd". It is one of six archetypical network structures they found to exist on Twitter. This study does not only confirm the deep political divide in the United States, it also demonstrates that people prefer to communicate with like-minded individuals in their personal "filter bubble" (Pariser 2011).

11.3 Mini-Publics and Polymediated Media Dynamics: Examples from the Field

Twitter and Mini-Publics

One of the most relevant social media for the creation and maintenance of mini-publics is Twitter. The brief format and the specific textual functions make Twitter an excellent tool for information distribution and political exchange.

> Though the 140-character format is a constraint, it need not be seen as a limitation; while participants often shorten and otherwise modify tweets to fit into 140 characters, this characteristic of Twitter can also be seen as an advantage.
>
> (Boyd, Golder, and Lotan 2010, 10)

Due to the limited space, Twitter constitutes a complex and semiotically loaded communication system. Users can constitute a multi-referential system, in which authors relate to one another via a specific sign system. This interrelatedness is one of the core elements of the formation of intergroup dynamics within the mini-publics. By addressing other users directly or by just mentioning them within a tweet (@-symbol + Username), Twitter users can build contacts and initiate wide-spread discussions with several participants who are either involved actively or just read along. The @-function helps establishing interactional "cross-turn coherence" (Honeycutt and Herring 2009, 2) and creates new options to participate in the political online discourse. The #-symbol is used to mark keywords or topics in a Twitter message and helps categorizing tweets semantically. Twitter users can follow

176 *Caja Thimm*

conversations regarding a certain topic and get a better overview of what is being discussed within the certain field of interest (content mapping). This communicative function of hashtagging stands for discourse organization and content contextualization.

Hyperlinks (each string headed by http://) help expand the 140-sign limit of a tweet and sequence the content. The communicative function of linking allows users to substantiate their argumentation within a discussion by inserting multi-modal content, such as photos, videos, or links to other websites. The users can link to online articles or blog postings in order to provide background information or give some "proof" of a claim by uploading a photo or video. Some of the visually stimulating hyperlinks like inserted photos are also used as narrative elements.

The fourth main communicative strategy is retweeting (RT). A user can re-send another user's tweet by either clicking the retweet-button (automatic retweet) or by putting RT at the beginning of the message. As the initiator of the re-tweeted tweet is informed about this activity, she or he can see who values the tweet. This "closeness-potential" is becoming a strategic factor of personalizing election campaigns on social media, not only on Twitter.

Summing up the following four main technological options based on Twitter's media logic and its underlying algorithms are open to the users:

1. addressing (@),
2. tagging (#),
3. linking (http://),
4. republishing (RT)

The image demonstrates the four functional *operators* (see Chapter 3 in this volume) in context of a tweet from the mini-public on #S21 (see below).

Figure 11.2 Tweet with four functional operators (mini-public #S21).

These four functional signifiers offer new opportunities for citizens to participate in political discourse via Twitter. The following *communicative functions* can be isolated:

- *Information distribution*: Sharing and distributing information, sometimes on the level of an "eye-witness medium"

The Mediatization of Politics and the Digital Public Sphere 177

- *Organizing*: Activating others (followers) to engage, sometimes in real life activities
- *(Re)Publishing:* Informing about events from other sources
- *Discussing:* Engaging in discussions with supporters or adversaries
- *Personal sharing*: Seeking comfort and support in case of tragedy
- *Group formation and maintenance*: Keeping in touch with members of the mini-public by social interaction

These diverse functions turn Twitter into a "discursive universe" (Thimm, Dang-Anh and Einspänner 2011). To show how in concrete political situations Twitter can serve as platform for mini-publics, two examples shall be given. Firstly, a case of an *ad-hoc and event instigated mini-public* (the explosion of the nuclear reactor in Fukushima) and secondly, the case an *over-time mini-public,* with a smaller audience group discussing a local political conflict. The cases illustrate the different dynamics, which constitute such mini-publics.

Mini-Publics on Twitter: the Cases of "Fukushima" and "S21" in German State Elections

The basis of analysis are tweets published by politicians, citizens and news media portals, which were collected during state elections in 2011 in the state of Baden-Württemberg, one the larger regions in southern Germany (11 million inhabitants). In this election the Green Party surprisingly won the election, which was even more sensational, as Baden-Württemberg is not only an industrial powerhouse with the car industry dominating the economy, but had also been ruled by a conservative majority for over fifty years. Since the election, and for the first time in its history, the state has had a green minister as its president. The case is, therefore, particularly interesting when trying to assess the impact of mini-publics on the logics of the political system. Two topics will be analyzed to show how differently mini-publics are being constituted, developed and maintained.

Shortly before the election in Baden-Württemberg in May 2011, the nuclear reactor in Fukushima exploded and resulted in millions of ad-hoc mini-publics worldwide. This *event-driven mini-public* was intensively publicized in Germany as well, as Germany has a long tradition of anti-nuclear protest. The second mini-public dealt with a local issue, an expensive construction project in the state capital of Stuttgart. This project, named "Stuttgart 21", or abbreviated as "S21", refers to a plan to put the main train station of the city underground, a project which had been contested due to its costs and destructive potential for the inner city for years. The group of citizens engaged in this conflict, undertook intensive activities in online media, but were also involved in fierce street battles with the police, which is rather unusual conduct for the southern German population. This mini-public is characterized by its local nature, a tight within-group organization and

178 Caja Thimm

the political backing of the Green Party, which was opposed to the project from the beginning (for details see Thimm and Bürger 2013).

The data for the study of state-focused mini-publics were collected in four state elections in the years 2010 and 2011 in order to differentiate, for comparative purposes, between local mini-publics on local issues with local protagonists on the one hand and state-wide formations on the other. The analysis is based on tweets posted by politicians (personal accounts selected candidates of each party), political parties (party accounts), citizens ('public sphere') and media accounts during in the time frame of three weeks before and one week after the election. The data can be summarized in the following table:

Table 11.1 Overview of collected Twitter data (German State Elections in 2011)

	North Rhine-Westphalia	*Baden-Wuerttemberg*	*Rhineland-Palatinate*	*Saxony-Anhalt*
	Election day: 9.5.2010	*Election day:* 27.3.2011	*Election day:* 27.3.2011	*Election day:* 20.3.2011
	Enquiry period: 18.4.-16.5.2010	*Enquiry period:* 6.3.-3.4.2011	*Enquiry period:* 6.3.-3.4.2011	*Enquiry period:* 27.2.-27.3.2011
Public Sphere	8,769	21,288	21,055	15,089
Politicians	3,080	981	1,610	1,833
Parties	1,316	1,829	1,682	1,109
Media	5,496	1,997	2,749	1,434
Total	18,661	26,095	27,096	19,465

The results show that Baden-Württemberg had at the time neither a very active digital public (citizens), nor very digitally engaged politicians. This is part due to the fact that Twitter only picked up a larger user group in the more recent election (see Einspänner-Pflock *et al.* in this volume).

The Twitter agenda in Baden-Württemberg will be assessed by *topic frequency count* in order to isolate the most important mini-publics. Regarding topic engagement, intensity and time (frequency over time), the hashtag analysis yielded the following results.

Whereas the high frequency of hashtags like #LTW11 or #LTWBW, which both refer to the German abbreviation for the election in question, is not surprising, the high number of references to "Fukushima", "Atom" and "S21" give a clear indication of political issues discussed at the time of the election. Comparing these hashtags over time, the following dynamics were found.

Comparing the three hashtag frequencies, two interesting dynamics can be observed. Whereas Fukushima was more important than "Atom" right after the accident, this changed toward election day (March 27, 2011). The participants lost interest in the event itself, while the underlying political

The Mediatization of Politics and the Digital Public Sphere 179

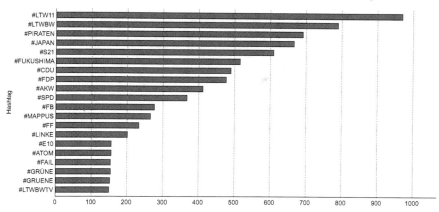

Figure 11.3 Topic intensity by hashtags in Baden-Württemberg's state election 2011.

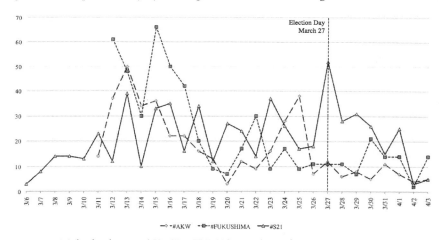

Figure 11.4 The hashtags "AKW", "FUKUSHIMA" and "S21" in comparison.

issue nuclear energy (#Atom) ranked highly. These dynamics demonstrate a typical event-driven ad-hoc mini-public: the more time passes the less participation it receives. The new mini-public, evolving out of the event-driven mini-public "Fukushima", is a much more political one with a topic of general interest for the election itself.

The dynamics of the mini-public on "#S21", the construction project, are quite different. From the level of frequency participation rates stay relatively balanced until election day itself: the high increase of tweets with the hashtag "S21" is a clear indication of an election-related campaign and a get-out-the-vote strategy with the protagonist calling their supporters to the urns.

11.4 Conclusion

The approach developed in this paper leads us to argue that the notion of fragmentation does not reflect the role of the net-based publics properly.

180 Caja Thimm

Instead, we need to regard the dynamics and value of the activities of interest groups and the ad-hoc formation of publics from a new perspective. Although the two examples described briefly in the chapters above only offer a first glimpse on the dynamics of these mini-publics, they underline the value of such polymediated activities. It is evident, however, that we need to know more about people's motivation, perception or interest for participation in these smaller circles to understand their value for the public sphere in general.

Mediatization of politics, it has been argued, is a process that is strongly determined by the social nature of the Internet. But when looking at mediatization as a meta-process, it needs to be made clear which elements of this process are having which kinds of effects on society as a whole. All signs indicate that due to its high complexity, the Internet is no longer merely a digital reflection of the real world. Online worlds are quickly developing their own rules of engagement that go above and beyond any in the real world. The Internet has become a mediatizator by its own right, enhancing social complexity and even putting our value system to a test. This is true for the public sphere as well, which is currently changing its nature, conditions and manifestations.

Note

1. Edited by Frank Esser and Jesper Strömbäck, *Mediatization of Politics*, published 2014 by Palgrave Macmillan. Reproduced with permission of Palgrave Macmillan.

Works Cited

Allard, Laurence, and Vandenberghe, Frédéric. 2003. "Express yourself! Les pages perso." *Réseaux*, 117(1):191–219.

Altheide, David, and Snow, Robert. 1979. *Media Logic*. Beverly Hills: Sage.

Anastasiadis, Mario and Caja Thimm (eds.). 2011. *Social Media: Theorie und Praxis digitaler Sozialität*. Frankfurt/New York: Lang.

Bächle, Thomas Christian, und Thimm, Caja (eds.). 2014. *Mobile Medien —Mobiles Leben. Neue Technologien, Mobilität und die mediatisierte Gesellschaft*. Münster: Lit.

Baym, Nancy. 2010. *Personal connections in the digital age*. Chichester: Polity Press.

Beck, Ulrich. 1997. *Was ist Globalisierung*. Frankfurt a. M.: Suhrkamp.

Bieber, Christoph, Härthe, Constantin, and Thimm, Caja. 2015. *Erregungskampagnen in Politik und Wirtschaft: Digitale Öffentlichkeit zwischen Shit- und Candystorms*. Schriftenreihe der Bonner Akademie für Forschung und Lehre praktischer Politik Bonn (BAPP). Bonn.

Bohman, James. 2004. "Expanding Dialogue: The Internet, the public sphere, and prospects for transnational democracy". *The Sociological Review* 52: 131–155.

Boyd, Danah, and Ellison, Nicole. 2007. "Social Network Sites: Definition, History, and Scholarship". *Journal of Computer-Mediated Communication*, 13:210–230.

Boyd, Danah, Golder, Scott, and Lotan, Gilad. 2010. "Tweet, Tweet, Retweet: Conversational Aspects of Retweeting on Twitter." *Proceedings of the Forty-Third*

The Mediatization of Politics and the Digital Public Sphere   181

Hawai'i International Conference on System Sciences. Accessed April 18, 2015. http://www.danah.org/papers/TweetTweetRetweet.pdf.

Breese, Elizabeth B. 2011. "Mapping the Variety of Public Spheres". *Communication Theory*, 21:130–149.

Bruns, Axel. 2008. *Blogs, Wikipedia, Second Life and Beyond: From Production to Produsage.* New York: Peter Lang.

Carpentier, Nico. 2011. "The concept of participation. If they have access and interact, do they really participate"? *Communication Management Quarterly* 21:13–36. Accessed April 18, 2015. http://www.costtransforming-audiences.eu/system/files/pub/CM21-SE-Web.pdf.

Carr, Nicholas G. 2010. *The Shallows: What the Internet is Doing to Our Brains.* New York: W. W. Norton & Company.

Castells, Manuel. 2005. "The Network Society: From Knowledge to Policy". In *The Network Society: From Knowledge to Policy,* edited by Manuel Castells and Gustavo Cardoso, 3–21. Washington, D.C.: John Hopkins University.

Castells, Manuel. 2008. "The New Public Sphere: Global Civil Society, Communication Networks, and Global Governance(s)" *Annals of the American Academy of Political and Social Science*, 616: 78–93.

Chayko, Mary. 2008. *Portable Communities. The Social Dynamics of Online and Mobile Connectedness.* Albany: State University of New York.

Christensen, Henrik S. 2011. "Political activities on the Internet: slacktivism or political participation by other means"? *First Monday* 16(2–7): February 2011.

Couldry, Nick. 2008. Mediatization or mediation? Alternative understandings of the emergent space of digital storytelling. *New Media and Society 10(3)*, 373–392.

Couldry, Nick, and Hepp, Andreas. 2013. "Conceptualizing Mediatization: Contexts, Traditions, Arguments". *Communication Theory* 23(3): 191–202.

Dahlberg, Lincoln. 2007. "The Internet, Deliberative Democracy, and Power: Radicalizing the Public Sphere". *International Journal of Media and Cultural Politics,* 3(1): 47–64.

Dahlgren, Peter. 2009. *Media and Political Engagement: Citizens, Communication, and Democracy.* Cambridge: Cambridge University Press.

Donk van de, Wim, Loader, Brian, Nixon, Paul, and Rucht, Dieter (eds.). 2005. *Cyberprotest: New Media, Citizens and Social Movements.* London: Routledge.

Downey, John and Fenton, Natalie. 2003. "New media, counter publicity and the public sphere". *New Media & Society*, 5(2): 185–202.

Einspänner-Pflock, Jessica, Dang-Anh, Mark, and Thimm, Caja (eds.). 2014. *Digitale Gesellschaft – Partizipationskulturen im Netz.* Berlin: Lit.

Frame, Alex, and Brachotte, Gilles. 2015. "Of 'Tweets', 'Twits' and 'Twats'. Use of Twitter by Leaders' Partners during Election Campaigns." In *Political Leadership in Western Democracies,* edited by Francois Vergniolle De Chantal and Agnès Alexandre-Collier. London: Palgrave Macmillan.

Goodin, Robert E., and Dryzek, John S. 2006. "Deliberative impacts: the macropolitical uptake of mini-publics." *Politics and Society,* 34: 219–244.

Gruzd, Anatoliy, and Wellman, Barry. 2014. "Networked Influence in Social Media: Introduction to the Special Issue". *American Behavioral Scientist, 58:* 1251–1259.

Habermas, Jürgen. 1989. *The Structural Transformation of the Public Sphere: An Inquiry Into a Category of Bourgeois Society.* Cambridge: Polity Press.

Hepp, Andreas, and Krotz, Friedrich (eds.). 2014. *Mediatized Worlds: Culture and Society in a Media Age.* London: Palgrave.

182 Caja Thimm

Hjarvard, Stig. 2008. "The Meditatization of Society. A Theory of the Media as Agents of Social and Cultural Chance". *Nordicom Review*, 29(2): 105–135.

Hjarvard, Stig. 2013. *The Mediatisation of Culture and Society*. London: Routledge.

Honeycutt, Courtenay, and Herring, Susan C. 2009. "Beyond Microblogging: Conversation and Collaboration via Twitter". *Proceedings of the Forty-Second Hawai'i International Conference on System Sciences*. Accessed April 18, 2015. http://ella.slis.indiana.edu/~herring/honeycutt.herring.2009.pdf.

Krotz, Friedrich. 2007. "The Meta-Process of mediatization as a Conceptual Frame". *Global Media and Communication* 3(3): 256–60.

Krotz, Friedrich. 2009. "Mediatization: A Concept With Which to Grasp Media and Societal Change". *Mediatization: Concept, Changes, Consequences*, edited by Knut Lundby, 19–38. New York: Peter Lang.

Lindgren, Simon, and Lundström, Ragnar. 2011. "Pirate culture and hacktivist mobilization: The cultural and social protocols of #WikiLeaks on Twitter". *New media and society*, 13(6): 999–1018.

Lundby, Knut (ed.). 2009. *Mediatization: Concept, Changes, Consequences*, New York, NY: Lang.

Lunt, Peter, and Livingstone, Sonia. 2013. "Media studies' fascination with the concept of the public sphere: critical reflections and emerging debates" *Media, Culture and Society*, 35(1): 87–96.

Madianou, Mirca, and Miller, Daniel. 2013. "Polymedia: Towards a new theory of digital media in interpersonal communication". *International Journal of Cultural Studies*, 16(2): 169–187.

Mercier, Arnaud. 2014. "Twitter l'actualité : usages et réseautage chez les journalistes français". *Recherches en communication*, 39: 111–132.

Mororov, Evgeny. 2011. *The net delusion. The Dark Side of Internet Freedom*. Philadelphia: Perseus Book.

Norris, Pippa. 2001. *Digital Divide: Civic Engagement, Information Poverty, and the Internet Worldwide*. Cambridge: University Press.

Papacharissi, Zizi, and De Fatima Oliveira, Maria. 2012. "Affective News and Networked Publics: The Rhythms of News Storytelling on #Egypt". *Journal of Communication*, Vol. 62: 266–282.

Pariser, Eli. 2011. *The Filter Bubble: What The Internet Is Hiding From You*. New York: The Penguin Press.

Rheingold, Howard. 2000. *The Virtual Community: Homesteading on the Electronic Frontier*. Cambridge, MA: MIT Press.

Sayre, Ben, Bode, Leticia, Shah, Dhavan, Wilcox, Dave, and Shah, Chirag. 2010. "Agenda Setting in a Digital Age: Tracking Attention to California Proposition 8 in Social Media, Online News, and Conventional News". *Policy & Internet*, 2(2): 7–32.

Shirky, Clay. 2011. "The Political Power of Social Media: Technology, the Public Sphere, and Political Change". *Foreign Affairs*, 90(1), 28–41.

Smith, Marc, Rainie, Lee, Himelboim, Itai, and Shneiderman, Ben. 2014. "Mapping Twitter Topic Networks: From Polarized Crowds to Community Clusters". PEW Internet Research online. Accessed April 7, 2015. h.ttp://www.pewInternet.org/files/2014/02/PIP_Mapping-Twitter-networks_022014.pdf

Strömbäck, Jesper. 2008. "Four Phases of Mediatization: An Analysis of the Mediatization of Politics". *The International Journal of Press/Politics*, 13(3): 228–246.

The Mediatization of Politics and the Digital Public Sphere   183

Strömbäck, Jesper, and Esser, Frank. 2014. "The mediatization of Politics: Towards a Theoretical Framework". In *Mediatization of Politics. Understanding the Transformation of Western Democracies,* edited by Jesper Strömbäck and Frank Esser, 3–29. Basingstoke: Palgrave.

Sunstein, Cass. 2001. *Echo Chambers: Bush v. Gore, Impeachment, and Beyond.* Princeton and Oxford, Princeton University Press.

Surowiecki, James. 2005. *The Wisdom of Crowds.* New York: Anchor.

Thimm, Caja. 2008. "Technically mediated interpersonal communication". In *Handbook of Interpersonal Communication,* edited by Gerd Antos and Ejia Ventula, 331–354. Berlin: De Guyter.

Thimm, Caja. 2012. "Political Conflict, Microblogging and the changing Role of the Citizens: Examples from Germany, Tunesia and China". *Proceeedings oft the 4th International Conference on Mobile Media for Development,* 388–398.

Thimm, Caja, and Bürger, Tobias. 2013. "Digitale Partizipation im politischen Kontext – 'Wutbürger' online". In *Liquid Democracy Digitale Politikvermittlung – Chancen und Risiken interaktiver Medien,* edited by Mike Friedrichsen and Roland A. Kohn, 255–272. Wiesbaden: VS.

Thimm, Caja, Dang-Anh, Mark, and Einspänner, Jessica. 2011. "Diskurssystem Twitter: Semiotische und handlungstheoretische Perspektiven". In *Social Media: Theorie und Praxis digitaler Sozialität,* edited by Mario Anastasiadis and Caja Thimm, 265–286. Frankfurt/New York: Lang.

Thimm, Caja, Dang-Anh, Mark, and Einspänner, Jessica. 2014. "Mediatized Politics – Structures and Strategies of Discursive Participation and Online Deliberation on Twitter". In *Mediatized Worlds: Culture and Society in a Media Age,* edited by Friedrich Krotz and Andreas Hepp, 253–269. Basingstoke: Palgrave Macmillian.

Tufekci, Zeynep, and Wilson, Christopher. 2012. "Social Media and the Decision to Participate in Political Protest: Observations From Tahrir Square". *Journal of Communication,* 62(2): 363–379.

Webster, James, and Ksiazek, Thomas. 2012. "The Dynamics of Audience Fragmentation: Public Attention in an Age of Digital Media". *Journal of Communication* 62(1): 39–56.

12 Alternative Media Spaces
The Case of Russian LGBT News Blogging Community

Evgeniya Boklage

Introduction

The decision of the Russian government to ban the so-called "propaganda of homosexuality" made headlines worldwide in 2013. The bill passed by the parliament prohibited "propaganda of sodomy, lesbianism, bisexualism and transgenderness among minors" (Wilkinson, 2013). In practice, this legal initiative, which was a consolidation of previous regional-level initiatives, criminalized any public expression of homosexuality and, therefore, proscribed public association and assembly for sexual minorities (Johnson, 2011).

Homosexuality was decriminalized in Russia in 1993. This was not, however, a deliberate step toward greater liberation of Russian society. No media coverage or public discussion followed this event. The annulment of anti-sodomy legislation was rather a compulsory measure for Russia to meet the minimum requirements for membership in the Council of Europe (Kon, 2009). After that, politicians have been trying to keep LGBT people within the confines of "zones of Internet and commerce" and away from the political debate (Healey, 2008: 175). In many ways, homosexuality in Russia remains marginalized and strongly embedded in the aura of depravity and illegality. Open public discourse of LGBT issues remains virtually inexistent, while "the silence and secrecy surrounding it for so long means that Russian has never developed a gay vocabulary" (Kondakov, 2013: para.15).

Furthermore, the political climate in Russia has changed considerably since the rise to power of Vladimir Putin in 2000. The new conservative developments have negatively influenced the Russian LGBT community. Homophobia and discrimination have been intensifying (Poushter, 2014). More deliberate attempts to restrain sexual minorities from entering the realm of public debate evolved in the "new politics of homophobia" (Healey, 2008: 175). Gays and lesbians started being portrayed in mainstream media as dangerous invaders aggressively trying to "LGBT-ize" the heterosexual majority (Lenskyj, 2014).

Today, the Russian LGBT community faces a number of challenges in regard to mainstream media coverage of its affairs. On the one hand, it has dealt with years of almost complete media invisibility, which helped to maintain the group's powerlessness and its position "at the bottom of the

Alternative Media Spaces 185

social heap" (Gross, 2001). On the other, there is a growing tendency in the mass media to demonize LGBT people as threatening the values of conservative morality and traditional family.

When achieving social visibility through mainstream media becomes a challenge for a minority group, its members can try to take control of communication streams by producing their own media (Rodriguez, 2001). The Internet and associated technologies can offer underrepresented groups alternative spaces of self-representation and at least some media visibility. This article argues that LGBT bloggers play an important role as alternative media producers in the Russian context. Grassroots bloggers can act as citizen journalists when they engage in the process of information gathering and dissemination. In this case they perform the function traditionally carried out by professional journalists and can become important news sources besides the mainstream media.

This paper is set to analyse the *AntiDogma* blogging community, which is an open media outlet with orientation toward dissemination of LGBT-related information. Anyone with a *LiveJournal (LJ)* account can post entries on the web page. The purpose of this study is to examine to what extent authors use the blog as a media outlet to report about current political and social events and what reporting practices and routines they employ. The research question is concerned with how the *AntiDogma* blogging community operates as an alternative news medium, alongside mainstream Russian media, trying to fill the gap in coverage of LGBT issues in the latter and provide its critique.

12.1 Citizen News Making

The advent of the Internet represents a critical point in the evolution of alternative media in general and citizen journalism in particular. Easy-to-use technology changed the previously existing relational dynamics between the news media and their audiences. The one-to-many way of communication characterized by a strict hierarchy and unidirectional information flow from media organizations to the citizens shifted towards a many-to-many mode of communication (Jensen & Helles, 2010: 2–4). This brought about a significant flattening of the communicative hierarchy, weakened the position of traditional media, and ended its complete monopoly on the production and propagation of news content.

Allan & Zelizer (2010: 18) defined citizen journalism as "a type of journalism in which ordinary citizens adopt the role of journalist in order to participate in news-making." This is the kind of journalism where amateurs rather than professionals play the central role. It gives the audience, equipped with mobile devices and Internet access, an opportunity to speak back to the media (Andén-Papadopoulos & Pantti, 2011). With little to no expenses other than their time, citizens can create their own media narratives.

186 *Evgeniya Boklage*

There are two interweaving tendencies which led to the emergence and strengthening of the phenomenon of citizen journalism. Socially, it is rooted in the need for the mass media to display greater sensitivity towards ordinary citizens and their problems (Kern & Nam, 2009: 639). Commercial mass media in the West spent the past few decades focusing on the maximization of profits, rather than trying to become more inclusive for the various social clusters. In their striving for an ever larger audience, mass media succumbs to bad news, scandals, and sensationalism causing disappointment and cynicism on the part of the citizens (Newton, 1999: 577). Deregulation of the media industry led to the concentration of ownership, cross-ownership and control by non-media companies (Herman & Chomsky, 1988). As a result, citizens were left feeling alienated from media institutions.

Another was a technological tendency of proliferation of digital gadgets and Internet access which reinforced citizen journalism (Bai, 2007: 133). Communicative infrastructure in which ordinary citizens can act as media reporters was described by Castells (2004: 3) with the term *network society*, "whose social structure is made of networks powered by microelectronics-based information and communication technologies". The emergence of the networked society changed the previously existing institutional power relations. Together with an opportunity for mass self-communication, social actors gained capacity to challenge institutionalized power relations (Castells, 2007). In the context of the relationship between mass media organizations and their audiences, it means that the former lose their exclusive control over the means for news dissemination. Neither can they any longer make unanimous decisions about the interpretational context of the events and the construction of social meaning.

Citizen journalists challenged the mass media function of gate-keeping defined as "selecting, writing, editing, positioning, scheduling, repeating and otherwise massaging information to become news" (Shoemaker et al, 2008: 73). The function of gate-keeping was a way for professional reporters to filter information and influence the construction of society's knowledge about the world. With the loss of a monopoly on news-making, news media have shifted from the process of gate-keeping towards gate-watching (Bruns, 2005). In the environment where information is neither scarce nor hard to produce and publish (Lewis et al., 2010), gate-watching is not concerned with deciding on the issues that can enter the mediascape, but rather with navigating the stream which is now beyond direct control of professionals.

The growing number of media producers has led to the increase in diversity of the media content, which is crucial in terms of the representation of a heterogeneous society. Citizen journalists are engaged in a range of practices which encompass news blogging, photo and video sharing, posting eye-witness commentary as well as reposting, tagging, "liking", rating, adapting and commenting on professional news content (Goode, 2009: 1288). They have been particularly instrumental in expanding representations of various social groups worldwide. Their work has targeted a vast selection of issues from local community problems to community emancipation and empowerment to coverage of military conflicts (Rodriguez, 2001; Hamdy, 2010). Citizen journalists in some cases offered greater news content diversity than mainstream media (Carpenter, 2010). In doing so, they helped to close the gaps left by the traditional media institutions whose content tends to target a large homogeneous audience and is embedded in grand meta-narratives socially and politically.

12.2 Russian Blogosphere

The Russian blogosphere emerged in the context of increasingly restricted system of mass media which resulted from the intensifying authoritarian tendencies. Today, state-controlled television channels remain the main source of news and entertainment for 73 per cent of the Russian population (Orttung & Walker, 2013). Yet, freedom of expression in the mass media has been compromised by a variety of measures. To prevent criticism, the Kremlin will resort to anything "from energy-sapping charges of defamation and checks for 'extremism' to the newly reinstated article of the Criminal Code on defamation, which attracts astronomical fines" (Arapova, 2012: para. 3). There is also a complex system of informal media regulations in place, such as recommendations and curatorship coming from public officials (Arutunyan, 2009; Mayr et al., 2012).

At the same time, the internet has been the fastest-growing branch of the Russian media system over the past decade. While only about 8 per cent of the population went online from time to time in 2003, ten years later this figure crossed the 60 per cent threshold with people going online for a variety of purposes including news, entertainment and communication with friends (Volkov, 2012). In a country where mass media discourse is determined by the political elite while the Internet remains relatively unrestricted, it is inevitable that the blogosphere be utilized as a venue for debate and criticism focusing on burning political and social issues. The study by Etling et al. (2010) found a dynamic blogosphere on the Russian internet. Russian-speaking people write and read some 65 million blogs on a variety of subjects including domestic and international politics (Koltsova & Koltcov, 2013).

It was observed that increased blogging activity – writing and sharing political posts – has had its effects reaching outside the realm of online communication (Koltsova & Shcherbak, 2013). This was exemplified by the role of political blogs, along with social networking sites, as viable political agents during the public protests following parliamentary and presidential elections in 2011–12 (Popkova, 2014). The blogosphere became the only available space for political self-expression where citizens would come together to create a "self-generated public opinion" (Koltsova & Koltcov, 2013: 207).

188 *Evgeniya Boklage*

Etling et al. (2010) argued that there are certain unique features particular to the Russian blogosphere. It is highly segmented and has a hyperactive core of bloggers mostly within *LiveJournal*, which constitutes a central hub for online activism and political and social discussions (Etling et al., 2010; Alexanyan & Koltsova, 2009). The bloggers within the core appear to be less isolated into "echo-chambers", less ideologically clustered, and less polarized along the liberal-conservative axis compared to the U.S. blogosphere (Adamic & Glance, 2005). Instead, Russian bloggers demonstrated an inclination toward "independent intellectual postures" and abstained from a distinct group affiliation (Etling et al., 2010: 19).

On a less optimistic note, Rohozinski (1999) maintained that adoption of new communication technologies would inevitably be guided by the existing social and cultural norms of a given society, rather than transform it unilaterally towards a more open and democratic political system. Similarly, Gorny (2009: 8) has written about the Russian blogosphere that it "reproduces the fundamental structural features of the Russian society, such as social atomization, negative attitudes to official institutions (and, more generally, to any 'Other') and a strong dependence on personal networks as a source of information, opinion and support". The study by Fotasso et al. (2008) regarded it as an unlikely event that bloggers could be significant actors of social change. Opposing the Western rhetoric of the web as an instrument of democratization, it claimed the web was more likely to attune itself to the existing political norms. Although the study emphasized the web's role in the dissemination of political information, it was not found to be a mobilizing force for broad masses and those involved in online activism were "mainly closed clusters of like-minded users who only on rare occasions are able to and willing to cooperate with other groups" (ibid: 53). Similarly, Kyria (2013) claimed that in the Russian context, the system of entanglement between online media, such as blogs and social networks, and traditional media creates a situation of isolation, marginalization and polarization of oppositional groups, which prevents them from achieving meaningful political goals.

12.3 Citizen News-Making in *Antidogma* Blogging Community

This paper turns now to an exploration of the LiveJournal-based blogging community called *AntiDogma*. The case study is based on an in-depth reading of 212 selected entries from *AntiDogma* blog and their 2,203 comments. It used the theoretical sample proposed by Altheide & Schneider (2013: 55), which means that the data-gathering procedure starts with an initial inspection of available material and the researcher moves step by step, delineating the spectrum of relevant data with a certain degree of flexibility.

Alternative Media Spaces 189

Data gathering for this study started with an overview of the *AntiDogma* blog and its contents. The data analysis was conducted in early 2014 when the blogging community active for nearly seven years and contained 7,322 journal entries, which had received 180,261 user comments. From this number, a smaller primary sample of 212 blog entries together with their comments (2,203) was selected for closer qualitative analysis on the level of individual blog entries and reader commentaries. These were all the posts which appeared in four fifteen-day periods. Two of these periods were chosen intentionally: February 29 – March 14, 2012 were approximately two weeks surrounding the passing of "homosexual propaganda" law in Saint Petersburg; June 23 – July 7, 2013 were the days near the time President Putin signed the nationwide ban. Two further periods, January 8 – January 22, 2013 and August 20 – September 3, 2013, were picked randomly. In addition, following the principle of theoretical sampling, the study examined materials linked to by bloggers, when considered necessary. For instance, outbound links to Facebook or VK groups, mainstream media, other blog posts and so forth were surveyed. The meta-data about the community was collected from the archive page, profile and organizational documents that appeared as blog entries at various moments during community's life span.

The overall method of this study lies along the lines of qualitative content analysis, discourse analysis, and social constructivism (Berger & Luckmann, 1971; Fairclough, 2003; Mayring, 2004). The main purpose is to analyse the available texts in order to offer a detailed account of news blogging practices as presented in the blog's content.

AntiDogma describes itself as "*[t]he largest in ZheZhe* [Russian for equivalent for "*LJ*"] *independent community of LGBT (lesbians, gays, bisexuals, transgenders* [sic]) *and their friends*" and displays no formal ties to any official organization, thus emphasizing its grassroots, bottom-up structure. In February 2014, it totalled 2,532 members (number of users eligible to post blog entries and see protected posts) and was watched by 3,178 *LJ* users. These are two overlapping groups, meaning the members are also listed as watchers. In order to become a member, one has to have an *LJ* account and send a request to join the community. The first blog entry – its mission statement – was posted in April 2006 by one of its moderators. The number of entries totalled 180,261 in early 2014. The blog posts are publicly accessible with or without an *LJ* account.

The community's mission statement expresses its ideological orientation as a news-producing and disseminating community. *AntiDogma* states its main goals to be delivery of "information, analysis, overview, and insight" and clearly steers away from being an outlet for publishing fiction or poetry, visual artwork or religious commentary unrelated to the LGBT advocacy. Thus, it situates itself on a level with professional news media, whose main objective is to deliver relevant, factual rather than fictional, noteworthy information.

190 *Evgeniya Boklage*

Alternative News and Agendas

Broadly defined, alternative news is information about current affairs which comes from channels other than mainstream media. In this sense, the Russian blogosphere is a critical source of alternative news, for the news makes up around 25 to 30 per cent of all content in the form of blog posts, reposts, and comments of other media material (Pankin et al., 2011).

Alternative news media is expected to oppose traditional mass media in terms of its agenda, content and editorial approach (Joye, 2010). How a media outlet is organized, and in particular how editorial decisions are made, is one of the ways to separate alternative from mainstream. In this sense, *AntiDogma* blog is self-organized, lacks a clear hierarchy of editors and completely relies on the contributions from citizen bloggers for its content. Due to the policy of post-publication moderation – all blog entries are published immediately and evaluated by the moderators later – the authors of *AntiDogma* enjoy a high degree of autonomy. In practice, any news content can be made instantly available to the few-thousand-large blog audience.

The community rules stressed the production of alternative news as one of the blog's main objectives. Suitable content is described as

> news, which for one reason or another went unnoticed but nonetheless is important (especially in regard to photographic reports from the scene and eyewitness reports).

This statement articulates the challenge to mass media that they are insufficient in their representation of LGBT issues. But it also claims to set the news agenda, focusing on the events which have been omitted in the mainstream news.

One such example was *AntiDogma*'s coverage of a gruesomely violent homophobic murder which went remarkably unnoticed in most mass media outlets. A blog post from November 26, 2013 reported a development in the case which happened in Russia earlier that year. The murder of a 23 year-old occurred during a drunken brawl, after a young man allegedly confessed his homosexuality to his companions:

> Yesterday in Volgograd Regional Court started a trial of Vlad Tornovoy case, who was murdered on homophobia grounds, regardless of whether he was gay or not. In the news – not a word ... ACTIVISTS IN VOLGOGRAD, I REALLY HOPE IT WILL BE POSSIBLE TO SHAKE SOMEONE UP TO GO THERE. WON'T LET THEM DOWNPLAY THIS AS BITOVUHA.[1]

The author expressly blamed the mainstream news media for failing to pay attention to the growing social problem of homophobic crime. He pointed to further damage done by mass media: influenced by the official political agenda which perpetuates the invisibility of LGBT community, mass media

Alternative Media Spaces 191

framed the case as a random act of violence, unrelated to the widespread homophobic attitudes in the general Russian population.

This post exhibited another evident tendency that, for many *AntiDogma* authors, the body of work in blogging is determined by their experiences of balancing media work and real-life activism. Many of them are active in the public protest scene and feel like their stories must be a part of news discourse. They pick up where the mainstream media stop, in order to deepen coverage by providing different angles and mobilizing information about events (Atton, 2002). This study has found that the community has extensively reported activist events. The most popular type of activist news was the coverage of public demonstrations, when the texts were supplemented with the photographs. Other posts provided additional details and follow-up information, which could be relevant for the LGBT movement. For instance, a blog entry from June 29, 2013 covered a pride event to support sexual minorities' rights, that took place in St. Petersburg:

> The participants of the fourth St. Petersburg pride – APPROVED and LEGITIMATE action on Marsovo Polye for protection of LGBT from persecution, were arrested today, the organizer Yury Gavrikov is still held by the police.

It continued by describing other uninvited but not unexpected attendees of the event – the opponents of LGBT activists from the ranks of religious activists, alleged nationalists and Cossacks, Russia's conservative minority – followed by an account of police brutality. The report, for the most part, was written in dispassionate language, and it remained unclear whether the author was an active participant, an eyewitness, or whether information was gathered from the participants. At one point the author reported that

> people were literally pushed out of the square which had been especially allocated in advance, and squeezed into buses.

After that, the blogger provided three links, one to the website of a mainstream newspaper, and two to *YouTube* videos filmed at the scene.

This blog entry can be contrasted with the news piece of the mainstream outlet found under a web link provided by the blogger. The brief, mainstream article stated in a manner similar to a police report that "*3 LGBT activists were arrested*". The blogging piece instead offered a more personal account of the events by giving the names of the arrested activists. In this way, for a blogger, the audience is not just an anonymous group of people who are given some news facts. The readers are perceived as a community who share not only experiences but also concerns. It implies that they not only care about the activists being arrested, but also about who these people are. The blogger thus performed the double function of being a news provider and an active community-builder. In general, such functional convergence was

192 *Evgeniya Boklage*

a common feature found in the blog entries. Often, the news posts incorporated the elements of commentary, opinion, calls for discussion, community building and activism.

News Commentary

News commentary from the beginning has been a central practice in the blogosphere and it contributes a significant proportion of blog content (Reese et al., 2007). Bloggers routinely repost materials found in the mainstream media which they incorporate with blog commentary (McKenna & Pole, 2008; Woodly, 2008; Vraga et al., 2011). For many bloggers who write in their spare time and without financial compensation, the mainstream media remains the predominant source for original news content. There are situations where citizens can gain access to public events and become reporters, such as in the case of activist rallies or public protests, but they are still limited in terms of the access they have to institutional politics. It means that most bloggers will get their information about economic and political elites from the professional news organizations (Bruns, 2007).

This tendency to rely on traditional media was also found in the news content of *AntiDogma*. A large proportion of analysed content did not feature original reporting, but "recycled" the relevant news published in the mass media resources. Yet, indiscriminate copying of materials was rare and most, if not all, of the reposted content was expanded on with the blogger's commentary. The importance of providing commentary was also mentioned in the community rules, which stated that:

> [T]he project does not have a purpose of becoming a "twin-brother" for other news websites by blindly circulating their materials. However, if it seems to you that news or an article are especially interesting for community members and can lead to lively opinion exchange – make a brief announcement with a link to the original source, and necessarily provide your own opinion on the topic.

The recommendation acknowledges the dependency of *AntiDogma* bloggers on mainstream media for information, while highlighting the power struggle between the alternative and traditional news. Media organizations control the means of information and communication, which gives them symbolic power – the "capacity to intervene in the course of events, to influence the actions of others and indeed to create events" (Thompson, 1995: 17). They can easily dominate public discourse to the point where represented social groups have little say over their media image. Nevertheless, the dynamics of these power relations are complex and versatile and "resistance remains always a possibility, even against hegemonic articulations" (Carpentier, 2011: 146). News commentary on the blog becomes the tactic of resistance and direct challenge to the hegemonic communication of the mainstream media.

Alternative Media Spaces 193

The following analysis is based on two examples of the way bloggers interacted with mass media content by providing critical commentary. In July 2013, one blogger reposted the news from a mainstream source about the investigation by Pavel Astakhov – Russia's Children's Rights Commissioner – of the case of an American gay couple who sexually abused a child born from a Russian surrogate. Astakhov, already previously known in Russia as a celebrity lawyer, gained international publicity after he proposed a ban on foreign adoption of Russian children, proclaiming frequent abuse and murders as the main reason for such a measure (Herszenhorn, 2013). He has been criticized by bloggers and public commentators for being a publicity seeker who incites panic while ignoring the needs and safety concerns of Russian orphans inside Russia. The blogger on *AntiDogma* commented on the article:

> Amazingly hypocritical bastard. This is dismaying, of course. The most revolting is that in Russia, it seems, no efforts are being made to shed light on cases of violence against children. The most abominable, beyond anything human, cases about which I read all appear in the local crime sections [of newspapers].

The comment criticized the bias in both the work of ombudsman Astakhov and in its coverage by mainstream news outlets. It moved from the particular case reported in the article to focus on the broader social matter: that the government tried to score political points internationally (the ban on adoption came immediately after the United States signed the Magnitsky Act[2]) while completely disregarding the real problems inside Russia. Moving from a specific case toward more general issues, the blogger opened up "focal points of broader political discussion" (Xenos, 2008: 487), debating the welfare of children inside Russia and pointing to how little attention is being paid to a profound social problem by mainstream media. The author argued that official news failed to systematically scrutinize the issue and downplayed it from a clear social pathology to the level of random crime reports. In effect, it also challenged the effort in the mass media to relate crimes against children to the LGBT community and to polarize public opinion by promoting negative stereotypes about LGBT people, which is characteristic of the Russian mass media at large (Umland, 2012).

The second example of bloggers' interaction with the mass media material shows their concern with the lack of LGBT voices in it, even in instances when they provide positive overall coverage of the community. One post offered a direct critique of professional media, which routinely exclude LGBT representatives from media discourse. In March 2012, the blog entry *"Material about homophobic law in Afisha[3]"* was posted. It linked to an article that examined the possible consequences of the St. Petersburg "gay propaganda" law on the city's cultural landscape. The material in Afisha asked whether it would jeopardize the upcoming concert of German music

194   Evgeniya Boklage

band *Rammstein* and inquired few public figures to comment on it. The blogger offered his reading of the article and the following critique:

> On the website of "Afisha" they put material about homophobic law. I liked the statement by Shklowsky. But it is anyway striking how the journalists manage to interrogate the "experts" on the matter, graciously forgetting about any representatives of LGBT. In general, the article is positive, but very much "Afisha" style. In short, [it is written] so that hipsters don't get bored.

This is an account of the obvious disappointment the blogger felt about the editorial bias, and how the LGBT community was deliberately deprived of the possibility to speak for itself. Decades ago, Robert Giles expressed the same concern in the context of the United States saying that: "no voice is regularly heard that looks at life from a gay perspective" (quoted in Alwood, 1996: 304). The author of the post could not intervene with the *Afisha's* editorial process and confront the representation he felt dissatisfied with. Moreover, a web page with the original article did not feature a commentary section for the readers. Thus, the blogger reposted the news and turned passive reading into an act of opinion expression. He publicly articulated his awareness of the bias and, using the blog's own reader comment function, challenged it in a dialogical manner together with other users.

Networked Newsgathering

Social networks dramatically transform the news gathering practices of professional journalists (Bruno, 2011). Professional journalists use social media for sourcing increasingly often (Broersma & Graham, 2013; Kristensen & Mortensen, 2013). Given the lack of resources available to the media organizations, citizen bloggers can also benefit from the networked communities as information sources. They bring together large numbers of people, all of whom can share what they know, see and record.

Many posts from the *AntiDogma* blog show how the networked structure of *LJ* helps to assemble information which would otherwise never reach the public. As in the case of the murder of Vlad Tornovoy, the information about the trial featured in a personal *LJ* diary of a freelance journalist who had made contact with the press service of the Volgograd Regional Court. Moreover, in the conversation on the comment board, the author said that the service "*didn't even know about it* [the date of the hearing], *they checked their database ...*" Although the news still did not appear in the mainstream media, it was disseminated in the blogosphere and published on *AntiDogma*.

While the citizen bloggers have little access to institutional media or the political elite, they can take advantage of the online technologies available to them. Concerning such practices Castells (2009: 65) contended that "as people [...] have appropriated new forms of communication, they have built

Alternative Media Spaces 195

their own systems of mass communication." In the case of *AntiDogma*, bloggers were found to make use of online social networks to gather information which was later shared with the readers. The social-networking websites *VK* and *Facebook* acted as rich, even if imperfect, information sources about people, communities and events. One such instance was found when bloggers used the pages of the Russian social network *VK* to gather information about homophobic groups in Russia in order to publicize their mostly delinquent activities against LGBT people.

In 2013, two related grassroots groups derived from the Russian skinhead movement, *Okkupay Pedofiliay* and *Okkupay Gerontofiliay*. While claiming to fight "against paedophiles and perverts", in practice, both are vicious groups that target LGBT people. One usual tactic of *Okkupay Pedofiliay* is to engage in an online conversation with unsuspecting users posing as teenagers, usually as sixteen-year-old young men, and arrange a meeting during which the victims, deemed paedophiles by the *Okkupay*-ers, are brutally beaten and degraded while the act is being filmed on mobile camera. The final measure is publishing the video on the *VK* group's page, to prompt stigmatization and further bullying of the attacked. In the second case of *Okkupay Gerontofiliay*, the victims were usually gay youngsters who were similarly approached on the Internet and promised a financial reward for sexual services. The police were astonishingly reluctant to start criminal investigations of the numerous chapters of the movements throughout the country, and the mainstream media was for the most part silent on the issue (Turovsky, 2013).

Close reading of *AntiDogma* entries found a strong interest on the part of community members in this movement. Many blog posts were discovered in which the authors have written about attacks on LGBT people by morally and physically abusive *Okkupay* activists. Reporting on this subject also illustrated how bloggers engage in a kind-of investigative work by means of social-networking sites.

The blog post from 21 August, 2013 named "*New attacks on gay teenagers. Gerontofiliay in Irkutsk*" chronicled the actions of seven *Okkupay Gerontofiliay* activists who abused an eighteen-year-old gay teenager. The entirety of the blog post was based on information the author sourced from the group's *VK* page. She provided a *VK* video and a transcript of the conversation between the abusers and their victim. In anticipation that the video might be taken down from the social network, the author gave a *YouTube* link to a copy of the video saying: "*if these monsters will try to delete the proof, the video is copied* here". Below the transcript, the author gave a list of attackers with their names and links to *VK* profiles against each name. The collection of photographs of abusers was posted in which the blogger identified each youngster by their name and indicated whether the person "*took part in harassment*".

On the one hand, the diversity of content gathered by the blogger – personal information, photo and video content – was astonishing and

196   *Evgeniya Boklage*

showed the richness of social networks in the information they can provide, which is easily available to anyone with the *VK* account. The entire blog article was based on content from the social network.

On the other hand, this points to one of the central ethical issues which arise within the personalized communicative space of social media, namely the question of user privacy. Many users of social networking sites are unaware about their degree of visibility to others, for the internet "places private information about private people into the public view" (Whitehouse, 2010: 322). In the given example, the perpetrators were visibly minors, fourteen- to fifteen-year-old teenagers. Potentially harmful information about them (association with neo-nazi organization, involvement in violent acts) could have long-standing negative consequences. Similarly, the video depicting the victim of the attack was copied and further publicized. The fact that it was being proliferated in the blogosphere without concern for the privacy of all those involved in the event indicated that citizen bloggers could be driven by passion and the sense of rage in their reporting rather than ethical values. In a way, the blogger has done the same thing as the young hooligans did to their victims: it was an act of public shaming. The rage can be explained by the sense of lawlessness in the face of authorities staying passive, which results in mob justice. The ethical question, therefore, remains: "Does the value of information gained outweigh the harm done to the individual's sense of privacy [and] the public understanding of privacy ..." (Whitehouse, 2010: 320).

12.4 Conclusion

This chapter examined the news blogging practices of *AntiDogma* blogging community. The literature has pointed to the fact that Russia's mainstream media has become increasingly restrained and fails to provide adequate coverage of various social issues and groups. In the atmosphere of growing homophobia supported by the official ban on the "propaganda of homosexuality", this especially concerns the Russian LGBT community. The absence of LGBT topics in the news is detrimental to the community by keeping it socially invisible. It means that abuses of the rights of LGBT people, be it on the individual level of discrimination and hate crimes or on the higher level of anti-gay legislation, go largely unnoticed by the general population. In such a situation, grassroots online media becomes a vehicle for public discourse and an alternative news outlet that offers a selection of topics, either ignored by the mass media or offered negative coverage that intensifies stigmatization of sexual minorities.

The mission statement describes *AntiDogma* as an information outlet set to provide LGBT-related news, among other things. The news media work of bloggers consists of focusing on relevant events that were omitted by the mainstream media and filling the information gap that would otherwise lead to LGBT citizens remaining invisible. Bloggers challenge their hegemony, which consists in stereotyping and demonizing sexual minorities. The most straightforward way to contest the hegemony of mass media is to engage in a public critique of their professional integrity. *AntiDogma* bloggers have offered public commentary of mass media work and addressed specific examples of media content, e.g., television programs or newspaper articles, which were either deficient or damaging to the image of LGBT people.

Another solution is to reject grand meta-narratives used to authorize and legitimize traditional beliefs and institutions, usually promoted by the mass media. *AntiDogma* authors accomplish this by engaging in postmodern journalistic practices that concentrate on personal stories written in less formal language. Bloggers' experiences take central place in the news coverage, as the boundary between reporting subjects and objects gets blurred. Many *AntiDogma* bloggers were found to report the events in which they were active participants. For instance, in cases of protests and rallies, writing a news piece about the event was often a part of an activist project: the author would help to organize it, participate in it, and finally write a report for a blog.

However, a complete break from meta-narratives and the media organizations that convey them was not possible, in particular due to the remaining dependency of citizen bloggers on mass media content. The *AntiDogma* regulations reinforce these meta-narratives as they apply the traditional criterium of trustworthiness based on the outlets' reputation: prospective *AntiDogma* bloggers are instructed to link to "*reliable*" media outlets.

Lacking the resources available to the professional media, citizen bloggers were found to make use of networking tools, by exploiting the vast wealth of information they provide. Online social networks offer information about events and individuals, which is easily accessible to any Internet user and which bloggers can use as sources in their posts. Whereas the practice facilitates the work of citizen bloggers, it also prompts the question about the ethics of amateur reporters. Many private details become publicly available on social networking sites, and users may have little awareness of just how much personal information they disclose. Without editorial control and professional ethical guidelines, bloggers can engage in controversial newsgathering practices that not only yield unverified information but also pose threats to the privacy of users.

Finally, it is important to point out that the media work of *AntiDogma* blogging community is defined by its grassroots character and lack of formal organization. The advantage of the considerable degree of autonomy enjoyed by its authors is counterbalanced by insufficient editorial control guided by professional journalistic values. As a result, the contribution of this media project must be seen as emergent through collectively practiced random acts of journalism rather than an outcome of consistent activist endeavours.

198 Evgeniya Boklage

Notes

1. *Bitovuha* (Rus.) is slang for violent crimes (battery, murder) happen which in a private setting between family, friends or acquaintances. Can be vaguely translated as domestic abuse, but it also covers cases when people involved are not family or intimately related. The connotation often implies that alcohol consumption was among the triggering factors for a brawl which ended in violence.
2. The Magnitsky Act sanctioned a number of Russian officials as punishment for human rights violations in Russia.
3. Afisha is a fortnightly Moscow entertainment magazine.

Works Cited

Adamic, Lada, and Glance, Natalie. 2005. "The political blogosphere and the 2004 U.S. election: divided they blog". Accessed January 15, 2014. http://scedu.unibo.it/roversi/SocioNet/AdamicGlanceBlogWWW.pdf.

Alexanyan, Karina, and Koltsova, Olessia. 2009. "Blogging in Russia is not Russian blogging". In *International blogging: Identity, politics, and networked publics*, edited by Adrienne Russel and Nabil Echchaibi. New York: Peter Lang.

Altheide, David, and Schneider, Christopher. 2013. *Qualitative media analysis*. Thousand Oaks, CA: Sage Publications.

Alwood, Edward. 1996. *Straight news: Gays, lesbians, and the news media*. New York, NY: Columbia University Press.

Arapova, Galina. "Media freedom in Russian regions? You must be joking …". *OpenDemocracy*, August 23, 2012, accessed February 10, 2014. http://opendemocracy.net/od-russia/galina-arapova/media-freedom-in-russian-regions-you-must-be-joking%E2%80%A6.

Arutunyan, Anna. 2009. *The media in Russia*. Berkshire, UK: Open University Press.

Atton, Chris. 2002. *Alternative media*. London: Sage Publications.

Bai, Matt. 2007. The argument: Billionaires, bloggers, and the battle to remake democratic politics. New York, NY: The Penguin Press.

Berger, Peter, and Luckmann, Thomas. 1971. The social construction of reality: A treatise in the sociology of knowledge. Harmondsworth, UK: Penguin.

Broersma, Marcel, and Graham, Todd. 2013. "Twitter as a news source: How Dutch and British newspapers used tweets in their news coverage, 2007–2011". *Journalism Practice*, 7(4): 446–464.

Bruno, Nicola. 2011. "Tweet first, verify later? How real-time information is changing the coverage of worldwide crisis events". Research paper, Reuters Institute Fellowship, University of Oxford, accessed January 20, 2014. https://reutersinstitute.politics.ox.ac.uk/fileadmin/documents/Publications/fellows__papers/2010-2011/TWEET_FIRST_VERIFY_LATER.pdf.

Bruns, Axel. 2005. *Gatewatching: Collaborative online news production*. New York, NY: Peter Lang Publishing.

Bruns, Axel. 2006. "The practice of news blogging". In *Uses of Blogs*, edited by Axel Bruns and Joanne Jacobs. New York: Peter Lang.

Cammaerts, Bart. 2011. "Mediation and resistance". In *Critical perspectives on the European mediasphere*, edited by Ilija Tomanić Trivundža, Nico Carpentier, Hannu Nieminen, Pille Pruulmann-Vengerfeldt, Richard Kilborn, Tobias Olsson and Ebba Sundin. Ljubljana: Faculty of Social Sciences: Založba FDV.

Carpentier, Serena. 2010. "A study of content diversity in online citizen journalism and online newspaper articles". *New Media & Society,* 12(7): 1064–1084.

Castells, Manuel. 2004. "Informationalism, networks, and the network society: a theoretical blueprint". In *The network society: A cross-cultural perspective,* edited by Manuel Castells. Northampton, MA: Edward Elgar.

Castells, Manuel. 2007. "Communication, power and counter-power in the networked society". *International Journal of Communication,* 1: 238–66.

Castells, Manuel. 2009. *Communication power.* New York, NY: Oxford University Press.

Etling, Bruce, Alexanyan, Karina, Kelly, John, Faris, Robert, Palfrey, John, and Gasser, Urs. 2010. "Public discourse in the Russian blogosphere: Mapping RuNet politics and mobilization". Berkman Center Research Publication 2010–11, accessed January 10, 2014. http://cyber.law.harvard.edu/sites/cyber.law. harvard. edu/files/Public_Discourse_in_the_Russian_Blogosphere_2010.pdf.

Fairclough, Norman. 2003. Analysing discourse: Textual analysis for social research. London: Routledge.

Fotasso, Floriana, Lloyd, John, and Verkhovsky, Alexander. 2008. "The web that failed: How opposition politics and independent initiatives are failing on the internet in Russia". Paper by Reuters Institute for the Study of Journalism, accessed January 20, 2014. http://reutersinstitute.politics.ox.ac.uk/fileadmin/documents/Publications/The_Web_that_Failed.pdf.

Goode, Luke. 2009. "Social news, citizen journalism and democracy". *New Media & Society,* 11(8): 1287–1305.

Gorny, Evgeny. 2009. "Understanding the real impact of Russian blogs". *Russian Analytical Digest* 69: 8–11.

Gross, Larry. 2001. *Up from visibility.* New York, NY: Columbia University Press.

Hamdy, Naila. 2010. "Arab media adopt citizen journalism to change the dynamics of conflict coverage". *Global Media Journal Arabian Edition,* 1(1): 3–15.

Healey, Dan. 2008. "'Untraditional sex' and the 'simple Russian': Nostalgia for Soviet innocence in the polemics of Dilia Enikeeva". In *What is Soviet now? Identities, legacies, memories,* edited by Thomas Lahusen and Peter Solomon Jr. Berlin: LIT Verlag.

Herman, Edward, and Chomsky, Noam. 1988. *Manufacturing consent: The political economy of the mass media.* New York, NY: Pantheon Books.

Herszenhorn, David. "Russia backs off claim of murder in death of adopted boy in Texas". *The New York Times,* February 21, 2013, accessed February 10, 2014. http://nytimes.com/2013/02/22/world/europe/russia-backs-off-claim-of-murder-in-death-of-adopted-boy-in-texas.html?_r=0.

Jensen, Klaus, and Helles, Rasmus. 2011. "The internet as a cultural forum: implications for research". *New Media & Society,* 13(4): 517–533.

Johnson, Paul. "Russian ban on propaganda violates human rights". *Jurist,* December 1, 2011, accessed February 12, 2014. http://jurist.org/hotline/2011/12/paul-johnson-russia-lgbt.php.

Joye, Stijn. 2010. "Reflections on Inter Press Service: Evaluating the importance of an alternative news voice". *Global Media and Communication,* 6(1): 121–25.

Kern, Thomas, and Nam, Sang-hui. 2009. "The making of a social movement: Citizen journalism in South Korea". *Current Sociology* 57(5): 637–660.

Koltsova, Olessia, and Koltcov, Sergei. 2013. "Mapping the public agenda with topic modeling: The case of the Russian LiveJournal". *Policy & Internet* 5(2): 207–227.

200 Evgeniya Boklage

Koltsova, Olessia, and Shcherbak, Andrey. 2013. "'LiveJournal Libra!' The influence of the political blogosphere on political mobilisation in Russia in 2011–12". Working paper, accessed January 28, 2014. http://hse.ru/data/2013/10/03/1277867593/LJ%20Libra%20site.pdf.

Kon, Igor. 2009. "Homophobia as a litmus test of Russian democracy". *Sociological Research* 48(2): 43–64.

Kondakov, Alexander. "Do Russians give a damn about homosexuality"? *Open Democracy*, June 20, 2013, accessed January 14, 2012. http://opendemocracy.net/od-russia/alexander-kondakov/do-russians-give-damn-about-homosexuality.

Kristensen, Nete, and Mortensen, Mette. 2013. "Amateur sources breaking the news, metasources authorizing the news of Gaddafi's death: New patterns of journalistic information gathering and dissemination in the digital age". *Digital Journalism*, 1(3): 352–367.

Kyria, Ilya. 2013. "Sotsialniye media kak instrument politicheskoy izolyatsii v Rossii [Social media as an instrument of political isolation in Russia]". In *Smeyushchayasya nerevolutsiya: Dvizheniye protesta i media (mifi, yazik, simvoli)* [Laughing nonrevolution: Protest movement and the media (myths, language, symbols)], edited by Anna Kachkaeva. Moscow: Fond "Liberalnaya Missiya".

Lenskyj, Helen. 2014. *Sexual diversity and the Sochi 2014 Olympics: No more rainbows* [Kindle edition]. Basingstoke: Palgrave Macmillan.

Lewis, Seth, Kaufhold, Kelly, and Lasorsa, Dominic. 2010. "Thinking about citizen journalism: The philosophical and practical challenges of user-generated content for community newspapers". *Journalism Practice*, 4(2): 163–179.

Mayr, Walter, Neef, Christian, and Schepp, Matthias. "Shadow economy and media control: Russians fed up with Putin's manipulations". *Spiegel Online International,* March 2, 2012, accessed March 3, 2014. http://spiegel.de/international/europe/shadow-economy-and-media-control-russians-fed-up-with-putin-s-manipulations-a-818930.html.

Mayring, Philipp. 2004. "Qualitative content analysis". In *A companion to qualitative research,* edited by Uwe Flick, Ernst von Kardorff and Ines Steinke. London: Sage Publications.

McKenna, Laura, and Pole, Antoineette. 2008. "What do bloggers do: an average day on an average political blog". *Public Choice,* 134(1–2): 97–108.

Newton, Kenneth. 1999. Mass media effects: Mobilization or media malaise? *British Journal of Political Science,* 29(4): 577–99.

Orttung, Robert, and Walker, Christopher. 2013. "Putin and Russia's crippled media". *Russian Analytical Digest* 123: 2–5.

Pankin, Alexei, Fedotov, Andrei, Richter, Andrei, Alekseeva, Anastasia, and Osipova, Daria. (2011). "Mapping digital media: Russia. Open Society Foundations". A report by the Open Society Foundations, accessed January 20, 2014. http://opensocietyfoundations.org/reports/mapping-digital-media-russia.

Poushter, Jacob. "Russia's moral barometer: Homosexuality unacceptable, but drinking, less so". *Pew Research Center,* February 6, 2014, accessed March 7, 2014. http://pewrsr.ch/1fWnAVU.

Reese, Stephen, Rutigliano, Lou, Hyun, Kideuk, and Jeong, Jaekwan. 2007. "Mapping the blogosphere: Professional and citizen-based media in the global news arena". *Journalism* 8(3): 235–261.

Rodríguez, Clemencia. 2001. Fissures in the mediascape: An international study of citizens' media. Cresskill, NJ: Hampton Press.

Rohozinski, Rafal. 1999. "Mapping Russian cyberspace: Perspectives on democracy and the net". *UNRISD* Discussion paper 115, accessed January 17, 2014. http://unpan1.un.org/intradoc/groups/public/documents/UNTC/UNPAN015092.pdf.

Shoemaker, Pamela, Vos, Tim, and Reese, Stephen. 2008. "Journalists as Gatekeepers". In *Handbook of Journalism Studies,* edited by Karin Wahl-Jorgensen and Thomas Hanitzsch. New York, NY: Routledge.

Thompson, John. 1995. The media and modernity: A social theory of the media. Cambridge, UK: Polity Press.

Turovsky, Daniil. (2013, July 5). "Obraztsovo-pokazatelnoe unizhenie: Kak Okkupay-Pedofiliay boretsya s 'izvreschentsami' na Urale [Exemplary humiliation: How Occupy-Pedofiliay fight 'perverts' in Ural region]". *Lenta,* July 5, 2013, accessed February 5, 2014. http://lenta.ru/articles/2013/07/05/kamenskuralsky/.

Umland, Andreas. "Do Russians love their children too"? *Transitions Online*, July 16, 2012. Accessed January 30, 2014. http://tol.org/client/article/23258-do-russians-love-their-children-too.html.

Volkov, Denis. 2012. "The internet and political involvement in Russia". *Russian Education & Society* 54(9): 49–87.

Vraga, Emily, Edgerly, Stephanie, Wang, Bryan, and Shah, Dhavan. 2011. "Who taught me that? Repurposed news, blog structure, and source identification". *Journal of Communication,* 61(5): 795–815.

Whitehouse, Ginny. 2010. "Newsgathering and privacy: Expanding ethics codes to reflect change in the digital media age". *Journal of Mass Media Ethics,* 25(4): 310–327.

Wilkinson, Cai. 2013. "Russia's anti-gay laws: the politics and consequences of a moral panic". Accessed March 15, 2014. http://thedisorderofthings.com/2013/06/23/russias-anti-gay-laws-the-politics-and-consequences-of-a-moral-panic/.

Woodly, Deva. 2008. "New competencies in democratic communication? Blogs, agenda setting and political participation". *Public Choice* 134(1–2): 109–123.

13 Online Lobbying of Political Candidates

Paula Keaveney

Introduction

This chapter focuses on the way citizens engage with politicians and attempt to participate in politics in the online world. The specific focus is on engagement with political candidates in the run-up to major election contests. Election contests, particularly those of national importance, create an arena in which citizens theoretically have the opportunity to play many roles. These range from being simply consumers of, or reactors to, political messages to being active participants in influencing politicians' decisions and behaviour. This chapter looks at the latter and at how citizens, and their organisations, attempt to lobby election candidates. While between elections there are a finite number of political decision-makers to attempt to influence, the emergence of candidates in the run-up to a poll means there are new and extra people to contact as well as an environment in which contact should be welcomed.

The author of this chapter is an experienced parliamentary candidate as well as an academic teaching public relations and politics[1]. The data is drawn from two specific elections. The first is the police and crime commissioner (PCC) elections, which took place in England and Wales in 2012. The second is the current UK general election (scheduled for May 7, 2015). As, at the time of writing, the UK general election has still to take place, the data for this is necessarily less complete than that for the PCC contest. It is included, however, because it shows changes in approach and sophistication, which could be relevant to the questions being posed. In both cases, lobbying activity taking place online has been analysed. Where possible, citizens taking part in the lobbying have been questioned and motivations and approaches considered. In both specific elections, the citizen lobbying data is based on a particular constituency, although some broader information has also been collected.

Given the ease with which citizens can contact political candidates online, and the increase in policy promotion and development which an approaching election brings, it would be natural to assume that citizens would be more engaged and that engagement would be more meaningful. In addition to looking at methods and motivations, this chapter asks whether the online environment and the possibilities that brings is making citizens more or less meaningfully engaged in the process.

The lobbying of candidates, rather than actual office holders, is not new. Stephen, in *Anti-Slavery Recollections*, writes of a lobbying campaign during the 1832 UK parliamentary election (republished in 1971 by Routledge). This campaign used techniques of pledge collection, questions to candidates and media coverage in a way that would be recognisable today. Candidate lobbying and candidate comment publishing also took place during campaigns against the UK death penalty in Victorian times (Gregory 2012) and as part of the work of the Anti-Corn Law League (Hollis 1974).

Zetter (2011) makes the point that there is no agreed-upon definition of lobbying. He does, however, go on to provide his own definition, which he gives as "the process of seeking to influence government and its institutions by informing the public policy agenda. It is also, of course, the art of political persuasion". Thomson and John (2006) say there are four basic reasons to lobby. These are to protect an organisation, to help identify new opportunities, to help build support and to raise profile.

However, despite candidate lobbying being common and, based on author observation between 1997 and 2015, growing, there is little general literature today about the how-to or even the why of lobbying candidates. Zetter (2011), Colvin (2011) and Thomson and John (2006) all identify target audiences that, in a UK context, jointly include members of the European Parliament, local councillors, assembly members, members of the Scottish Parliament, civil servants, Westminster MPs and peers, but none highlights candidates for political office. The only how-to literature found is that prepared by campaign groups and voluntary organisations aimed at their own supporters. UK charity Christian Aid, for example, produces material telling its supporters that "meetings with constituents make a real impact on prospective politicians" (Christian Aid Briefing Document, n.d.). Campaign organisation Amnesty International UK's guide for supporters says, "In the run-up to the election politicians will be engaging with their constituents (you) a lot more than they normally do and all the main political parties will have candidates canvassing for votes in your constituency. We are looking to use this opportunity to show all candidates, and through them their political party, that Amnesty is a movement of passionate and committed members who care about how the next government and parliament acts on human rights" (Amnesty International, n.d.). The umbrella body, the National Council for Voluntary Organisations (NCVO), organised a conference (September 2014) and a publication specifically to help its voluntary sector members think about how best to lobby in the run-up to the 2015 general election. While the voluntary sector material is clearly useful for existing supporters, the lack of more general material about lobbying candidates could mean that citizen engagement is limited to those who happen to have connections with, or know about, existing campaigning bodies. This in turn poses a question of motivation and real engagement. Supporters of existing bodies are prompted, sometimes repeatedly, to lobby. By definition, people who are not supporters are not. There is, of course, no way of

204 *Paula Keaveney*

knowing if the prompted person would have lobbied independently anyway, but the author has so far not identified a policy-related lobbying approach that cannot be traced back to an organisation of some sort.

While some may see lobbying as a corporate activity that goes on behind closed doors involving a small group of 'those in the know', lobbying can range from the highly secret to the extremely open. Any individual contacting a politician to urge a particular point of view is, in fact, lobbying. And the openness of some politicians to this, particularly in the run up to elections, means this is a simple way in which citizens can engage, albeit in an initially limited and choreographed way. For some, this can be the way into more active participation, as urging a point of view at election time is an activity that has a very obvious purpose.

13.1 The Elections Studied

The first election featured is the 2012 police and crime commissioner contest in Merseyside, in which the author was a candidate. Merseyside is in North West England and is home to the City of Liverpool. The police and crime commissioner posts were new in 2012. Each commissioner covers a UK police force area, which is considerably larger than a Westminster parliamentary constituency. The elections are, however, similar to Westminster parliamentary elections in that one individual is elected for a defined area. A supplementary vote method was used, meaning voters had a first and second choice. The second choice would only come into play if no candidate achieved 50 per cent plus one of the total votes cast. There is evidence (observed at the election count and also reported by colleagues elsewhere) that some voters did not understand or want to use the second choice element, either deciding to vote for the same candidate twice or simply leaving the second choice blank. In Merseyside, the winning candidate gained enough votes for transfers not to be needed.

In the second election, the constituency is Sefton Central, in which the author is a parliamentary candidate. Sefton Central is a Merseyside area to the north of Liverpool. The constituency is held by the UK Labour party, although has previously been seen as marginal.

The phrase "online lobbying" here refers almost entirely to email (although later trends show some campaigns are incorporating a Twitter 'ask' into the e-mail and there are limited attempts to lobby via tweets). While it would clearly be possible for Facebook users to take part in online candidate discussions, with all candidates or with one or some, the author has yet to experience this happening in any organised way. Interestingly, one of the participants in the survey carried out for this research remarked that she was surprised there was no standard local online debate for this election or for others. This may be a case of political parties, and likely debate organisers, being less imaginative than potential voters. It may, however, be a case of organisers and parties not wanting to lose control of a forum or event. There is a growth of Twitter Q and A (question and answer) sessions featuring UK politicians, but these are less suitable as lobbying opportunities partly because of the nature of Twitter which, given its character limits, can make it hard to ask complex questions or suggest complex solutions. The Twitter Q and As also tend to be "owned" by the politician himself or herself, whereas lobbying activity is usually initially owned by the lobbyist even if it does then become shared with some politicians.

In terms of citizen engagement, it could be argued that lobbying candidates, as opposed to simply concentrating on office holders, potentially increases engagement as it brings more voices to the debate and means that a "go away" from a politician of one colour may be matched by a "tell me more" from another. Candidates who are not already office-holders do not face collective responsibility or whipping restrictions, and although party discipline can be tight among those likely to win, it can still be easier to engage with a candidate than with an incumbent. It is also the case, in the author's experience, that challenger candidates are naturally more open to certain lobbying approaches as it is in their interests to build support bases where they can. The culture of a particular party can play a role, too, in terms of responsiveness. The research data for the PCC election showed a large difference in the responsiveness of candidates. Respondents (the constituents who had been in touch) were asked which candidates replied to their emails, with the least responsive candidate replying to only 14 per cent while the most replied to 84 per cent (see Table 13.1). As a new post, the PCC position had no defending candidate and, therefore, no challengers. This means that party culture is more likely to be the significant factor here.

Table 13.1 Party response rates to lobbying emails

Party	Response Rate to Lobbying e mails
Conservative	14%
English Democrat	39%
Independent	73%
Labour	69%
Liberal Democrat	84%
UKIP	16%

In the lobbying seen so far (as of March 7 2015) for the general election 2015, there is evidence that some challenger candidates in the Sefton Central constituency are already markedly more responsive than the incumbent MP[2].

13.2 Candidate Lobbying is Different

In my experience as a parliamentary candidate, organised lobbying of candidates is increasing, taking up a growing proportion of a candidate's time if

206 *Paula Keaveney*

s/he chooses to engage. Even before I had properly announced my candidacy for the 2015 election, I started receiving lobbying approaches on issues as diverse as Palestine and support services for children with autism. During the police and crime commissioner elections it was not uncommon for there to be several screens full of new lobbying emails waiting for me when I logged on. Yet I have never won a parliamentary election. Arguably then, those constituents wasted their time. This is what makes candidate lobbying different. The main purpose of public affairs work is to influence decision-makers. When lobbying officeholders (whether elected or appointed) the public affairs practitioner knows who they are and whether or not they are influential. He will focus on those who have decision-making power or who have influence over those with decision-making power. Yet those lobbying candidates are obliged to be more broad-brush. The mathematics of a UK parliamentary election is that most candidates will lose. In some cases we are not sure who the winner will be, but we can be absolutely sure that more will lose than will win. This gives candidate lobbying a range of purposes. The lobbyist may well want to influence a future decision-maker, but he may also want to influence public opinion, make friends for the future, influence party policy processes and so on. In the case of the UK voluntary sector, members of which are very active in candidate lobbying, there is also a need to ensure the appearance of political neutrality, which in turn can lead to the lobbying of those destined to lose badly. For this research I spoke to a campaign officer at *Barnardos*, a UK-based child-care charity, who explained that making friends for the future and developing new contacts was very important to them, and a losing candidate could still be a valuable stakeholder whether then or in the future.

I have been aware of the organised lobbying of candidates for some time. My experience includes working in PR (pubic relations) on lobbying campaigns for charities but also being the recipient of lobbying. Since 1997, the first time I was a candidate in a parliamentary election, I have seen a change in the way lobbying is carried out. This has happened in two ways: method and communication channel. In 1997 there was heavy reliance on providing candidates with "manifestos" on certain subjects. Mail-outs included a "manifesto for dentistry" and a "refugee manifesto". There were questionnaires and other attempts to assess candidates' views, but these appeared to be a relatively small proportion of the whole. Since then there has been a change in the proportion of types of communication, with questionnaires and other attempts to seek out views or gain clear support for very specific propositions taking up a much greater 'market share' than those communications aimed simply at informing or attempting to influence through information provision. Along with this change in method has gone a change in channel, with written (print) communications being almost entirely replaced by online communications.

Of course, this channel change could also be part of, or be an influence on, other changes in the lobbying relationship between candidate and elector or

Online Lobbying of Political Candidates   207

candidate and organisation. The lobbying so far in 2015 shows a significant development. It is normal for major organisations to ask local representatives to make contact with local candidates. These approaches typically ask questions or ask for support for a particular initiative. This year, however, I am seeing an increasingly integrated approach. Local supporters are contacting candidates to let them know of the imminent arrival of a request (usually a link to pledge support) from a national organisation. Local supporters are also asking candidates to tweet their support with hashtag details provided. At the time of writing, in mid-March 2015, integrated approaches like this have arrived from a mental health charity, a cancer charity, an organisation supporting local pubs and a campaign against tax dodging. The suggested use of Twitter not only gives the campaign more visibility, it helps reward engagement by local supporters as the effect of their work can be apparent almost immediately. For the politician, these approaches feel as if there may be an attempt to set up two-way communication as opposed to simply asking a question or providing an argument and then disappearing.

There are common software systems used now to make it much easier for organisations to ask their supporters to contact candidates and for individuals to do so. Gone are the days when names and addresses would have to be looked up and letters written. This should of itself mean an increase in lobbying with many of the time and effort barriers removed. It could, however, be argued that this very ease of contact means the level of commitment to the cause is lower, and there is evidence that some of those lobbied recognise this to be the case. After the police and crime commissioner election an interview took place with Jane Kennedy, the election winner. She expressed some surprise at the number of approaches that were word-for-word identical and that didn't feel like an attempt to engage. While her response rate to approaches was good (see Figure 13.1), the repetitive nature of approaches may make candidates less concerned about the individual contact. Standard email messages can retain phrases which make it clear that little or no actual local thought has been applied, such as the one I received including the phrase "if you are in England" or the other retaining the phase "put in your own example here or delete this paragraph". Data from research into the 2012 lobbying showed that the link between voting intention and the policy positions being urged or asked for is not as strong as some of the wording would have candidates believe. This has the potential to undermine the credibility of future approaches and is significant for understanding the real meaning of the engagement.

13.3 Dialogue?

One way of looking at types of communication and categorising them is that devised by Grunig and Hunt (1984). This approach is clearly not new but it has the benefit of simplicity. Grunig and Hunt look at four models of public relations communication ranging from the press agency

208 *Paula Keaveney*

model (loosely translated as getting stories in the newspapers) through to two-way symmetric communication. Whatever the detail of this, and whatever the more recent adaptations, the implication is that two-way communication is to be preferred because it is more sophisticated, democratic and properly described as communication. If we take the view that it is better for voters and organisations to have two-way symmetric communication with candidates, then we would assume that the move to online lobbying, with technology meaning replies can be quick and dialogue possible, is part of the journey toward this form of communication. Actually the change in technology would appear to have made little or no difference in the 'dialogue' element of candidate lobbying. In 2010, when I was a general election candidate, I was surprised that not a single one of my replies to lobbying approaches was acknowledged, queried or replied to. In 2012 the election at which I deliberately collected the data, only one organisation appeared to have encouraged its supporters to acknowledge and thank, let alone query and discuss. In 2015, a larger number of organisations are encouraging thanking and responding, but these remain in the minority. It seems then that this form of lobbying remains rather unsophisticated and the changes possible through speed and technology are resisted or at least not used. It also implies that what is being seen as engagement is not really such. Of course, if the purpose of lobbying a candidate is simply to get an answer, get a signature or try a simple piece of persuasion, then this may not matter. But it perhaps points to the way that this change in technology is not affecting method or approach in the way it could do.

13.4 The Police and Crime Commissioner Research Results

The data for the remaining sections of this chapter is mainly taken from organised lobbies during the police and crime commissioner election in Merseyside. The organisational lobbies chosen were the four with the most initial emails. Communications about individual or area specific issues (usually anti-social behaviour in some districts) have been omitted, as have communications, which did not involve more than one person (for example, questionnaires from a headquarters). In some cases those emailing made it clear that they were doing so on behalf of an organisation. In others it was clear, because of identical wording or a reference to a request, that although an organisation was not being named, this was organised lobbying. Some of the issues raised are not ones for which the police and crime commissioner would be responsible. In some cases the request is to identify with an opinion or to press someone else for change. The fact that lobbies raise issues like this is more evidence of the multi-functional nature of candidate, as opposed to office-holder, lobbying. It is also evidence of the recognition by some that an election is a PR "news peg" in the same way as other events and can be used for various PR and organisational ends.

Online Lobbying of Political Candidates   209

Against privatisation of police services and the use of a particular contractor – Organised by 38 degrees. 38 degrees is a UK organisation that encourages individuals to campaign on a range of issues. It has run high-profile campaigns on particular pieces of legislation and has the capacity to fasten quickly onto controversial live topics. The name 38 degrees is based on the theory that a 38-degree angle is a tipping point.

For the prioritisation of action on wildlife crime – more than one organisation but mainly the League Against Cruel Sports. The League Against Cruel Sports is a campaigning membership organisation with a record of political lobbying.

Various free speech issues – Christian organisations. No one organisation was named by these lobbyists but the wording on each email was identical.

For more action against child trafficking - Barnardos, which is a large national child care charity founded in Victorian times. It provides services but also campaigns on issues of child welfare and poverty. Like many large UK charities, it has local support groups and individual supporters.

After the election, those who had been in touch were contacted with a link to a short survey. It was explained that that the results would hopefully be of some use for organisations wanting to think about improving their lobbying activities and increase political responsiveness. The survey was created in December 2012 with answers being received in December 2012 and January 2013. Survey questions included why individuals had been in touch, what effect the responses had on them (or on their organisation) and whether there would be or had been any follow up. A few individuals appeared on more than one list. In these cases they were included with the larger of the groups they appeared in.

The potential questionnaire respondents were all individuals who had emailed the author in her role as candidate. This means that anyone emailing other candidates but omitting the author would not receive a questionnaire. It is unlikely that this number would be large, however.

The questionnaire looked at motivation and asked which of these potential motivating factors, and there could be more than one, applied:

1 To make candidates aware on a particular subject
2 To find out a policy position to help me decide how to vote
3 To collect information about candidates' views for an organisation or group (this could be to help a national lobby collate material or decide who to follow up)
4 To attempt to persuade candidates of a point of view
5 To find out a policy position to help me decide who not to vote for (ie to help with elimination of possibilities)

At this point some will query the approach taken to the definition of lobbying. It could be argued that asking policy questions is not, in itself, an attempt to influence. However, it is clear to the author as an experienced

210 Paula Keaveney

candidate that a set of questions from, for example, the League Against Cruel Sports, is not a neutral communication and at the very least is an attempt to get the candidate to perceive animal rights as important.

Of the motivating factors, number 4 (see Table 13.2) is the most straightforward lobbying approach but all have elements of lobbying about them.

Table 13.2 Results of question on motivation

Response	Aggregated	38 Degrees	Animal rights	Christians	Barnardos
1	43	17	21	2	3
2	55	36	15	3	1
3	29	24	4	1	0
4	19	10	8	0	1
5	35	28	5	2	0

It is interesting here that the straightforward lobbying motivation is the one selected the least. This could be because of the nature of the communication, usually phrased as a question or response to support X.

Given the organised nature of this lobbying, it is also surprising that response 3 does not get a higher score. Many of the emails were of a national campaign nature which implies the information being provided to an HQ or central point of some sort. It is of course possible that those doing local lobbying did not fully understand how collated replies could be used in pursuit of a broader policy effort.

One of the benefits of using email and other online methods is that it enables much quicker sharing of information and feedback. For candidates of course this means a comment sent to one individual can very quickly be passed on. For lobbying campaigns this is useful as it can identify targets for follow up (particularly keen or interested people for example) but it brings with it an increasing likelihood of self-censorship on the part of candidates, leading perhaps to blander answers or to a restriction to "yes/no" comments. It is interesting that many of the individual comments provided by respondents found candidate replies rather "standard" or "bland" or not really to the point. This may of course simply be due to pressure of time, or unrealistic expectations from individuals who are part of an electorate of millions. But it does again hint at self-censorship. In my experience, at public meetings, those with more to lose (for example the challenger candidate in a marginal constituency or the defending candidate) self-censor more than others. However, the growth of the ability for risky comments to "go viral" may now mean that everyone self-censors more.

Respondents were questioned on what effect, if any, the candidate replies had on actual voting. It is worth bearing in mind that the turnout for this election was very low. The question asked, among those who did vote, what role the answers received played in decision-making. The options were:

1 Only one candidate replied satisfactorily and the issue is so important for me I voted for him/her.
2 Several candidates replied satisfactorily and the issue is so important for me that I made a short list based on this and then decided on other factors.
3 The replies had an effect on my decision-making process, but it wasn't a major one.
4 Frankly, I was always going to vote the way I did regardless of the answers.
5 Not applicable. (This was included in case some non-voters attempted to answer this question, but it may understate the abstention rate.)

Table 13.3 Effect on voting

Response	Aggregate	38 Degrees	Animal Rights	Christians	Barnardos
1	17	8	5	2	2
2	27	19	8	0	0
3	9	4	1	2	2
4	7	3	4	0	0
5	15	7	8	0	0

The survey asked whether respondents were involved in any follow-up lobbying or had contact with the newly elected PCC. Options offered were:

1 Yes.
2 No.
3 No, but I plan to do so in the future.
4 No but I am aware this is being raised/dealt with at national level.

Table 13.4 Follow up intentions

Response	Aggregate	38 Degrees	Animal Rights	Christians	Barnardos
1	14	8	5	0	1
2	33	19	11	2	1
3	24	15	8	1	0
4	13	6	4	1	2

The study did not seek to determine whether those who said they would lobby in future actually did so; however, feedback from the successful candidate, interviewed several months after the election, showed a lack of

212 *Paula Keaveney*

follow-through that throws some doubt onto the value placed on the issue by those doing the lobbying.

Respondents were asked to give their own comments about how they viewed the experience and their own motivation. There was a great deal of disquiet about the very existence of the election, which had become controversial; however, some comments illustrate general points. The first is about the general lack of online opportunities. As respondent 1 put it:

> I would have liked to have been able to join an "on line question time" facilitated by a respected third party (such as Radio Merseyside) which would have given all the candidates an opportunity to impress or disappoint me. I really do not understand why such an arrangement could not be made for all elections? (Respondent 1, online survey Jan 2013.)

At the time of writing I am not aware of any attempts to set up such an opportunity locally for 2015. There are arrangements being made for a local TV hustings, for radio debates with phone-in segments and for various published newspaper pieces. The fact that these plans are fairly well advanced highlights the lack of obvious online thinking. Perhaps the online environment is seen as too informal for something as structured as a hustings. Or perhaps this again is an issue of ownership.

As a candidate, I take the view that anyone can contact me about anything. Like many others I publish email addresses and my home address. I also publish my mobile phone number and would always consider myself accessible; however, I was interested in one response that showed whatever politicians might think, people do not necessarily think they have the opportunity, or the "permission", to approach to lobby.

> Were it not for the fact that I am a member of 38 Degrees I doubt that an opportunity to lobby candidates prior to election would have been available to me as an ordinary voter. I am grateful to them for that and so should the candidates be. There is a national groundswell as yet unpublicised and untapped of public antipathy towards professional lobbyists and political consultancies and the financial clout they wield at the highest levels of political decision making and indeed candidate selection and backing too. Every opportunity should be made by public representatives to tap into the ideas and aspirations of their constituents on a regular basis irrespective of political affiliation and as opposed to special interest groups. (Respondent 2, online survey Jan 2013.)

The fact that very few people contacted me independently (by which I mean finding out my contact details separately and writing their own email) highlights the suggestion that without organisations such as 38 degrees making it easy to lobby and suggesting topics, the average citizen would not think to do it. This raises a huge question around engagement. If it takes an organisation to tell someone what to write and to give them a 'two clicks' way of doing it, is this really engagement in any meaningful sense?

However there is evidence from another reply that simply going through this exercise could lead to more meaningful engagement later on.

> I was surprised by the number of candidates who replied. One of the candidates demonstrated in their reply that they had not read my email properly, however that candidate surprised me as it was the fifth time I had written to them and it was the first time they replied. This was very helpful. ... The responses I received were interesting, some were very detailed, others far more brief and 'standard', it has definitely made me want to contact future candidates in 'proper' elections. (Respondent 3, online survey Jan 2013.)

This comment does not, unfortunately, elaborate on whether the "surprise" was because the replies were from many candidates or from few. The paragraph, however, seems to imply a large proportion of replies. If a citizen enters the exercise expecting to be ignored, this goes some way toward illustrating how even those attempting to engage may also feel disengaged.

Finally, one respondent had a more direct message.

> Candidates should get their act together and reply to e-mails. I believe that is the future in elections in the years ahead, keep in touch with your electorate and you will get votes, common sense in my view. (Respondent 4, online survey Dec 2012.)

This is certainly the view of many practicing politicians who set great store by developing email lists and providing regular communications (both proactive and reactive) by email. This is not new. As Cornfield put it in 2004, "Where politics is concerned, a flimsy email list will outperform a sterling website ninety-nine days out of one hundred".

13.5 General Election 2015; Some Early Thoughts

Because the police and crime commissioner election was unusual in many ways, it is hard to make a direct comparison between it and the 2015 general election. It is possible, however, to look at lobbying activities in 2015 and draw some very early conclusions. Based on what I have seen so far, there are points about speed, dialogue and sophistication that can be made. All of these bear in different ways on questions of citizen engagement and participation.

On 11 February 2015, campaign organisation 38 degrees published a blog on the HSBC "tax dodging scandal". (This is a story about part of HSBC enabling the very rich to dodge tax and about some governments

214 *Paula Keaveney*

doing little about it.) The 38 degrees blog remains but has since been edited to remove a link to a standard letter and to a table of results.[3] I viewed the blog previously and so am aware of the previous link to the letter text, of the form which enabled participants to enter their details to get a template letter which would go automatically to know candidates and of what the text said. The first email to me as candidate, using the text word for word, arrived at 1.18pm on 11 February. This was followed swiftly by (at the time of writing) thirty-seven others using the same wording. Participants are asked to fill in a form to log replies from their candidates. As the table of results link is, at the time of writing, not available, it is impossible to see how many have been logged so far; however, this is a good illustration of the speed which systems such as this make possible. How seriously candidates take these messages, when they are clearly word-for-word identical, is open to question and it may be the case that the very speed of contact throws doubt onto its sincerity. As a candidate I answered every email carefully and would have been interested to see how quickly my response appeared on the 38 degrees site. It could be argued that the lack of a real time display of responses by 38 degrees throws some doubt on whether a two way dialogue is taking place or is desired.

In January 2015, local supporters of Cancer Research UK contacted candidates to warn them that the national campaign would be in touch to lobby for support and to ask candidates to sign a particular pledge to "Cross Cancer Out". The national email arrived on 13 February containing a link to pledge. Candidates pledging support online were directed to a form asking them what further information or help they would like. This included infographics, a draft press release, constituency specific information and so on. There was also suggested text for a tweet. Once the form was filled in, another link was provided to take the candidate to the selected resources. This gives useful material for candidates, but is also another way of the charity knowing who is interested in what. It will be interesting to see if the loop is closed by emails from local supporters saying thank you (at the time of publication this has not happened). This approach is the most sophisticated I have seen so far. It enables local volunteers to engage in a way which helps their organisation while providing elements of dialogue and benefits for all parties.

The findings to date do not show that these methods of online lobbying increase citizen engagement in politics or make that engagement more meaningful. They certainly make contact speedier and easier but arguably that speed and ease devalues the effort. In the 1800s more than half a million women in the UK signed an anti-slavery petition (the Affectionate Address or Stafford House Address) to be sent to the United States. Only women were eligible to sign, and this was hard copies for which signers had to be in particular places. Today we view 100,000 electronic signatures (the trigger figure for a potential parliamentary debate in the UK) as a large number. Could technology in fact be showing us to be less engaged than ever?

13.6 Areas for Further Research

This discussion has raised a number of issues that would repay further exploration. There are issues around how candidates respond to or engage with online lobbying. There is already anecdotal evidence, and in some case press reports, of parties attempting to pre-screen tweets and other communication online. There is also anecdotal evidence of candidates attempting to persuade others to agree to jointly not reply to certain organisations. The dangers of 'hostage to fortune' type quotes in material that can easily be shared is clear. It would be interesting to look at how parties plan to manage this, whether they plan to manage this or whether in fact the opening up of social media channels means a change in the power relationships between parties and individual candidates or between parties, their members and others. Lilleker, in Scullion et al. (2013), highlights the potential tension for those parties for which internal democracy and member participation matter. If my rights as a member are important, will I want non-members to have an equal say?

The issue of lobbying follow-up was identified. Clearly in this case we do not know if respondents who said they would follow up actually did, although this is supplemented by comments from the actual police and crime commissioner. It would be worth in future looking at a pre-election lobby and then examining the follow up with elected office holders after a twelve-month period.

The police and crime commissioner election was unusual in a number of ways. As a 'first' and an unpopular first, participation and awareness rates were lower than the norm for a UK election. It would be worth carrying out this exercise again for the Westminster parliamentary election in 2015 to see if this has an effect on the motivations of lobbyists and the likelihood of follow-up.

Notes

1. This combination of personal experience with academic study means that the author makes clear by using "I" when she is commenting specifically from personal experience or including a personal reflection.
2. This data is incomplete but is gained by viewing responses posted on organisational websites, such as the International Fund for Animal Welfare, which tend to not only display what individual candidates have said but which candidates have not replied. The author plans to carry out or encourage an interview and analysis exercise post-election and it will be interesting to see if response rates change nearer polling day.
3. The current content is at http://blog.38degrees.org.uk/2015/02/11/tax-dodging-where-do-candidates-stand/#comments [accessed 9 March 2015].

Works Cited

38 degrees. Accessed 9 March 2015. http://www.38degrees.org.uk/.
Amnesty International. Accessed 9 March 2015. https://www.amnesty.org.uk/actions/uk-election-2015-join-fight-rights.

Association of Police and Crime Commissioners. Accessed 10 February 2015. http://apccs.police.uk/role-of-the-pcc/.

Cancer Research UK. Accessed 15 February 2015. http://scienceblog.cancerresearchuk.org/2014/10/24/its-time-to-cross-cancer-out-our-general-election-campaign/.

Christian Aid. Accessed 19 December 2012. http://www.christianaid.org.uk/.

Colvin, Scott. 2011. How to Use Politicians to Get What you want. London. Biteback.

Cornfield, Michael. 2004. *Politics Moves On line*. New York. Century Foundation.

Gregory, James. 2012. Victorians Against the Gallows. Tauris.

Grunig and Hunt. 1984. *Managing Public Relations*. Holt, Rhinehart and Winston.

Hollis, Patricia. 1974. *Pressure from Without in early Victorian England*. London. Hodder and Stoughton.

Merseyside Police and Crime Commissioner. Accessed 10 February 2015. http://www.police.uk/merseyside/pcc/.

National Council for Voluntary Organisations. Accessed 14 February 2015. https://www.ncvo.org.uk/component/redshop/24-ncvo-member-publications/P150-general-election-2015-how-to-campaign-in-your-local-area?Itemid=0.

Scullion, Gerodimos, Jackson and Lilleker. 2013. *The Media, Political Participation and Empowement*. London. Routledge.

Stephen, George. 1971. Anti-Slavery Recollections: in a series of letters written to Mrs Beecher Stowe. Routledge.

Thompson and John. 2006. *Public Affairs in Practice*. London. Kogan Page.

Zetter, Lionel. 2011. Lobbying: *The Art of Political Persuasion*. Petersfield. Harriman House.

Concluding Note

Geoff Craig

This volume of research, drawn from presentations at a wonderful conference at the University of Burgundy in Dijon, serves the important function of taking us beyond traditional narratives about the roles of online media and social networking sites (SNS) in political communication that either singularly champion their emancipatory power or denounce their erosion and trivialization of off-line politics and citizen engagement. Instead, the studies, spanning a broad range of national political situations, force us to adopt a more sober view about the uses and power of the Internet and social media. They are valuable contributions to the field of study because they 'de-centre' the technologies, requiring us to ground our appraisals of social media in the contexts of pre-existing media environments, the machinations of the political field, and also the existing dynamics of everyday life and forms of political engagement by citizens.

For those of us who would want to see greater dialogue between politicians and their constituents and invigorated forms of political engagement, these studies may not always yield a greater sense of hope. Instead, they remind us that progress in democratic accountability and participation is a hard fought political achievement that exists beyond the mere communicative potential of online media and SNS. Equally, however, they do show how the political communication landscape is rendered more complicated by these online technological innovations, that the public visibility and scrutiny of politicians is enhanced, and that the 'produser' status that is afforded by such forms of media do provide citizens with greater opportunities to more publicly engage with traditional mass media and the discourse and images of politicians.

The studies in Part 1 that examine how politicians use online media and SNS are cumulatively a powerful reminder of the way that the logics of the political field govern practice. As Bourdieu (1991) reminds us, politicians are influenced by both an internal, relational logic of the political field whereby all discourse and actions are evaluated against political opponents, and an external logic where discourse and actions must also appeal to groups and individuals outside the political field. The studies in Part 1 of the volume often reveal a strongly strategic use of Web 2.0 applications where politicians seek primarily to promote themselves, and when they do

218 *Geoff Craig*

interact online it is with fellow party members, other politicians, or other actors within the formal political field. Elena Cebrián Guinovart, Tamara Vázquez Barrio and David Sarias Rodriguez note how both of the studied Spanish political leaders mainly use Twitter to promote themselves and their policies, and in particular they reveal that links in Prime Minister Mariano Rajoy's Twitter account primarily directed readers to the prime minister's web page or events in which Rajoy was participating, and never towards other social networks. Sharon Haleva-Amir found that Israeli politicians on Facebook tended to interact more with party members and people they already knew. We see across these studies how online media and SNS do not implement fundamental changes to the dynamics of the political field; rather they are mobilized to serve the already existing requirements to manage the political field through the control of the politician's self-image for public consumption and also control of the circulating discursive interactions between political and media players.

The studies from Part 1 of the volume show a common tendency of politicians not to exploit the dialogical potential of Web 2.0 applications and instead use them primarily for simple dissemination of information. In this sense the logics of broadcast mass media are applied and the public are posited more as the consumers of political messages. In their study of Twitter communication in the 2013 Italian election, Guido Di Fraia and Maria Carlotta Missaglia conclude that in most cases politicians were not interested in building stronger relationships with citizens or engaging with them about political problems. The studies reveal that politicians are keen to be able to reach constituents so that they can garner support but they are also equally keen not to open up dialogue in a way that could undermine their public authority and provide an advantage for political opponents. In this way the highly disciplined and 'risk-averse' methods of modern political communication management are replicated in these case studies. This mode of political communication is now a generalized practice given we live in the age of the permanent campaign although it could be argued that such strategies and practices are even more pronounced during formal election campaigns, as we see in a number of the studies from Part 1 of the volume.

The studies in Part 2 of the volume reveal a more promising perspective on the uses of online media and SNS by members of the public in acts of political communication. Again, there is tremendous value in the cumulative force of the studies as they variously demonstrate the complicated relationships that exist between online and offline political participation, online and offline media, and the flow of information within and between niche publics and a singular public sphere. As Darren Lilleker observes, we firstly need to adopt "a more nuanced perspective" on what constitutes political behavior in the uses of online media and SNS. Such a perspective would emphasize both the communicative basis of politics as well as the nature of the relationship between online communication and offline political participation. Jaromír Mazák and Václav Štětka's study of clicktivism in the Czech

Concluding Note   219

Republic highlights the positive character of online political expression and its relationship to offline political participation, including the link between online political expression and a belief in political efficacy. The multi-faceted relationship between traditional mass media and activist-based online media is well illustrated in Evgeniya Boklage's study of the Russian LGBT news blogging community. The AntiDogma community was able to challenge mainstream news media through its coverage of otherwise unreported events and its adoption of the more personal modes of 'native reporting', but it also engaged with mass media content in its commentary, where it both 'recycled' content and also offered critique through meta-commentary. We do see across such research the ways that the traditional gate-keeper function of mainstream mass media has been diminished, giving way to the task of trying to monitor the flow of information from online and SNS sources.

The research in these studies also highlights the different kinds, levels and temporalities of public formation that occur with online media and SNS. Caja Thimm invokes Ulrich Beck's (1997) idea of 'sub-politics', which helpfully reminds us that so much of the political energy that we see manifested in the studies in Part 2 of the volume have arisen from frustration with the specialization and bureaucratization of party politics and that as a result we are seeing the landscape of politics becoming broader and more fragmented. Thimm provides us with a categorization of types of mini-publics (user-initiated mini-publics, event-driven mini publics and commercially launched mini-publics), while also distinguishing between mini-publics that exist only on one media platform and polymedia mini-publics, and also differentiating between ad-hoc mini-publics and those that have a longer existence. This work raises important questions about how such formations facilitate political action and the character of such formations. How, and to what extent, should such mini-publics engage with the broader public sphere, and alternatively how important is it that such collectivities are able to carve out their own spaces for identity confirmation? How does the facility for ad-hoc publics to engage in strategic forays into political participation work with, and impact upon, more sustained public terrains and political orders?

I believe the research that has been conducted here and elsewhere in the field gives us a sense of the complex, evolving landscape of citizen participation and political communication but it also propels us to further consider the question of how we characterize the agglomerations of citizens who congregate, usually both passionately and precariously, around claims and rights. How do we describe the clusters or nodes where such citizens are collected, and the networks that facilitate myriad connections that variously consolidate and challenge regimes and apparatuses of power? And how should we evaluate the public expressions that occur through such media and on such sites in terms of rationality, rhetoric, affect, spectacle, virtual presence and embodiment?

220 *Geoff Craig*

There are no easy solutions here, no prescriptions for success for acts of political communication in a digital world, but rather the studies offer a vista on the struggles of people where the potential of Web 2.0 applications are often mapped on a political field where a Web 1.0 approach persists. In this sense, the studies remind us that online media technologies and SNS are often shaped and used for particular purposes in the contexts of the political field. That said, the studies also show us how people are negotiating the dilemma of acting politically in a world where the pace of public life is increasing and there is a greater ephemerality to the flow of political issues. In such situations people are trying to establish networks, grow communities, challenge authority and bring about change. We should not be dispirited by such struggles – they are the necessary hard political work that will always have to be done – but we do now have a better understanding of how the technological tools we possess can help us in the task of building a more interactive and democratic politics.

Works Cited

Beck, Ulrich. 1997. *The Reinvention of Politics: Rethinking Modernity in the Global Social Order.* Trans. M. Ritter. Cambridge: Polity.
Bourdieu, Pierre. 1991. *Language and Symbolic Power.* Oxford: Polity.

Contributors

Mario Anastasiadis is a Research Assistant at the University of Bonn, Germany, Department of Media Studies. His research interests are social media and political communication, media and popular culture, popular music in the media, extremism on the Internet, and qualitative methods (online and offline). In the research project "Deliberation on the Net", which is part of the priority program "Mediatized Worlds" (funded by the German Science Foundation), he is dealing with questions of how deliberative discourses evolve on Twitter. anastasiadis@medienwissenschaft.uni-bonn.de.

Dr Lluís Anyó was awarded a PhD in film studies from Ramon Llull University with a thesis about video games, narrative and identity. He holds a degree in cultural anthropology from the University of Barcelona. Anyó is currently associate professor of film studies at the Blanquerna School of Communication and International Relations at Ramon Llull University, and director of the master's degree in cultural production and communication at the same university. His research focuses on the relationship between identity and narrative, with particular emphasis on game studies and cultural practices. He has published articles on cultural practices, fan culture, identity and video games.

Dr Tamara Vázquez Barrio is Lecturer in Public Opinion at San Pablo CEU University (Spain). She holds a master's degree in audio-visual production from the Complutense University of Madrid (UCM 2003), and a further MA in needs and rights of children and youths from the *Autonomous University of Madrid* (2006). She also holds a degree as expert in design and statistical treatment of market research from UNED (2007). Her research interests include political communication, with a special attention to digital politics and politainment, and on the effects of the mass media in childhood and young people. In the latter field her particular interests are digital literacy, parental mediation and social responsibility of the mass media.

Dr Evgeniya Boklage is currently a Researcher at the Institute for Media and Communication Studies at the Free University of Berlin, working in the field of science journalism and communication. Her doctoral dissertation

222 *Contributors*

focused on Russian LGBT community and their use of social media for the purposes of self-representation and mobilization of social action. She has been teaching master's-level courses at the Free University of Berlin and University of Helsinki and has published on blogging and media activism. She spent one year as an author at the European Journalism Observatory.

Dr Gilles Brachotte is Associate Professor in Communication Science at the University of Burgundy, member of the CIMEOS/3S research team (EA 4177) and teaches at the web design department of Dijon-Auxerre Technological Institute (IUT Dijon-Auxerre). After starting his career as an IT networks teacher, his research has taken him into the field of communication science and more specifically ICT usage. He focuses on the way ICT is used in practice and more generally on social change resulting from the adoption and integration of ICT in society, notably among young people and in the political sphere. His research centres on the discursive, social, ergonomic and technical dimensions which are sources of meaning and contribute to complexify the communication processes involved. Gilles. brachotte@u-bourgogne.fr

Prof. Geoffrey Craig is Professor of Communication Studies and Head of Research at Auckland University of Technology in New Zealand. He was previously professor of journalism in the Centre for Journalism at the University of Kent. Geoffrey is the author of *The Media, Politics and Public Life* (Allen & Unwin 2004), the co-author of *Slow Living* (Berg 2006) and the co-editor of *Informing Voters? Politics, Media and the New Zealand Election 2008* (Pearson 2009). He has published broadly across a range of international journals in the areas of political and environmental communication.

Jessica Einspänner-Pflock is a Research Assistant at the University of Bonn, Germany, Department of Media Studies. Her research interests are social media and political communication, online privacy, online journalism, and digital methods. In the research project "Deliberation on the Net", which is part of the DFG priority program "Mediatized Worlds" (funded by the German Science Foundation), she deals with questions of how deliberative discourses evolve on Twitter. Email: jep@uni-bonn.de.

Dr Guido Di Fraia is Associate Professor at IULM University (Milan) and Coordinator of the Board of Professors for the Doctoral Course in Communication and New Technologies. He is scientific director of the IULM master in social media marketing & web communication. His research interests include: Web 2.0 and corporate communication; political communication; media narratives; innovative methods in social and market research. He has a degree in political science from the University of Milan. As Fulbrighter, he studied social psychology and methodology of social research in a Ph.D. program at the University of Los Angeles (UCLA).

Contributors 223

Dr Alex Frame is Associate Professor in Communication Science at the Languages and Communication Faculty of the University of Burgundy (Dijon, France), where he runs the MA course in Intercultural Management. Born in Britain, he graduated from the University of Oxford in 1998, before settling in France and completing his PhD in communication science at the University of Burgundy, in 2008. He is a member of the TIL ("Texte, Image, Langage") research group (EA 4182), where he specialises in intercultural communication and comparative cross-cultural communication studies. He is currently leading the research project "TEE2014", looking into the use of Twitter by candidates during the European parliamentary elections in 2014, involving forty researchers from five European countries, concentrating on their respective national corpora. alexander.frame@u-bourgogne.fr.

Dr Elena Cebrián Guinovart is a Lecturer at CEU San Pablo University, in Madrid (Spain), where she teaches Communication and Information Theory. Her research interests include political communication in social media, political infotainment and religion in the media. She is actively participating in the international research project "Twitter at the European Elections 2014" (TEE2014) and in the Spanish national project "El Infoentretenimiento político en Televisión e Internet. Formatos, audiencias y consecuencias en la comunicación política Española" (CSO2012-34698). She was a visiting researcher at Pontificia Università della Santa Croche (Rome, Italy) in 2007 and 2009.

Dr Sharon Haleva-Amir is a Lecturer in Tel Aviv University and Beit Berl College and a Research Fellow at the Haifa Center of Law and Technology (HCLT). Sharon holds a bachelor degree in law (LLB) from Tel-Aviv University; a master's degree (MA) in information science (internet studies track) from Bar-Ilan University and a PhD in law from the University of Haifa. Her fields of research include e-Democracy, e-Politics, MPs' web practices, law and technology, websites content analysis and Internet ethics. She won a doctoral scholarship for excellence from the University of Haifa, a Transparency International (Israel) scholarship and the best paper award in 2013 from the Israeli Political Science Association.

Paula Keaveney is a Lecturer at Edge Hill University where she teaches Public Relations and Politics. She is active in politics having fought many, and won some, elections. She was the first female leader of the opposition on Liverpool city council. She is currently the Liberal Democrat parliamentary candidate for Sefton Central (2015). Paula's research interests include lobbying, political communication and communication by and for the voluntary sector. She is the co-editor of *Marketing for the Voluntary Sector* (2001) published by Kogan Page. Before joining Edge Hill, Paula worked as a PR practitioner for major national charities and as a BBC journalist.

224   *Contributors*

Dr Darren G. Lilleker is Associate Professor in Political Communication in The Media School, Bournemouth University. Dr Lilleker's expertise is in the professionalization and marketization of politics and its impacts on citizens, on which he has published widely including the textbook *Key Concepts in Political Communication* (Sage, 2006), monographs *Political Campaigning, Elections and the Internet* (Routledge, 2011) and *Political Communication and Cognition* (Palgrave, 2014) and has co-edited *The Marketing of Political Parties* (MUP, 2006), *Voters or Consumers* (CSP, 2008) *Political Marketing in Comparative Perspective* (MUP, 2005) and *The Media, Political Participation and Empowerment* (Routledge, 2013).

Jaromír Mazák is a PhD student, Lecturer and Researcher at the Department of Sociology, Faculty of Arts, at Charles University in Prague. He is a long-term collaborator of the PolCoRe group at the faculty of social sciences of the same university. His interests cover electoral and non-electoral political participation with special emphasis on social and political movements. Email: mazak.jaromir@gmail.com

Prof. Arnaud Mercier holds a PhD in Political Science from the Institute of Political Studies of Paris. He is a former director of the Communication and Politics Research Centre in Paris (CNRS). In 2005 he became full professor of information and communication science at the University of Lorraine in Metz, where he set up an MA course in journalism and digital media. He also founded a research program: the *Observatory of Web-journalism* (www.obsweb.net) to study the evolution of challenges facing journalism in the era of the Internet, including journalistic uses of social media. He is currently running a funded research project (ANR), entitled: *Flow of information through social media*. He created a barometer to monitor the tweet-campaign during the March 2014 municipal elections, in collaboration with French national radio (France Info) and is currently taking part in a comparative European project on the use of Twitter by the candidates in the 2014 European elections.

Maria Carlotta Missaglia is a PhD candidate in Communication and New Technologies at IULM University, in Milan. During 2014 she worked as a guest researcher at University of Oslo. She has attended and completed a master degree in television, cinema and new media, and she graduated cum laude. The graduation thesis was a work titled: "Social (Media) Politics: how Social Media are changing the national political communication". Her interests concern political communication, e-democracy, digital communication, change of communication paradigms and media narrative. She was junior researcher for the "Social Media Ability" of Italian companies with Professor Guido Di Fraia's research group. (http://www.osservatoriosocialmedia.com/).

Iasa Monique Ribeiro was born in Curitiba, Brazil. She is currently a journalist and a PhD student at Ramon Llull University (Barcelona, Spain).

She also completed a master's degree in cultural production and communications (2013) at Ramon Llull University, producing a thesis entitled "Collective and collaborative creation: a methodological proposal for the design of participatory projects". Ribeiro's current research work focuses on custom-built projects, innovation and quality control, networking, collaborative relations and social impact.

Dr David Sarias Rodríguez holds a PhD in American history from the University of Sheffield. His research interests focus on political thought and social movements in the United States and Europe since 1945 with a special interest in the Trans-Atlantic dimension of social and political change. David has published on American politics and social movements, is currently working on a book manuscript dealing with the American conservative movement and the presidency of Richard Nixon and on a book chapter re-assessing the characteristics of American law. David is a lecturer at Universidad CEU San Pablo where he teaches public opinion and history of political thought and culture.

Dr Christelle Serée-Chaussinand is Senior Lecturer at the University of Burgundy (Dijon) where she teaches contemporary Irish literature, civilization and culture. Her research interests lie in autobiographical writings and portraiture or self-portraiture in literature as well as in the visual arts. She has published several articles on contemporary Irish literature and art, in particular on such writers and artists as Sean O'Faolain, Sebastian Barry, Derek Mahon, Paul Muldoon, Seamus Heaney, Sinéad Morrissey or Louis le Brocquy. She runs a research seminar on contemporary creation in its relation to critical theory. She is a member of the editorial board of *Interfaces*, an international bilingual journal dedicated to intermediality word and image.

Dr Václav Štětka is Senior Researcher and Leader of the PolCoRe research group at the Institute of Communication Studies, Faculty of Social Sciences, at Charles University in Prague (http://www.polcore.cz). Between 2009 and 2013 he was senior research fellow at the department of politics and international relations, University of Oxford, working on the ERC-funded project "Media and Democracy in Central and Eastern Europe". His research interests encompass political communication and the role of new media, transformation and democratization of media systems, media ownership and globalization. Email: vaclav.stetka@fsv.cuni.cz

Prof. Dr Caja Thimm is Full Professor at the University of Bonn/Germany and the Head of the Department for Communication, Music and Media. She has done extensive research on social communication on the web, e-learning and e-democracy. Her most recent work is on Twitter and on mobile media.

Angelia Wagner is a PhD candidate in the Department of Political Science at the University of Alberta in Edmonton, Canada. Her dissertation investigates the role of gender and municipal context in the political communication strategies of Canadian municipal candidates. In addition to political communication, her research interests include women in politics, gendered mediation, and representation. She has authored and co-authored papers in the *International Journal of Press/Politics*, *Journalism Practice*, and *Canadian Political Science Review*.

Prof. Simeon Yates is Director of the Institute of Cultural Capital. His research on the social, political and cultural impacts of digital media includes a long-standing focus on digital media and interpersonal interaction. He currently researches digital inclusion and exclusion and projects exploring digital arts. Simeon's work has often been interdisciplinary and has predominantly involved creative and digital industry partners. He has undertaken research on the impacts of the Internet and new/digital media on language and culture since 1990. This includes large-scale linguistic comparison of speech, writing and online interaction, and analyses of gender differences in computer-mediated communication.

Index

abstention 2, 142, 211
activism x–xvii, 120–2, 125–36, 148–9, 188–97; art as form of 153–65; "mediactivists" 141; *see also* clicktivism; *see also* slacktivism
agenda-setting 37, 46, 168, 171, 190–2
algorithms 171, 176
Allard, Laurence 140, 168
Altheide, David 169, 188
Altmaier, Peter 50–7
Anastasiadis, Mario xiii, 6, 42–59, 168, 221
Anyó, Lluís xv, 8, 153–66, 221
argumentation 44, 47, 51, 55, 95, 120–1, 139, 141, 146, 150, 175–6
armchair activism *see* clicktivism
authenticity xvi, 35, 99–101

Bakhtin, Mikhaïl xi, xvi, 102
Bauman, Zygmunt 157, 160
Baym, Nancy K. 154, 168, 171
Beck, Ulrich 168, 219
Bennett, Lance W. 3, 125, 139
Berlusconi, Silvio 33–7
blogosphere (political): in Russia 187–97
blogs 17, 34, 88, 97, 115, 119, 140, 143, 149, 156, 167, 173, 176, 184–97, 213–4
Blumler, Jay G. 1, 30
Boklage, Evgeniya xv, 8, 184–201, 219, 221
Bourdieu, Pierre 142, 217
Boyd, Danah 139, 168, 171, 175
Brachotte, Gilles 3, 6, 167, 222
branding (personal) 34, 99–100
broadcasting (as communication strategy) xiii, 2, 28–9, 37–8, 81, 87, 91, 148, 185, 218
Bruns, Axel 43–4, 125, 167, 186, 192
Burgess, Jean 43–4, 141

Cameron, David 100–1
campaigns: electoral 27–38, 45–57, 60–3, 72–4, 81–92, 109–111, 125–36, 139, 144–51, 176, 179; negative 87; on Facebook 161; Scottish referendum 118–21; *see also* lobbying
Canada (political participation in) 81–94, 149
candidates: challengers 49, 87, 205, 210; incumbent 84–7, 205
Cantijoch, Marta 114, 125, 127
Castells, Manuel 13, 30, 125, 154, 170, 186, 194
Cebrián Guinovart, Elena xiii, 6, 60–80, 218, 223
celebrity politics 96–7, 99, 102
censorship 140, 172; self-censorship 210
Christensen, Henrik Serup 3, 126, 173
citizen journalism / citizen media *see* journalism (citizen)
clicktivism 2, 5, 112–3, 125–36, 173; *see also* slacktivism
cognitive surplus 155–165
community 115–7, 158, 184–97; affinity-based 142, 149; hashtag *see* hashtag (community); online engagement 143; page on Facebook 18, 117; peg 161–2; politics 15, 128, 132; strong or weak 155, 157, 164; virtual 160–2; *see also* LGBT; *see also* blogging; *see also* publics
connective action 139
constituency service 14–15
content analysis 17, 26–7, 32–3, 37, 47, 189
control (over communication / discourse) xiv, 61, 99–101, 140–1, 153, 169, 185–7, 192; lack of / loss of 76, 89, 186, 204; *see also* empowerment

228 *Index*

controversy *see* polemics
Couldry, Nick 1–2, 167, 169
counterpublics *see* publics
Craig, Geoff 217–220, 222
Czech Republic (political participation
in) 143–36

Dahlgren, Peter 2–3, 142, 170
Dang-Anh, Mark 43, 45, 47, 171, 177
debates (televised) *see* second screen
decision-making (process of) 15, 116–7,
167–72, 190, 202, 206–12
deliberation 42–3, 57, 59, 61, 65, 81–3,
89, 91, 141, 160, 172–3
democratization (political process of)
x–xi, 13, 16, 20, 30, 60–3, 70, 92,
109–10, 113, 122, 125–6, 141, 148,
154, 158, 171–2, 188; of access to
technology 153
Di Fraia, Guido xiii, 6, 25–41, 218, 222
digital activism *see* activism
digital public sphere *see* public sphere
(digital)
direct action (political) 109–10, 141–2
direct communication *see* one-to-one
communication
discussions: between politicians and
voters 2, 17–21, 55, 89, 204, 208;
online 33, 42–3, 46–9, 57, 76, 91,
130, 172–8, 192–3; as a form of
participation 118, 128
Dryzek, John 8, 172–3

Einspänner-Pflock, Jessica xiii, 6, 42–59,
171, 178, 222
election campaigns *see* campaigns
empowerment 2–4, 113, 116–8, 121,
143–5, 157, 159, 168, 171, 186–7;
see also community
engagement: 13, 18, 29, 35, 71, 90, 96,
103, 112–22, 125–7, 131–6, 142,
148, 158, 171–3, 177–8, 180, 202–8,
213–5, 217; cognitive 112–3
extremism (political) 126, 139, 143,
172, 187

Facebook 13–22, 27, 31, 70, 88–90,
110–15, 119, 121, 126–36, 150,
161–4; typology of political uses of
18–19
follow-up communication 49, 191,
211, 215
Frame, Alex ix, xii, xvii, 1–10, 167, 223
France (political participation in)
157–65, 167

Fuchs, Christian 3, 30, 43, 130
functional operator model 44–5, 176

gatekeeping 168, 171, 186
gender 83–5, 89, 129, 132, 161, 184
Germany (political participation in)
42–58, 167, 177–8
Gibson, Rachel K. 21, 82–3, 114, 125,
127
Goffman, Erving 140, 143
Graham, Todd 25, 27, 194
Great Britain (political participation in)
x, 14–15, 112, 202–16
Grillo, Beppe 28, 35–7

Habermas, Jürgen 141–2, 170
Haleva-Amir, Sharon xiii, 5, 13–24,
218, 223
hashtag 28–9, 33, 37, 43–9, 56–7
61–4, 68–9, 77, 140–1, 148–50, 161,
174–9, 207; community 43, 141
Hepp, Andreas 1, 167–8
Hermans, Liesbeth 2, 13–14, 20–1
Herring, Susan C. 17, 175
Hindman, Matthew 30, 110
Hjarvard, Stig 168–9
Hollande, François 101, 145–9
homosexuality *see* LGBT

ideology ix–xvii, 62–8, 71–7, 116,
139–43, 189
influence: of the media 46, 169, 171,
174, 186, 190; on the media 37, 46,
82, 95, 168; of citizens / politicians
through the media 56, 99, 101,
116–7, 120–1, 143, 159; on political
activity 103, 109–13, 118, 120, 141,
148, 202–3, 206, 217
informalization *see* personalization
Instagram 95–6, 99–100
insults 47, 75, 120, 143–6
interactivity (technical) 14, 20,
81, 89, 92; *see also* one-to-one
communication
interviews: in the media 18, 89, 97; as
research method 13, 84, 129, 207
irony 55, 139–50, 164
Israel (political participation in) 13–22
Italy (political participation in) 25–38

Jackson, Daniel 3
Jackson, Nigel A. 2, 13–15, 21, 27,
82, 125
Jakobson, Roman 34–6
Jenkins, Henry 30, 125, 159

journalism: citizen journalism 30, 185–7, 197; journalists 42–3, 52–7, 63, 82, 86–7, 90, 97–8, 101, 139, 143–50, 185, 194; *see also* mass media

Keaveney, Paula xv, 8, 202–16, 223
Krotz, Friedrich 1, 167–9
Künast, Renate 50–1, 55–7

Larsson, Anders Olof 2, 21, 25, 27, 75, 125
leaders (political) 21, 28, 32, 35–8, 60–4, 67–75, 95–103, 120–1, 139; *see also* public opinion (opinion leaders)
leadership 38, 87, 98
legitimacy (political) 113, 127, 136, 139
Lévy, Pierre 2, 157
LGBT (community) 184–97
Lilleker, Darren G. xiv, 2–3, 7, 13–15, 21, 27, 82, 109–24, 125, 141, 215, 218, 224
Loader, Brian 30, 168
lobbying 33, 89, 92, 110–11, 202–15
local politics 29, 81–92, 144–7, 177–8, 207, 212–4
Lundby, Knut 31, 167–8

mainstream media *see* mass media
Maireder, Axel 2, 44
Mannheim, Karl x–xi, xvii
marketing (political) 22, 29, 100, 126, 150
mass media 25–9, 37–8, 82, 86, 168, 171, 174, 185–93, 196–7, 217–9
Mazák, Jaromír xiv, 7, 125–38, 218, 224
media logic 37, 44, 57, 169–70, 174–6
mediatization 4, 31, 167–80
Mercier, Arnaud xv, 2, 7, 139–52, 167, 172, 224
Merkel, Angela 48–53, 56, 145
microblogging *see* Twitter
Missaglia, Maria Carlotta xiii, 6, 25–41, 218, 224
mobilisation (internet as a tool affecting) 60–1, 114–6, 139, 150
Morozov, Evgeny 2, 7, 30, 112, 125–6, 171
municipal elections *see* local politics

news: breaking 43, 149; coverage of political actions 82, 87, 95, 141, 208; gathering 194–7; online 16,

52, 115, 185, 191; sensationalism 5, 186; social media influence on 35–6, 45, 168, 185, 190; television 112, 187; *see also* agenda setting; *see also* gatekeeping
Norris, Pippa 2, 128, 141, 170

Obama, Barack 60, 82, 97–102
offline political participation 3–4, 112, 114, 118, 125–8, 131–6, 160, 163
one-to-many communication *see* broadcasting (as communication strategy)
one-to-one communication 2–5, 17–19, 25–7, 31, 35–8, 47, 51–2, 55–7, 60, 63, 78, 82–3, 97, 175
operators (on Twitter) 6, 44–55, 176; *see also* functional operator model
opponents (political) *see* opposition (political)
opposition (political) 33–4, 37, 52, 57, 67–71, 87, 120, 139, 149, 177, 188, 217–8

parody *see* irony
partisans *see* supporters (political)
party line 15, 67, 205
Pérez Rubalcaba, Alfredo 61–78
personal branding *see* branding (personal)
personal profiles (on social media) 16–18, 20–1, 89, 95, 159, 178
personalization (of politicians) 15–16, 19–20, 33–5, 87, 139–40; *see also* proximity
photographs 18, 20, 47–8 52, 95–103, 112, 155, 161–2, 176, 186, 191, 195
planned behaviour (theory of) 117, 121
polemics 52, 56–7, 139–51, 172, 209
political agenda 20, 28, 34, 76, 78, 147, 203
political efficacy 126, 128–9, 134–5, 157
political parties 13, 15, 20, 27, 29–36, 57, 66–9, 77–8, 98, 103, 208, 215; online presence of 20, 46, 52, 62, 70, 82, 125–8, 178; showing allegiance to 19, 117, 128; small 61; *see also* party line
posters 89, 97, 143
power: political 95–103, 110, 141, 206; of the media 169, 192; *see also* empowerment
private sphere 2, 5, 96–7, 117, 140, 154–5, 160, 167, 196–7

230 *Index*

professionalization (of social media use for politics) 21–2, 56, 60–1, 83, 89, 141
propaganda 38, 102–3, 143, 184
protest movements 109–12, 120–1, 139–47, 150, 153, 159, 161, 163, 167–8, 172, 177, 187, 191–2, 197
proximity (between politicians and voters) 5, 21, 38, 98, 101–2, 176
public opinion 18, 42, 141, 162, 170, 178, 193, 206; opinion leaders 63, 148
public sphere (digital) 2–3, 17, 42–3, 57, 110, 114, 139, 141–6, 154, 157, 167, 74, 178, 180, 218–9; *see also* publics
publics: ad hoc publics 42–58, 141, 173–4, 177–80, 219; mini-publics 42–58, 167, 173–80, 219; counterpublics 139–151; 172, 184–97
Puig-i-Abril, Eulalia 114, 127–8

radicality *see* extremism (political)
Rajoy, Mariano 61–78
recognition: social 143–5, 153, 161; name 82, 87
research methods xv, 26, 44, 46–7, 63–5, 83–4, 115, 128–9, 153–5, 189, 209; qualitative 17, 26, 32, 44, 47, 51, 89, 129, 189; quantitative 26, 28, 32, 44, 47, 83, 119
Rheingold, Howard ix, 2, 110, 154, 168, 171
Ribeiro, Iasa Monique xv, 8, 153–166, 224
Rojas, Hernando 114, 127–8
Russia (political participation in) 184–198

Sarias Rodríguez, David xiii, 6, 60–80, 218, 225
Sarkozy, Nicolas 145–50
Scottish Referendum 118–20
second screen communication 47–9, 56–7
Segerberg, Alexandra 3, 125, 129
self-expressivity 99–100, 140, 144, 168, 187
selfies 95–103
self-promotion 64, 70, 77–8, 96, 103
Serée-Chaussinand, Christelle xiv, 7, 95–106, 225
Shirky, Clay 30, 125, 158–9, 162, 167
slacktivism 112, 122, 125–6, 128, 130, 148; *see also* clicktivism
Spain (political participation in) 60–78
Stanyer, James 14–15, 97

Steinbrück, Peer 47–56
Štětka, Václav xiv, 7, 125–38, 218, 225
stigmatisation 143, 147, 195–6
Strandberg, Kim 13, 83, 125
Strömbäck, Jesper 1–2, 5, 21, 169–70
supporters (political) 15–19, 81–2, 90, 111, 177, 179, 203, 207–9, 214
surveys *see* research methods

Thimm, Caja xiii, xv, 1, 6, 8, 42–59, 167–83, 219, 225
traditional political participation *see* offline political participation
trust 2, 19, 141, 146, 197
tweeting styles 44–56, 63
Twitter styles *see* tweeting styles
Twitter xii–xiv, 3, 25–38, 42–58, 60–78, 88, 90, 92, 95–7, 101, 115, 119, 139–51, 161, 168, 172, 174–8, 204–5, 207
two step flow 25–38
two-way communication *see* one-to-one communication
typologies: of mini-publics on Twitter 172–4; of online political expression vs voting behaviour 133–4; of political uses of Facebook 18–19

United Kingdom *see* Great Britain (political participation in)
utopia ix–xvii

Vandenberghe, Frédéric 140, 168
Vázquez Barrio, Tamara xiii, 6, 60–80, 218, 221
Vergeer, Maurice 2, 13–15, 20–1
violence 142–4; physical 190–1, 196; in language use 89; *see also* insults
viral (communication) 4–5, 35, 47–8, 98, 142–3, 210
virtual communities *see* community (virtual)
visibility (public/media) 2, 32, 56, 64–9, 82, 86–8, 90, 98–9, 103, 141–8, 155, 158, 161–4, 172–3, 184–5, 190, 196

Wagner, Angelia xiv, 6, 81–94, 225
"web 2.0" 2, 4, 14–15, 21, 25, 30–1, 114, 125, 153–9, 164
working class 142–3

Yates, Simeon ix–xvii, 2, 226
YouTube 88, 92, 174, 191, 195

Zittel, Thomas 13, 110